Developing AI, IoT and Cloud Computing-based Tools and Applications for Women's Safety

In a world increasingly driven by technology, this book explores the intersection of artificial intelligence (AI), IoT, and Cloud Computing and women's safety, highlighting the transformative potential of technology in safeguarding women's well-being in the physical and the digital world. As the safety and security industry embraces technological advancements, the need for inclusive and gender-centric solutions has become increasingly evident. This reference book delves into this critical area, showcasing the development of AI, IoT, and Cloud applications specifically tailored to address the unique safety challenges faced by women.

- Provides a comprehensive exploration of how AI and related technologies are reshaping the future of women's safety.
- Emphases the utilisation of AI to tackle the specific challenges women encounter in various contexts.
- Introduces innovative solutions such as wearable technology, AI-powered surveillance systems, and mobile applications designed for emergency responses.
- Discusses ethical implications of deploying technology for personal security and navigates the evolving legal landscape surrounding data privacy.
- Bridges the gap between theoretical discussions and practical implementations, offering a guide to developing technology for the improvement of women's safety.

It is an invaluable resource for professionals and researchers interested in the transformative role of AI, IoT, and Cloud in shaping the future of women's safety.

Developing AI, IoT and Cloud Computing-based Tools and Applications for Women's Safety

Edited by

Parul Dubey,
Gurpreet Singh Chhabra,
Bui Thanh Hung, and
Umashankar Ghugar

CRC Press
Taylor & Francis Group
Boca Raton London New York

CRC Press is an imprint of the
Taylor & Francis Group, an **informa** business
A CHAPMAN & HALL BOOK

First edition published 2025
by CRC Press
2385 NW Executive Center Drive, Suite 320, Boca Raton FL 33431

and by CRC Press
4 Park Square, Milton Park, Abingdon, Oxon, OX14 4RN

CRC Press is an imprint of Taylor & Francis Group, LLC

ISBN: 978-1-032-88455-4 (hbk)
ISBN: 978-1-032-88511-7 (pbk)
ISBN: 978-1-003-53817-2 (ebk)

DOI: 10.1201/9781003538172

Typeset in Times LT Std
by Apex CoVantage, LLC

Contents

Foreword

Amidst a swiftly progressing technological environment, the convergence of Artificial Intelligence (AI), the Internet of Things (IoT), and Cloud Computing has materialised as a promising prospect for confronting critical societal issues. Out of the various challenges at hand, the protection and well-being of women emerge as the most critical issue. It is crucial that, as we traverse the intricacies of the digital era, we leverage the capabilities of technology to establish more secure surroundings and enable individuals to assert their autonomy and rights.

Developing AI, IoT and Cloud Computing-Based Tools and Applications for Women's Safety, the title of the book in your possession, exemplifies the revolutionary capacity of technology to promote the safety and well-being of women. By virtue of its varied chapter composition, this volume presents an all-encompassing investigation into the ways in which artificial intelligence, the Internet of Things, and cloud computing can be harnessed to generate inventive resolutions customised to the particular obstacles and requirements encountered by women.

Every chapter in this book offers significant insights and perspectives regarding the technology's potential to improve the safety of women, ranging from theoretical foundations to practical applications. This book provides a wealth of knowledge and expertise, encompassing themes such as the integration of blockchain technology for secure platforms, the development of wearable devices for personal security, and the legal and ethical considerations associated with cybersecurity.

This volume is distinguished by its steadfast dedication to fostering inclusivity and empowerment. Through its exploration of the experiences of transgender people and women, among other marginalised groups, the book emphasises the criticality of technology in nurturing a culture of safety and equality for all and dismantling barriers.

As we commence this intellectual exploration of *Developing AI, IoT and Cloud Computing-Based Tools and Applications for Women's Safety*, I urge readers to approach every chapter with a receptive and collaborative mindset. With all sincerity, I hope that this book will stimulate substantial discourse, ingenuity, and proactive measures in the continuous pursuit of ensuring the safety and empowerment of women.

I would like to express my profound appreciation to the editors and contributors who have generously invested their time and expertise in the completion of this significant endeavour. Collectively, let us capitalise on the prospects that technology affords in order to forge a more promising and secure future for women on a global scale.

Dr. Pushkar Dubey
Assistant Professor and Head (Management),
Pandit Sundarlal Sharma (Open) University Chhattisgarh
MA (Economics), MBA (Gold Medallist)
Qualified UGC-NET (Management), PhD

Preface

An increasing number of individuals are beginning to recognise the interdependence between social welfare and technology, particularly with regard to matters such as the protection of women. The emergence of artificial intelligence (AI), the Internet of Things (IoT), and cloud computing has enabled the development of inventive approaches to address the unique challenges that women encounter in terms of self-protection. *Developing AI, IoT and Cloud Computing-Based Tools and Applications for Women's Safety* is the title of an edited collection that examines the numerous ways in which these technologies could be implemented to improve the world and safeguard women.

This book covers a lot of ground, from general theories to specific examples of how artificial intelligence, the Internet of Things, and cloud computing have improved women's safety. Giving readers a grounding in the topic, the voyage starts with an examination of how these technologies may be integrated for social benefit. Next, we'll take a closer look at some of the topics covered, such as how to build emergency response applications, the function of wearable tech in personal safety, and the use of blockchain technology for safe women's platforms.

Privacy and data security, ethical and legal issues, and the role of education and community involvement in creating a secure environment are all important topics covered in this collection. Additionally, it delves into the ways in which technology may shatter barriers and enable underrepresented communities, such as transgender people and women, to stand up for their own safety and autonomy.

This book highlights the use of AI, IoT, and Cloud Computing to improve women's safety via real-world examples and informative case studies. For those committed to using technology for social good and building a more inclusive and secure society, it is an exhaustive resource for academics, professionals, politicians, and campaigners.

Our deepest appreciation goes out to everyone who has contributed their knowledge and wisdom to make this collection a reality. In the never-ending fight for women's equality and empowerment, we pray that this book may serve as a catalyst for new ideas and partnerships.

Parul Dubey
Chief Editor

Editor Biography

Parul Dubey is currently working as an assistant professor in Symbiosis Institute of Technology, Nagpur Campus, Symbiosis International (Deemed University), Pune, India. The author's highest degree is the degree of master's in computer engineering. She is also a PhD research scholar in computer science and engineering at C.V. Raman University, Bilaspur, Chhattisgarh, India. She has good academic and research experience in various areas of CSE and IT. She has an experience of five years. She has been involved in research activities which include book chapters, books, conference papers, and journal articles. She has 17 Indian published patents and one Indian granted patent. She holds around 25 publications which are part of conferences, scopus, and other journals as well. The author is an AWS-Certified Cloud Practitioner badge holder, which is a proof for the expertise in AWS. She is currently guiding many engineering students to learn the AWS platform and complete their projects. She is currently working on three authored book proposals from international publishers. She is also an editor of two of these books.

Gurpreet Singh Chhabra (PhD CSE) has 16 years of teaching experience and is currently working as an assistant professor in the Computer Science and Engineering Department at GITAM School of Technology, GITAM Deemed to be University, Visakhapatnam. He has research interests in deep learning, machine learning, data science, and fog computing fields. He is a life member of the ISTE (Indian Society for Technical Education) and IAENG (International Association of Engineers). Also, he claims credit for many articles in international journals, book chapters, books, and patents.

Bui Thanh Hung received his MS degree and PhD degree from Japan Advanced Institute of Science and Technology (JAIST) in 2010 and in 2013. He was Director of Data Analysis Artificial Intelligence Laboratory—DAAI Lab, Thu Dau Mot university (2018–2021); Director of Artificial Intelligence Laboratory—AI Lab, Faculty of Information Technology, Ton Duc Thang University (2021–2022). Now, he works for Data Science Laboratory, Data Science Department, Faculty of Information Technology, Industrial University of Ho Chi Minh City. He has completed two projects, published two books, 22 journals, 22 book chapters, 39 International conference papers, and 16 domestic conference papers. He has received four best paper awards of FICTA 2018, RICE 2020, ICAIAA 2021, and CIEMA 2022. He was selected as Excellent Scientific Researcher of Thu Dau Mot University in 2019, 2020, and 2021 and received the CIEMA Research Excellence Award in 2022. He is a reviewer of many reputed journals and conferences. He has also been a keynote speaker of many domestic and international conferences. His main research interests are natural language processing, machine learning, machine translation, text processing, data analytics, computer vision, and artificial intelligence.

Umashankar Ghugar earned his full-time doctoral degree from Berhampur University, Odisha in 2021, and his MTech degree in computer science from Fakir Mohan University, Balasore, in 2012 and his BE degree in IT from Utkal University in 2006. He has ten years of teaching experience in different organisations and is currently working as an assistant professor in the School of Technology, Department of CSE at GITAM University, Visakhapatnam. He has published 14 articles in international journals. His research interests are in computer networks and network security in WSN. He is a reviewer of multiple international journals and also a member of IEEE, IACSIT, CSTA, and IRED.

Contributors

Pratik K. Agrawal
Symbiosis Institute of Technology, Nagpur Campus, Symbiosis International (Deemed University)
Maharashtra, Pune, India

Rahul Vinayak Bambodkar
JD College of Engineering and Management
Nagpur, Maharashtra, India

Devanand Bhonsle
Shri Shankaracharya Technical Campus
Bhilai, Chhattisgarh, India

Pushpa Birha
G. H. Raisoni Institute of Engineering and Technology
Nagpur, Maharashtra, India

Shashank Borikar
G. H. Raisoni College of Engineering
Maharashtra, India

Rajkumar Buyya
CLOUDS Lab, School of Computing and Information Systems
The University of Melbourne, Australia

Parul Dubey
Symbiosis Institute of Technology, Nagpur Campus
Symbiosis International (Deemed University), Pune, India

Pushkar Dubey
Pandit Sundarlal Sharma (Open) University
Chhattisgarh, Bilaspur (CG)

Suryya Farhat
Dr. Akhilsh Das Gupta Institute of Professional Studies
Shastri Park, Delhi, India

Hitesh Gehani
Shri Ramdeobaba College of Engineering and Management
Nagpur, India

Shivraj Guduri
G. H. Raisoni College of Engineering
Maharashtra, India

Amit Jain
OP Jindal University
Raigarh, India

Palak Keshwani
The ICFAI University
Raipur, Chhattisgarh, India

Sapna Singh Kshatri
Shri Shankaracharya Institute of Professional Management and Technology
Mujgahan, India

Manoj Kumar
Amity International Business School
Amity University
Noida, India

Rajendra Kumar
Kalinga University
New Raipur, Chhattisgarh, India

Roopesh Kumar
Banasthali Vidypith
Banasthali Rajasthan, India

K. Kushal
Amrita School of Computing
Karnataka, India

Alok Kumar Singh Kushwaha
Guru Ghasidas Vidyalaya,
Bilaspur, Chattishgarh, India

Supriya M.
Amrita School of Computing
Bengaluru, Amrita Vishwa Vidyapeetham, India

Biswajeet Mallick
G. H. Raisoni College of Engineering
Nagpur, India

Mamta
Chandigarh University
Punjab, India

Madhav Manoj
Amrita School of Computing
Karnataka, India

Manjushree Nayak
NIST University, Institute Ark, Palluhills
Golanthara Berhampur, Odisha, India

Rakesh Nayak
OP Jindal University
Raigarh, India

Shantipriya Parida
Silo AI
Helsinki, Finland

Peeta Basa Pati
Department of Computer Science and Engineering
Amrita School of Computing, Amrita Vishwa Vidyapeetham
Bengaluru, India

Anu G. Pillai
Kalinga University
Raipur, Chhattisgarh, India

Priyanka Prabhakar
Department of Computer Science and Engineering
Amrita School of Computing, Amrita Vishwa Vidyapeetham
Bengaluru, India

Shinu M. Rajagopal
Amrita School of Computing, Amrita Vishwa Vidyapeetham
Bengaluru, India

Soma Rajwade
Kalinga University
New Raipur, Chhattisgarh, India

Minakshi Ramteke
G. H. Raisoni College of Engineering
Maharashtra, India

Manas Rathore
Kalinga University
New Raipur, Chhattisgarh, India

Sujal Raut
G. H. Raisoni College of Engineering
Maharashtra, India

Kevansh Reddy
Amrita School of Computing
Karnataka, India

Tanu Rizvi
Shri Shankaracharya Technical Campus
Bhilai, Chhattisgarh, India

Thangam S.
Amrita School of Computing
Karnataka, India

Chandra Kumar Sahu
Kalinga University
New Raipur, Chhattisgarh, India

Kailash Kumar Sahu
Amity University
Chhattisgarh Raipur, Chhattisgarh, India

Monika Saxena
Banasthali Vidypith,
Banasthali, Rajasthan, India

Ruhi Uzma Sheikh
Anjuman College of Engineering and Technology
Nagpur, Maharashtra, India

Pratibha Singh
Guru Ghasidas Vidyalaya,
Bilaspur Chattishgarh, India

Anshul Srivastava
Amity International Business School, Amity University
Noida, India

Ajinkya Tamhankar
G. H. Raisoni College of Engineering
Nagpur, India

Araya Tripathi
G. H. Raisoni College of Engineering
Maharashtra, India

Arti Vaish
Department of Computer Science and Engineering
O. P. Jindal University
Punjipathra, Raigarh, Chhattisgarh, India

Praveen Kumar Yadaw
Kalinga University
New Raipur, Chhattisgarh, India

1 Introduction to the Integration of AI, IoT, and Cloud Computation for Social Welfare

Palak Keshwani, Hitesh Gehani, and Pratik K. Agrawal

1.1. INTRODUCTION TO ARTIFICIAL INTELLIGENCE

AI involves replicating human intelligence in machines and programming them to think, learn, and carry out tasks that typically require human cognitive skills (Arman Raj et al., 2023). The goal of AI is to build up systems that copy human functions like problem-solving, learning, perception, language understanding, and decision-making. AI technologies attempt to produce machines capable of autonomous task performance, adaptation to varying environments, and persistent upgrading. Figure 1.1 shows the components of AI in detail.

1.1.1. Key Components of AI

1. Machine Learning (ML): ML, a subset of AI, concentrates on allowing machines to learn from data with no explicit programming. It involves crafting algorithms that facilitate systems to recognize patterns, build predictions, and improve performance through experience (Bakshi & Bakshi, 2018).
2. Deep Learning: As a subfield of machine learning, deep learning includes artificial neural networks enthused by the human brain's structure and function. Deep learning algorithms, mainly deep neural networks, can learn hierarchical data representations, leading to notable achievements in areas like image recognition, natural language processing, and speech recognition (Alzubaidi et al., 2021).
3. Natural Language Processing (NLP): NLP, a branch of AI, concentrates on the communication between computers and human beings via natural language. It authorises machines to realise, interpret, and generate human language, facilitating meaningful and contextually relevant communication between computers and users (Khurana et al., 2022).

DOI: 10.1201/9781003538172-1

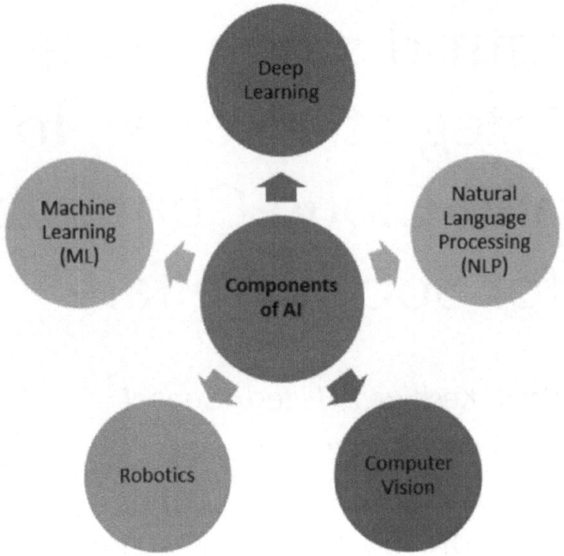

FIGURE 1.1 Components of AI.

4 Computer Vision: AI in computer vision facilitates machines to read and understand visual information from the world. It demands developing algorithms and systems competent of analysing visual data, such as images and videos, to build informed decisions (Wiley & Lucas, 2018).
5 Robotics: Robotics incorporates AI to design, build, and operate robots. AI in robotics enables machines to recognize their environment, make decisions, and carry out physical tasks autonomously, which is crucial for applications in manufacturing, healthcare, and various industries.

1.1.2. Types of AI

1 Narrow AI (Weak AI): Narrow AI is customised to execute specific tasks or closely related sets of tasks inside a limited domain, lacking the wide cognitive abilities found in humans. Examples include virtual personal assistants, image recognition systems, and language translation tools.
2 General AI (Strong AI): General AI pertains to machines with the ability to understand, learn, and apply knowledge across varied tasks, similar to human intelligence. Achieving true general AI remains a long-term goal and a subject of ongoing research.

1.1.3. Applications of AI

1 Healthcare: AI is useful in medical imaging, drug detection, personalized medicine, and patient care to improve diagnosis, treatment, and overall healthcare outcomes.

2 Finance: AI is employed in the financial sector for tasks such as fraud finding, algorithmic trading, client service, and risk management.
3 Education: AI finds value in adaptive learning platforms, personalised tutoring systems, and educational content creation, improving the learning experience.
4 Autonomous Vehicles: AI is essential in the development of self-driving cars and drones, allowing them to recognise their surroundings, make decisions, and navigate safely.
5 Customer Service: AI-powered chatbots and virtual assistants provide customer support, offering instantaneous responses and support.

1.1.4. Challenges

1 Bias and Fairness: AI systems may inherit biases from training data, leading to unjust outcomes. Addressing biases and ensuring justice in AI algorithms is a major challenge.
2 Transparency and Accountability: The lack of transparency in AI decision-making processes raises anxiety about accountability, particularly in critical applications like healthcare and criminal justice.
3 Privacy: AI often incorporates analysing vast amounts of personal data, raising concerns about privacy and data safety.
4 Job Displacement: The widespread adoption of AI technologies may result in job displacement, necessitating a proactive method for retraining and upskilling employees.

AI is a vigorously evolving field with noteworthy potential to transform various aspects of society.

1.2. INTERNET OF THINGS

The IoT is the idea of a network of interconnected things, including appliances, automobiles, and other real-world items that have sensors, software, and network connectivity built into them (Kumar et al., 2019). These gadgets can collect and share data. IoT's main goal is to create a smooth, intelligent environment where various gadgets can interact, exchange data, and make decisions based on that data—all of which will eventually increase productivity, convenience, and efficiency. Components of IoT can be seen in Figure 1.2.

1.2.1. Key Components of IoT

1 Sensors and Actuators: IoT devices are equipped with diverse sensors. These sensors allow IoT devices to measure various environmental elements such as temperature, humidity, motion, and light in real time. Actuators are a useful addition to this as they allow devices to perform physical actions based on data that is received.

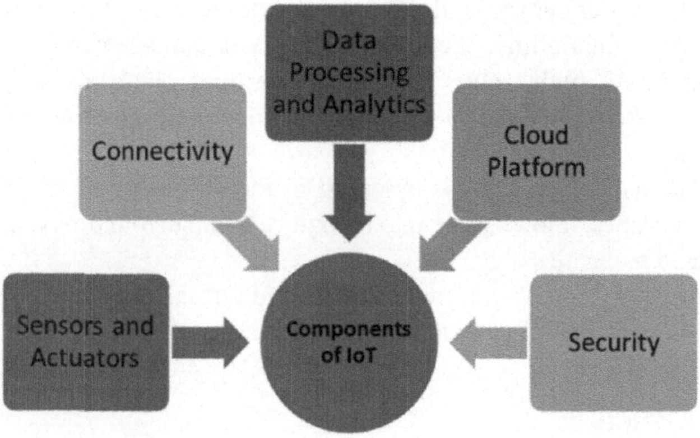

FIGURE 1.2 Components of IoT.

2 Connectivity: In order to enable communication between devices, IoT depends on connectivity. This connectivity encompasses wireless technologies like Bluetooth, Zigbee, Wi-Fi, and cellular networks in addition to traditional connections like Ethernet and USB. The individual needs of the IoT application determine which connectivity option is best.
3 Data Processing and Analytics: The data collected by IoT devices undergo processing and analysis to extract meaningful insights. This can occur locally on the device or be transmitted to a centralised cloud server for more extensive analysis. Advanced analytics generate actionable information from the substantial amount of data generated by IoT devices.
4 Cloud Platform: Cloud platforms play a pivotal role in IoT by providing storage, processing power, and scalable infrastructure for handling large volumes of data. Cloud services enable IoT applications to store and analyse data efficiently, facilitating remote monitoring and control of devices.
5 Security: Security is a paramount concern in IoT due to the sensitivity of the data transmitted between devices. Implementing robust security measures, including encryption, authentication, and secure protocols, is essential to protect against unauthorized access and potential cyber threats.

1.2.2. Applications of IoT

1 Smart Home: The IoT facilitates the creation of smart homes where devices like thermostats, lighting, security cameras, and appliances can be interconnected and controlled remotely, enhancing energy efficiency, security, and overall convenience.

2 Industrial IoT (IIoT): In industries, IoT is employed for monitoring and optimising manufacturing processes, predictive maintenance of equipment, and ensuring the efficient operation of supply chains, leading to improved productivity and reduced downtime.
3 Healthcare: IoT applications in healthcare include wearable devices, remote patient monitoring, and smart medical equipment. These technologies enable real-time health tracking, timely intervention, and personalised healthcare solutions.
4 Smart Cities: The IoT contributes to the development of smart cities by integrating technologies for traffic management, waste management, energy efficiency, and public safety, fostering more sustainable and livable urban environments.
5 Agriculture: IoT is utilised in precision agriculture for monitoring soil conditions, crop health, and irrigation systems, optimizing farming practices, conserving resources, and improving yields.

1.2.3. Challenges in IoT

1 Security Concerns: Ensuring the security of IoT networks is a significant challenge with the increasing number of connected devices. Exploiting device vulnerabilities can result in data breaches and privacy issues.
2 Interoperability: Different IoT devices often use diverse communication protocols and standards, posing a challenge to interoperability. Efforts are underway to establish common standards for seamless communication between devices from different manufacturers.
3 Scalability: As the number of connected devices grows, scalability becomes a concern. IoT platforms need to efficiently handle the increasing volume of data and support a large number of devices.
4 Privacy Issues: The extensive collection of personal data by IoT devices raises concerns about privacy. Striking a balance between collecting valuable data and respecting individuals' privacy is crucial.

The Internet of Things represents a transformative paradigm where the integration of smart devices and connectivity opens up new possibilities across various domains. As IoT evolves, addressing challenges and ensuring responsible deployment are essential to unlocking its full potential in shaping a connected and intelligent future.

1.3. CLOUD COMPUTING

Cloud Computing represents a groundbreaking technological shift that has revolutionised how businesses and individuals access and harness computing resources. Instead of relying on conventional on-premises servers and infrastructure, Cloud Computing provides access to a shared reservoir of resources, encompassing computing power, storage, and applications, all accessible over the internet (Parlinska & Petrovsk, 2017).

1.3.1. Key Components of Cloud Computing

1. On-Demand Self-Service: Cloud Computing empowers users to provision and manage computing resources autonomously, eliminating the need for direct intervention from service providers. This self-service feature fosters flexibility and scalability.
2. Broad Network Access: Cloud services are reachable over the internet through various devices, such as laptops, smart phones, and tablets. This broad network access ensures users can connect to cloud resources from virtually any location.
3. Resource Pooling: Cloud providers aggregate computing resources, serving multiple customers while simultaneously optimising resource utilisation and efficiency. Users enjoy cost savings and the ability to scale resources based on their requirements.
4. Rapid Elasticity: Cloud resources can be swiftly provisioned or released, allowing users to scale up or down in response to demand fluctuations. This elasticity ensures efficient resource allocation and cost-effectiveness.
5. Measured Service: Cloud Computing resources are metered, and users only pay for the resources they consume. This pay-as-you-go model offers cost transparency, enabling organisations to manage budgets effectively.

1.3.2. Service Models in Cloud Computing

The many approaches that organisations and individuals may take to use the resources and capabilities offered by the cloud are referred to as service models in the field. Users' degrees of agency, accountability, and adaptability with respect to their own computer resources are defined by these paradigms. Software as a service (SaaS), Infrastructure as a service (IaaS), and Platform as a service (PaaS) are the three main service models in cloud computing. Different models provide different degrees of abstraction and administration, each with its own set of benefits and drawbacks. If your company wants to reap the advantages of cloud computing and optimise your IT infrastructure to achieve your business goals effectively, you must understand these service models. Figure 1.3 shows the service models in cloud computing.

1. Infrastructure as a Service (IaaS): IaaS provides virtualised computing resources over the internet, granting users access to virtual machines, storage, and networking components. This flexibility allows users to manage and control the underlying infrastructure.
2. Platform as a Service (PaaS): PaaS furnishes a platform encompassing both hardware and software, enabling users to develop, run, and manage applications without grappling with the intricacies of the underlying infrastructure. This streamlines the development process and expedites application deployment.
3. Software as a Service (SaaS): SaaS delivers fully functional software applications over the internet. Users can access these applications through a web browser without concerning themselves with installation, maintenance, or infrastructure management.Figure 1.3 Service models in cloud computing.

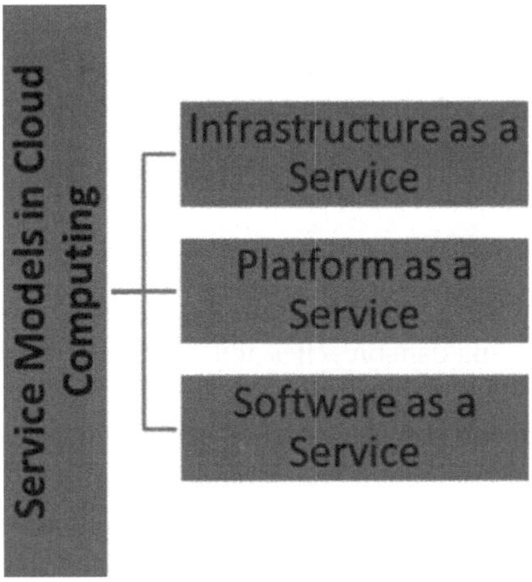

FIGURE 1.3 Service models in cloud computing.

1.3.3. Deployment Models in Cloud Computing

1. Public Cloud: Public cloud services, provided by third-party cloud service providers, are accessible to the general public. Resources are shared among multiple users, rendering it a cost-effective option for numerous organisations (Veni, 2018).
2. Private Cloud: Private cloud infrastructure is dedicated to a single organisation and can be hosted either on-premises or by a third-party provider. Private clouds provide enhanced control, security, and customisation.
3. Hybrid Cloud: Hybrid cloud amalgamates both public and private cloud resources, allowing data and applications to be shared between them. This approach provides greater flexibility, scalability, and optimisation of existing infrastructure.

1.3.4. Benefits of Cloud Computing

1. Cost Efficiency: Cloud Computing eliminates the need for substantial upfront investments in hardware and infrastructure. Users can pay for the resources they consume, making it a cost-effective solution.
2. Scalability: Cloud services can be easily scaled up or down based on demand, ensuring organisations can adapt to changing resource requirements.
3. Accessibility and Flexibility: Cloud services are accessible from anywhere with an internet connection, affording users the flexibility to work remotely and access resources on various devices.
4. Security: Cloud providers implement robust security measures to safeguard data and infrastructure. Many cloud services comply with industry standards and regulations, enhancing overall security.

5 Innovation and Collaboration: Cloud Computing accelerates innovation by providing a platform for the rapid development and deployment of applications. It also fosters collaboration among users by enabling seamless sharing and access to resources.

1.3.5. Challenges in CC

1 Security Concerns: Despite robust security measures by cloud providers, concerns persist regarding data breaches and unauthorised access. Organisations must carefully manage access controls and encryption to mitigate risks.
2 Data Privacy: Storing data on external servers raises concerns about data privacy and compliance with regulations. Organisations must ensure that their data handling practices align with legal requirements.
3 Downtime and Reliability: Dependence on internet connectivity and the reliability of cloud service providers can result in downtime. Organisations should consider service level agreements (SLAs) and redundancy strategies to minimise disruptions.
4 Data Transfer Speeds: The speed of data transfer to and from the cloud can be a limitation, especially for large datasets. Organisations need to assess their bandwidth requirements for efficient data transfer.

Cloud Computing has emerged as a transformative technology, providing organisations and individuals with a flexible, cost-effective, and scalable solution for accessing computing resources. As technology evolves, addressing challenges and leveraging its benefits will play a crucial role in shaping the future of IT infrastructure and services.

1.4. INTEGRATION OF AI, IoT, AND CLOUD COMPUTING

The convergence of AI, IoT, and Cloud Computing heralds a new era of technological synergy, reshaping our understanding and utilisation of interconnected systems. This amalgamation establishes a robust ecosystem where intelligent machines, real-time data exchange, and scalable computing resources seamlessly collaborate, presenting unparalleled opportunities for innovation and efficiency (Apo, 2021).

At the core of this integration is AI, which involves the emulation of human intelligence in machines. Machine learning algorithms within AI empower systems to analyse extensive datasets, discern patterns, and make informed decisions without explicit programming. The inclusion of AI enhances the capacity of interconnected devices to interpret and act upon data, contributing to heightened intelligent and autonomous functionalities.

Extending connectivity beyond traditional computing devices, IoT integrates sensors and communication capabilities into everyday objects. These interconnected devices collect and share data, establishing a network of physical entities that communicate and collaborate. The synergy with AI allows these devices not only to generate data but also to interpret and respond intelligently to their environment, ushering in a new level of automation and efficiency.

Serving as the foundation for this fusion, Cloud Computing provides a scalable and adaptable infrastructure. It furnishes on-demand access to a shared pool of computing resources, facilitating the processing and storage of the vast amounts of data generated by IoT devices. Cloud-based platforms also serve as an ideal environment for deploying AI algorithms, enabling distributed and efficient processing.

1.4.1. Key Components of the Fusion

1. AI-Driven Analytics: The infusion of AI into IoT devices amplifies their analytical capabilities. AI algorithms can process real-time data streams, identify meaningful patterns, and extract valuable insights, enabling more accurate decision-making and predictive functionalities across diverse applications (Liu et al., 2015).
2. Edge Computing: To address latency concerns and mitigate data transmission loads, edge computing comes into play. AI algorithms are deployed closer to the data source (at the network's edge), allowing faster processing and decision-making without solely relying on centralised cloud resources.
3. Autonomous Systems: The fusion empowers devices with the capability to operate autonomously. AI algorithms embedded in IoT devices enable them to adapt, learn from experiences, and make decisions without constant human intervention. This autonomy proves particularly valuable in applications like smart homes, industrial automation, and autonomous vehicles.
4. Scalable and Flexible Infrastructure: CC provides a scalable infrastructure that accommodates the dynamic demands of AI and IoT applications. It ensures efficient data storage, processing, and retrieval, allowing organisations to scale their operations seamlessly.

1.4.2. Applications of the Fusion

The combined influence of Artificial Intelligence (AI), Internet of Things (IoT), and Cloud Computing on social welfare is clearly evident in a spectrum of applications that redefine how societies confront challenges and uplift overall well-being. The following notable examples illustrate the collaborative impact of these technologies (Parlinska & Petrovsk, 2017; Nizetic et al., 2020; Cowls, 2021):

Healthcare Accessibility and Monitoring:

- *Telemedicine and Remote Patient Monitoring:* AI-driven healthcare applications, coupled with IoT devices, facilitate remote patient monitoring. Wearable devices and sensors collect real-time health data, analysed using AI algorithms. CC ensures secure storage and processing of health records, enabling timely interventions, and reducing the need for frequent hospital visits.

- *Disease Prediction and Prevention:* AI algorithms analyse large datasets, including IoT device data, to predict disease outbreaks and identify high-risk areas. Cloud-based platforms swiftly process this data, allowing authorities to take proactive measures to prevent the spread of diseases.

Precision Agriculture for Food Security:

IoT-enabled Agricultural Sensors: Smart agriculture integrates IoT devices like soil sensors and drones, gathering data on soil conditions, weather patterns, and crop health. AI algorithms process this data in the cloud, optimising irrigation, crop management, and resource allocation for heightened yields and reduced environmental impact.

Smart Cities for Urban Development:

Traffic Management: AI algorithms, integrated with IoT sensors, monitor and analyse real-time traffic patterns. CC processes this data to optimise traffic flow, reduce congestion, and enhance transportation efficiency in urban areas.

Public Safety and Security: AI-powered video analytics from surveillance cameras and IoT sensors contribute to crime detection and prevention. Cloud-based platforms facilitate the storage and analysis of vast amounts of video data, assisting law enforcement agencies in ensuring public safety

Education and Digital Learning:

Personalised Learning Platforms: AI-driven educational applications, seamlessly integrated with Cloud Computing, provide tailored learning experiences. IoT devices, such as tablets and interactive boards, foster interactive and adaptive learning environments personalised to individual student needs.

Access to Educational Resources: Cloud-based platforms make educational resources globally accessible. AI algorithms further optimise content delivery based on user preferences and learning styles, fostering inclusive and customised learning experiences.

Environmental Monitoring and Conservation:

Wildlife Conservation: IoT devices, encompassing animal tracking collars and camera traps, collect data on wildlife behaviour and habitat conditions. AI algorithms process this data in the cloud, aiding conservation efforts by identifying patterns, tracking endangered species, and detecting potential threats.

Climate Change Analysis: AI models, intricately connected with cloud platforms, analyse extensive datasets related to climate change. This information aids scientists and policymakers in developing strategies for mitigating the impact of climate change and adapting to environmental challenges.

Disaster Response and Management:

- *Early Warning Systems:* IoT sensors and AI algorithms integrate to create early warning systems for natural disasters. CC enables the rapid dissemination of alerts and coordination of emergency response efforts.
- *Resource Allocation:* During disaster situations, AI analyses real-time data from IoT devices and historical patterns to optimise resource allocation. Cloud platforms facilitate the sharing of critical information among response teams for efficient decision-making.

Social Services and Welfare Programs:

- *Automated Assistance:* AI-powered chatbots and virtual assistants, integrated with cloud services, provide automated assistance for social services. This includes answering queries, guiding users through application processes, and offering support for welfare programmes (Cowls, 2021).
- *Predictive Analytics for Social Trends:* AI algorithms analyse social data from various sources, including IoT devices and social media, to identify emerging social trends and issues. This information informs policymakers in designing targeted interventions for challenges and considerations.
- Privacy and Security: Ensuring the privacy and security of sensitive data collected from IoT devices is paramount. Robust encryption and access controls are necessary to protect individuals' information.
- Ethical AI Use: Implementing AI in social welfare should adhere to ethical guidelines to prevent bias and discrimination. Transparent AI algorithms and responsible data practices are essential.
- Infrastructure and Connectivity: Adequate infrastructure and reliable connectivity are crucial for the successful implementation of AI, IoT, and Cloud Computing in socially beneficial initiatives.
- Community Engagement: Inclusion of communities in the development and deployment of these technologies is essential to address specific needs and ensure acceptance.

These applications vividly demonstrate the collective impact of AI, IoT, and Cloud Computing in social welfare, providing innovative solutions that tackle diverse challenges and contribute to the establishment of more resilient, efficient, and equitable societies.

1.4.3. Challenges

1. Security Concerns: The integration of these technologies raises concerns about data security and privacy. Safeguarding interconnected systems from cyber threats and ensuring secure data transmission are critical challenges.

2 Interoperability: Ensuring seamless communication and compatibility among diverse AI, IoT, and Cloud Computing devices and platforms is a challenge that requires standardised protocols.
3. Data Overload: The fusion generates vast amounts of data, necessitating efficient data management strategies to prevent overwhelming cloud resources and ensuring timely processing.

The integration of AI, IoT, and Cloud Computing holds great potential for positively impacting social welfare by introducing innovative solutions that address various challenges. By leveraging these technologies responsibly, societies can strive towards more efficient, accessible, and equitable services for the well-being of individuals and communities.

1.5. ETHICAL CONCERNS

The incorporation of AI, IoT, and Cloud Computing introduce a multitude of ethical considerations that demand meticulous attention to guarantee responsible and advantageous implementation. Below are pivotal ethical considerations:

Privacy Concerns:

Data Collection and Storage: IoT devices generate copious amounts of data, and the involvement of Cloud Computing in storing and processing this data necessitates robust privacy measures, including encryption and secure storage, to safeguard individuals' sensitive information.

User Consent: Obtaining clear and informed consent from individuals regarding the collection, use, and sharing of their data is imperative. Transparency in data practices is pivotal for building trust and demonstrating respect for privacy.

Security Measures:

Cybersecurity Risks: The interconnected nature of AI, IoT, and cloud systems creates vulnerabilities. Implementing stringent cybersecurity measures, conducting regular audits, and ensuring timely updates are crucial to prevent unauthorized access and data breaches.

Device Security: Safeguarding IoT devices against potential hacking and unauthorised control is vital. Equipping devices with robust authentication mechanisms and providing regular security updates from manufacturers are essential practices.

Bias and Fairness:

AI Algorithm Bias: AI algorithms may inherit biases from training data, leading to discriminatory outcomes. Conducting regular audits and utilising diverse, representative datasets are necessary to identify and mitigate biases, ensuring fair and equitable treatment.

Impact on Vulnerable Communities: Consideration should be given to the potential disparate impact on vulnerable communities. Ethical AI deployment involves actively working to minimise negative consequences and promote inclusivity.

Transparency and Explicability:

Explicability of AI Decisions: AI systems often function as "black boxes", making it challenging to understand decision-making processes. Ensuring transparency and providing explanations for AI-driven decisions are critical for building user trust and ensuring accountability.

Data Processing Transparency: Cloud Computing processes vast amounts of data, and users should be informed about how their data is processed, who has access to it, and for what purposes. Transparency builds trust and aids users in making informed decisions.

Environmental Impact:

Energy Consumption: Cloud Computing infrastructure can have a significant energy footprint. Striving for energy efficiency and adopting sustainable practices, such as using renewable energy sources, can help mitigate the environmental impact.

Electronic Waste: The disposal of IoT devices contributes to electronic waste. Implementing recycling programs and designing devices with sustainable materials can reduce environmental harm.

Informed Decision-Making:

User Empowerment: Granting users control over the data collected about them is essential. Providing options for users to manage and control their data, including the ability to opt out of certain data collection practices, empowers individuals.

Education and Awareness: Ensuring that users and stakeholders are educated about the capabilities and limitations of AI, IoT, and cloud systems fosters informed decision-making and responsible use.

Legal and Regulatory Compliance:

Compliance with Data Protection Laws: Adhering to data protection regulations, such as GDPR, HIPAA, or other relevant laws, is essential. Compliance helps protect individuals' rights and ensures that organisations operate within legal frameworks.

Ethical Standards: Adopting and adhering to ethical standards and guidelines in the development and deployment of AI, IoT, and cloud technologies is essential for maintaining societal trust and promoting responsible practices.

Social Impact:

Job Displacement: The integration of AI may result in job displacement in certain sectors. Ethical considerations include implementing strategies for retraining and upskilling the workforce to address the potential social impact.

Access and Inclusion: Ensuring equitable access to AI, IoT, and cloud technologies is crucial. Efforts should be made to bridge the digital divide and avoid exacerbating existing inequalities.

Addressing these ethical considerations is vital for realising the full potential of AI, IoT, and Cloud Computing while minimising potential harms and ensuring the responsible and beneficial integration of these technologies into society.

1.6. ADDITIONAL ASPECTS

Beyond ethical considerations, there are several facets to explore concerning the amalgamation of AI, IoT, and CC in social welfare. Here are additional aspects to contemplate:

1 Collaborative Decision-Making: The integration of AI, IoT, and Cloud Computing streamlines collaborative decision-making processes. Real-time data and analytics empower policymakers, community leaders, and citizens to collectively contribute to well-informed decisions that address societal needs and challenges.
2 Efficient Resource Allocation: These technologies enhance the efficient allocation of resources in social welfare programs. AI-driven analytics, coupled with IoT data, and cloud processing, aid in identifying areas of need, optimising service delivery, and ensuring resources are directed where they can make the most impact.
3 Predictive Analytics for Social Trends: AI algorithms, when applied to data from IoT devices and various social sources, can predict emerging social trends. This foresight is invaluable for anticipating future challenges, planning interventions, and staying ahead of societal needs.
4 Streamlined Service Delivery: The integration streamlines the delivery of social services. AI-powered chatbots, virtual assistants, and automated processes, supported by cloud infrastructure, enhance the responsiveness and efficiency of service delivery, ensuring timely support for individuals in need.
5 Empowering Individuals: AI, IoT, and cloud technologies empower individuals by providing personalised services and information. Wearable devices, mobile applications, and online platforms enable individuals to access tailored resources and support, fostering a sense of autonomy and self-efficacy.
6 Innovation in Social Programs: The fusion of these technologies fosters innovation in the design and implementation of social programmes.

AI-driven solutions enhance the effectiveness of education programs, healthcare services, and employment initiatives, leading to more impactful outcomes.

7 Real-Time Monitoring and Evaluation: The combination of IoT devices and cloud-based analytics enables real-time monitoring and evaluation of social welfare programmes. This ensures that interventions are continuously assessed for effectiveness, allowing for prompt adjustments and improvements.
8 Community Engagement and Inclusion: AI, IoT, and Cloud Computing facilitate greater community engagement in social initiatives. Online platforms, social media, and IoT-enabled communication channels create opportunities for community members to actively participate, share feedback, and contribute to decision-making processes.
9 Data-Driven Policy Formulation: The integration supports data-driven policy formulation. Policymakers can leverage AI analytics on data collected through IoT devices to gain insights into societal needs, evaluate the impact of existing policies, and formulate evidence-based strategies for social welfare.
10 Educational Advancements: In the realm of education, these technologies enhance learning experiences. AI-driven educational applications, supported by cloud infrastructure, offer adaptive learning, personalized content, and interactive experiences, contributing to improved educational outcomes.
11 Enhanced Disaster Preparedness: AI, IoT, and cloud technologies play a crucial role in disaster preparedness and response. Early warning systems, real-time data analysis, and efficient resource allocation contribute to minimising the impact of natural disasters on communities.
12 Cross-Sector Collaboration: The integration encourages collaboration across different sectors. For instance, partnerships between technology companies, government agencies, non-profit organisations, and communities can leverage these technologies to create holistic solutions for social welfare.
13 Sustainable Development: The use of AI, IoT, and Cloud Computing can contribute to sustainable development goals. By optimising resource usage, improving efficiency, and addressing societal challenges, these technologies play a role in fostering sustainable and resilient communities.
14 Continuous Innovation and Adaptation: The dynamic nature of AI, IoT, and cloud technologies allows for continuous innovation and adaptation in response to evolving societal needs. This ensures that social welfare programmes remain relevant and effective over time.
15 Monitoring and Mitigating Inequalities: The integration helps in monitoring and mitigating inequalities. Through data analytics, it becomes possible to identify disparities in access to services, resources, and opportunities, enabling targeted interventions to address social inequities.

The integration of AI, IoT, and Cloud Computing in social welfare extends beyond ethical considerations to offer a multitude of benefits, ranging from streamlined service delivery to community empowerment and continuous innovation in addressing societal challenges.

1.7. CONCLUSION: UNLEASHING SYNERGY'S POTENTIAL

In delving into the amalgamation of Artificial Intelligence (AI), Internet of Things (IoT), and Cloud Computing within the sphere of social welfare, our exploration has taken us on a voyage through transformative technologies and their profound impact on the tapestry of societal well-being. Our narrative unfolded by navigating the foundational tenets of AI, IoT, and Cloud Computing—understanding their integration and exploring subsequent applications that redefine how societies tackle challenges and uplift communities.

1 Foundational Harmony: Our journey commenced by establishing a foundational understanding of each technology. AI, the realm of intelligent algorithms, and machine learning, endowed us with the cognitive prowess to decipher vast datasets. IoT, with its interconnected sensors, broadened the scope of connectivity to physical objects, creating a network of data-generating entities. Cloud Computing, the scalable and ubiquitous infrastructure, served as the linchpin for integration, providing the necessary computational power and storage.

2 Integration Dynamics: The integration of AI, IoT, and Cloud Computing transcended the sum of its parts. This fusion amplified the capabilities of each technology, birthing a dynamic ecosystem where intelligent algorithms could interpret real-time data from interconnected devices. All this was powered and supported by the scalable resources of cloud infrastructure. This synergy marked a departure from conventional approaches, ushering in a responsive, and interconnected paradigm for addressing societal challenges.

3 Impact on Social Welfare: The impact on social welfare manifested as a multi-faceted transformation across various facets of community life. From healthcare accessibility and predictive diagnostics to streamlined service delivery, these technologies showcased their potential to elevate efficiency, accessibility, and inclusivity. Smart cities optimised traffic flow and public safety, while educational advancements and personalised learning experiences reshaped the educational landscape. The integration played a pivotal role in disaster preparedness, environmental conservation, and predictive analytics of social trends.

4 Applications in Focus: Applications underscored the transformative power of this integration. In healthcare, remote patient monitoring and predictive diagnostics demonstrated how AI, IoT, and Cloud Computing could revolutionise patient care. Smart cities, fuelled by real-time data analytics, illustrated possibilities for efficient urban management. Educational advancements empowered students with personalised learning experiences, while disaster preparedness applications showcased the potential to mitigate the impact of unforeseen challenges.

5 Ethics as a Guiding Principle: Throughout this exploration, ethical considerations served as a guiding principle. Privacy concerns, bias in AI algorithms, security measures, and environmental impacts emerged as critical focal points. Acknowledging the ethical imperative ensured that the integration unfolded responsibly—respecting individual rights, fostering inclusivity, and mitigating potential harms.
6 A Vision for the Future: As we conclude this chapter, the integration of AI, IoT, and Cloud Computing in social welfare unveils a vision for the future. It envisions a world where technology is not merely a tool but a catalyst for positive change. Collaborative decision-making processes, efficient resource allocation, and continuous innovation form the building blocks of resilient communities. The integration aligns itself with sustainable development goals, contributing to a future where social welfare is synonymous with empowerment, inclusivity, and sustainability.
7 Continuous Learning and Adaptation: The integration recognises the dynamic nature of technology. Continuous learning, adaptation, and the willingness to address emerging challenges remain integral to its success. The journey does not conclude but evolves—lessons learned inform future initiatives, creating a culture of adaptability and progress.

The integration of AI, IoT, and Cloud Computing in the domain of social welfare represents a dynamic force reshaping the landscape of societal well-being, transcending mere functionality to become a potent catalyst for positive change. As we navigate the complexities of the future, this synergy stands as a testament to technology's potential to drive empowerment, foster inclusivity, and promote sustainability. It establishes groundwork for a future where innovation benefits all, with evolving technologies holding even greater promise for substantive contributions to human welfare. This integration not only heralds a new era of efficiency and connectivity but also signifies a shift towards a more equitable and inclusive society, where the dividends of technological progress are shared by all.

REFERENCES

Alzubaidi, L., Zhang, J., Humaidi, A., Al-Dujaili, A., Duan, Y., Al-Shamma, O., Santamaría, J., Fadhel, A., Al-Amidie, M., & Farhan, L. (2021). Review of deep learning: Concepts, CNN architectures, challenges, applications, future directions. *Journal of Big Data* 8(53):2–74.

Apo, B. (2021). Study on integration of cloud computing with artificial intelligence and its impact on education, defense and research sectors. *International Journal of Engineering Technology Research & Management* 5(2).

Bakshi, K., & Bakshi, K. (2018). Considerations for artificial intelligence and machine learning: Approaches and use cases. *IEEE Aerospace Conference*. https://doi.org/10.1109/AERO.2018.8396488.

Cowls, J. (2021). AI for social good: Whose good and who's good? Introduction to the special issue on artificial intelligence for social good. *Philosophy & Technology* 34(Suppl 1):S1–S5. https://doi.org/10.1007/s13347-021-00466-3.

Khurana, D., Koli, A., Khatter, K., & Singh, S. (2022). Natural language processing: State of the art, current trends and challenge. *Multimedia Tools and Applications* 82(6). https://doi.org/10.1007/s11042-022-13428-4.

Kumar, S., Tiwar, P., & Zymbler, M. (2019). Internet of Things is a revolutionary approach for future technology enhancement: A review. *Journal of Big Data* 6(111):1–21.

Liu, Y., Dong, B., Guo, B., Yang, J., & Peng, W. (2015). Integration of cloud computing and Internet of Things (IOT) in medical monitoring systems. *International Journal of Hybrid Information Technology* 8(12):367–376. http://doi.org/10.14257/ijhit.2015.8.12.28.

Nizetic, S., Solic, P., López-de-Ipiña González-de-Artaza, D., & Patrono, L. (2020). Internet of Things (IoT): Opportunities, issues and challenges towards a smart and sustainable future. *Journal of Cleaner Production*. https://doi.org/10.1016/j.jclepro.2020.122877.

Parlinska, M., & Petrovsk, I. (2017). Cloud computing and its benefits. *Information Systems in Management* 6(4):309–317. https://doi.org/10.22630/ISIM.2017.6.4.5.

Raj, A., Kumar, A., Sharma, V., Rani, S., Shanu, A., & Bhardwaj, H. (2023). Decipherable for artificial intelligence in medicare: A review. *2023 4th International Conference on Intelligent Engineering and Management (ICIEM)*. https://doi.org/10.1109/ICIEM59379.2023.10165690.

Veni, C. (2018). A study on social networks and cloud computing. *International Journal of Engineering Trends and Applications (IJETA)* 5(1).

Wiley, V., & Lucas, T. (2018). Computer vision and image processing: A paper review. *International Journal of Artificial Intelligence Research* 2(1):22. https://doi.org/10.29099/ijair.v2i1.42.

2 AI, IoT, and Cloud Overview With Respect to Women's Safety

Thangam S., Kevansh Reddy, K. Kushal, and Madhav Manoj

2.1. INTRODUCTION

Women play a vital role in contemporary society, contributing significantly to various domains, including home management, politics, economics, and nation-building. Ensuring the safety of women has become a paramount concern in today's world, with notable challenges, especially in India. Despite the implementation of various legislative measures aimed at curbing incidents, the pace of addressing these issues remains consistent and unchanged.

2.1.1. Increasing Concerns About Women's Safety

The latest data from the National Criminal Records Bureau (NCRB) reveals a worrisome trend, indicating a 15.3% increase in reported cases of crimes against women, rising from 3,71,503 in 2020 to 4,28,278 in 2021. Over the past decade, the vulnerability of girls and women to threats has surged by up to 44%. In response to this concerning scenario, numerous tools and applications have been developed for women's protection, including Hollaback, Fight Back, Guardly, On Watch, Family Locator, Sentinel, Street Safe, Circle of 6, B Safe, Cab 4 Me, and more. Despite the availability of various mobile apps designed to safeguard women, the challenge persists as these tools often require a touch, a click, or a shake, and carrying mobile gadgets at all times may not be feasible.

In Hawassa City, Ethiopia, a stark reality emerged: over 50% of the 199 surveyed women and girls reported experiencing multiple safety threats while using public transport. This isn't an isolated statistic; it echoes the alarming reality of violence against women and girls in public spaces globally. From verbal harassment and groping to physical assault and sexual violence, women and girls face a spectrum of threats that leave lasting emotional and physical scars. The fear of violence itself can deter W&G from using public transport altogether, restricting their access to education, employment, and essential services.

Closer to home, in Bengaluru, the bustling heart of India's tech industry, a different reality emerges for women navigating the city's roads. While the image of

DOI: 10.1201/9781003538172-2

progress and innovation shines bright, it casts a long shadow when it comes to women's safety. A 2023 study by Jana Urban Space paints a stark picture: 53% of female respondents reported feeling unsafe walking on footpaths, citing inadequate lighting, poor infrastructure, and harassment as constant threats. Public transport offers little solace, with a 2022 BMTC study revealing 42% of women experiencing verbal harassment and a shocking 18% facing physical assault on buses. Even the perceived freedom of driving isn't immune, with instances of stalking, road rage, and aggressive behaviour directed at women drivers documented all too frequently. The lack of dedicated lanes, poorly trained personnel, and inadequate street lighting further exacerbate the issue, creating an environment where fear becomes a constant companion.

The lack of safety for women on roads isn't just a statistic—it's a societal failing with far-reaching consequences. It limits women's mobility, stifles their opportunities, and casts a shadow of fear over their daily lives. This not only impacts their individual well-being but hinders the economic and social progress. Prioritizing women's safety on the roads isn't just about individual rights; it's about unlocking the full potential of everyone. By working towards safer roads by taking advantage of modern IoT solutions, we pave the way for a brighter future where all people, regardless of gender, can navigate with freedom and confidence.

2.1.2. Emergence of IoT-Based Solutions for Women's Safety

The integration of Internet of Things (IoT) solutions has emerged as a revolutionary approach, offering speed and feasibility in addressing security concerns. These innovative gadgets and devices, such as IoT-based Women Safety Gadgets (WSG), contribute to enhancing women's protection by leveraging advancements in technology. By seamlessly combining IoT gadgets with mobile phones, these solutions provide real-time communication and location tracking, empowering women to swiftly respond to threatening situations [1].

2.2. IOT-BASED WOMEN SAFETY GADGETS

2.2.1. An Overview and Examples of IoT-Based Women Safety Gadgets

A notable example of IoT in women's safety is the smart device designed for emergency scenarios. This device enables women to pinpoint their exact location and promptly inform law enforcement, enhancing their ability to receive timely assistance in critical situations [2]. Additionally, wireless IoT-based solutions leverage GSM and GPS technology, creating a portable alert system that communicates with concerned authorities, emphasising the importance of speed and efficiency in responding to safety threats [3].

Vahini [4] outlines that, in today's society, women confront an alarming rise in crime, especially among those aged 25 to 35, typically comprising full-time workers and students, compounded by health neglect due to busy schedules. To tackle this pressing issue, a smart and intelligent device is proposed, integrating wearable technology such as a smart-band and discreet webcam, linked via Bluetooth, and continuously monitoring vital signs and activities. The device's application tracks call logs, messages, movement, pulse, blood oxygen levels, and heart rate, securely recording data online. Featuring an SOS button, it triggers distress signals to predefined smartphones and the nearest police station, alongside precise location coordinates, while a discreet webcam captures the perpetrator's image for swift upload to a secure server. This innovative solution aims to bolster women's safety and security, offering real-time protection and evidence gathering capabilities in critical situations.

Harikiran et al. [5] advocates for the development of a groundbreaking device aimed at revolutionising women's safety paradigms. Central to this innovation is the integration of multiple hardware components, including a wearable "Smart band" in constant communication with internet-enabled smartphones. Operated through a sophisticated application programmed with comprehensive data on human behaviour and reactions, the device autonomously detects distress signals and initiates prompt rescue actions. Leveraging GPS and messaging services, the application swiftly dispatches help requests, along with precise location coordinates, to the nearest police stations, relatives, and individuals within the vicinity possessing the application. By seamlessly mobilising both law enforcement and community support, the proposed approach ensures rapid and accurate response mechanisms, fostering a safer environment for women in their daily lives.

SMARISA, a Raspberry Pi Based Smart Ring for Women is proposed by Sogi et al. [6] which is a smart security wearable device for women to enhance their safety. Comprising a Raspberry Pi Zero, Raspberry Pi camera, buzzer, and activation button, SMARISA is designed as a compact and portable smart ring. Activation of the device occurs with a simple button press, allowing the victim to swiftly alert authorities upon being assaulted. Upon activation, SMARISA automatically retrieves the victim's current location and captures an image of the attacker using the Raspberry Pi camera. This critical information, including the location and image link, is promptly transmitted to predefined emergency contact numbers or law enforcement agencies via the victim's smartphone. By eliminating the need for additional hardware devices/modules, the device remains compact and user-friendly, enhancing its practicality and effectiveness in safeguarding women against potential threats.

Venkatesh et al. [7] proposes the use of technologies like Global Positioning System (GPS) and Global Mobile Correspondence System (GSM) in the implementation of devices for women's safety. Specifically, they propose a device that is a wearable "Wrist band" that maintains continuous communication with a smartphone equipped with internet access. The paper delves into detailed insights regarding the design and functionality of the wristband. The device incorporates various components including a trigger, microcontroller (ATmega2560), GSM module (SIM800), GPS module (Neo-6M), IoT module (ESP-12E), neuro stimulator, buzzer, and vibrating sensor. In [8] situations where a woman perceives danger, she activates the trigger of the device. Upon activation, the device utilizes GPS technology to track the user's current location and sends an emergency message via GSM to pre-registered mobile numbers and nearby police stations. The IoT module facilitates efficient tracking and communication with internet platforms. In emergency scenarios, the neurostimulator delivers non-lethal electrical shocks to deter attackers, while the buzzer functions as an audible alarm to alert nearby individuals. Additionally, the vibrating sensor sends the last known location in case the device is tampered with or removed. The primary advantage of this project lies in the device's portability, allowing it to be carried everywhere due to its compact size.

Another proposal included the use of all Raspberry Pi, GPS, and GSM for a novel IoT-based women safety device, offering self-alert and protection functionalities. Sen et al. [9] proposes a device that operates as a three-way safety module, integrating self-defence mechanisms, evidence recording capabilities, and tracking functionalities. Employing a nerve stimulator for self-defence, the device administers shocks to potential attackers upon button activation, while an integrated buzzer provides audible alerts for immediate attention. Additionally, a video camera captures evidence upon button press, storing footage securely in the onboard Raspberry Pi. With GSM and GPS modules, activated via voice commands through a companion Android application, users can trigger emergency alerts by uttering the word "emergency", facilitating automatic SMS alerts with location details and dialling pre-set emergency contacts. Further enhancing communication during emergencies, the device features a microphone and speaker connected to the GSM module. Hardware components, including the Raspberry Pi 3 b+, GSM and GPS modules, relay module, buzzer, and nerve stimulator, synergize to create a comprehensive women's safety device, offering rapid assistance and support in critical situations.

Aljahdali et al. [10] discusses an alternative method to the LoRa technology proposed earlier by using ZigBee instead. ZigBee is a standards-based wireless technology developed to enable low cost, low-power wireless machine-to-machine and IoT networks [11]. It supports a mesh networking protocol to avoid hub devices and create a self-healing architecture. The advantages it offers are the fact that it can increase range on increasing the power source. Moreover, it is not affected by the weather unlike various other forms of signals. WiFi is another wireless communication technology that allows devices to connect to the internet [12]. The ESP8266 WiFi module is predominantly used for the development of IoT applications [13]. It has been designed to support both the TCP/IP capability and the access to any WiFi network for the microcontroller. The module has capabilities to work as a standalone device or as WiFi adaptor to any microcontroller. Manoj et al. [14] has shown the use of WiFi as the communication technology by using the above-mentioned module. He designed a system which uses Infrared (IR) [15] sensors to detect traffic density, and change signal lights overt the internet accordingly to provide a path for rapid response vehicles.

RFID [16] technology presents a promising avenue for bolstering women's safety on roads through its wireless capabilities and data transmission functionalities. By adapting the concept, RFID systems could include tags carrying personal identification or emergency contact details, which individuals, particularly women, could carry for safety purposes. RFID readers strategically positioned along roads or in public spaces could read these tags, transmitting information to central monitoring systems or authorities in case of distress. Integrating features like panic buttons or motion sensors could enhance these systems, providing rapid assistance and security alerts when needed. Leveraging RFID technology offers an innovative approach to address the urgent issue of women's safety in public areas, contributing to the creation of safer and more inclusive environments for everyone.

Moreover, the potential for Smart City technology in improving women's safety lies in its ability to swiftly address concerns and reduce the fear of crime. These solutions, grounded in IoT principles, encompass features that contribute to faster response times, making them a viable and effective choice for safeguarding women in urban environments. As the technology landscape continues to evolve, the speed and feasibility offered by IoT solutions play a crucial role in creating a safer environment for women, aligning with the urgent nature of addressing security threats.

2.3. LoRa TECHNOLOGY IN WOMEN'S SAFETY

2.3.1. Introduction to LoRa Technology

LoRa (Long Range) technology, a low-power, long-range wireless communication protocol, has emerged as a groundbreaking solution for enhancing women's safety. This technology utilises a unique modulation technique that allows for extended communication ranges, making it particularly advantageous in scenarios where widespread coverage is crucial. LoRa-based systems can operate over several kilometres, providing efficient communication even in remote or challenging environments.

2.3.2. Advantages of LoRa in Women's Safety

In the context of women's safety, LoRa technology offers distinct advantages. Its long-range capabilities facilitate swift and reliable communication, ensuring that distress signals or alerts can reach help centres, authorities, or designated contacts promptly. This speed and efficiency are paramount in emergency situations where every moment counts. Moreover, LoRa devices are known for their energy efficiency, enabling prolonged battery life and reducing the need for frequent maintenance. This aspect is crucial for women's safety gadgets, as they can operate seamlessly without the inconvenience of frequent charging or replacement.

The introduction of Intelligent LoRa-based Women Protection and Safety Enhancement solutions exemplifies the practical application of this technology. These innovative devices leverage LoRa to address women's daily safety concerns, emphasising how technology, specifically LoRa, can play a pivotal role in providing swift and effective solutions to enhance women's safety in various situations [8]. Additionally, the use of LoRa in emergency assistance systems, such as those designed for mountaineering or remote scenarios, further underlines its efficiency in ensuring safety in diverse environments [17].

Table 2.1 shows the comparison between popular wireless standards based on their power, range, and data rates highlighting the benefit of using LoRa technology.

TABLE 2.1
Comparison Between Popular Wireless Standards

Name	Power	Range	Data Rates
LoRa	Low	10 km	0.3 to 50 kbps
Wi-Fi	Medium	100 m to 2+ kms	10 to 100+ Mbps
ZigBee	Low	10 to 100 m	20 to 250 kbps
RFID	Low	300 m	40 kbps

2.4. PROPOSED ARCHITECTURE

2.4.1. Design Specifications

1) Hardware Requirements:
   a) *Atmega328P:* is an 8-bit microcontroller Atmel, now a part of microchip technology. They are widely used on the Arduino UNO board. It works up to 20MHz. 32KB flash memory, 2KB SRAM, 1KB EPROM is used. With advanced RISC architecture, it offers efficiency and low energy consumption.
   b) *LoRa SX1278:* 433MHz or 868MHz, operates in 433MHz or 868MHz, using the SX1278 transceiver for long-range communication, reaching several kilometres. Its low power consumption and versatile features, such as error correction and encryption, make it ideal for IoT applications and wireless sensor networks.
   c) *LED:* light emitting diode, is a semiconductor a device that emits light when an electric current passes through it that. It is used to indicate traffic lights.
2) Software Requirements:
   a) Arduino IDE: It is a platform with open-source hardware and software, converting inputs like sensor data into outputs through its user-friendly programming language and IDE. Supporting C and C++, it employs the Wiring software library for efficient input/output procedure.

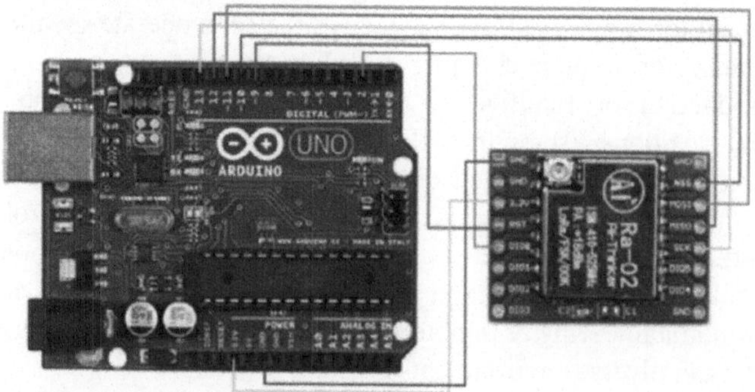

FIGURE 2.1 LoRa connection diagram.

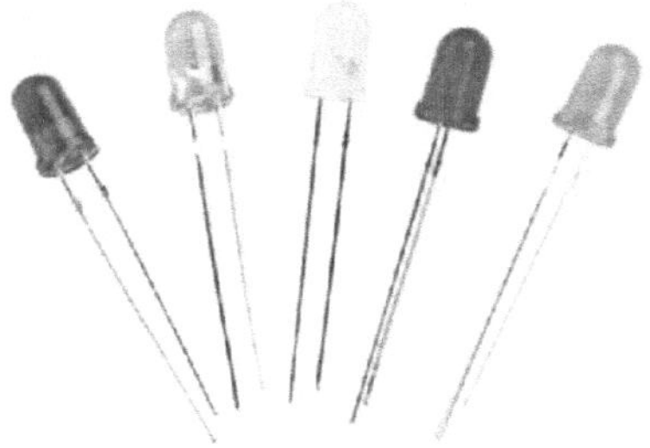

FIGURE 2.2 Led lights.

2.4.2. Methodology

In this advanced security alert system, the integration of two Arduino boards equipped with LoRa (Long Range) modules serves as a sophisticated mechanism for addressing distress situations in public transportation vehicles. The sender Arduino, acting as a transmitter, detects and responds to security incidents by transmitting a specific LoRa packet containing the message "RED" to the receiver Arduino.

The decision to use LoRa technology offers distinct advantages over alternative communication modes, such as mobile networks and WiFi. LoRa's long-range capability ensures that the sender and receiver Arduino boards can maintain connectivity over considerable distances, a critical feature in a transportation context where incidents may occur at varying distances from the traffic intersection. Unlike WiFi, which has limited range, and mobile networks that might face signal issues in certain locations, LoRa provides a robust and reliable connection even in challenging environments.

Furthermore, the low power consumption of LoRa modules is a key factor in the system's design [18]. The energy-efficient operation of LoRa allows the Arduino boards to operate on minimal power, making it suitable for continuous monitoring and swift response. In contrast, mobile networks may consume more power, and WiFi modules often demand higher energy resources, making LoRa a more sustainable choice for prolonged and autonomous operation in a security-focused context.

Upon reception of the "RED" signal, the receiver Arduino, following approval from the traffic controller, promptly triggers the activation of all red lights at the corresponding traffic intersection. This immediate response effectively halts all vehicular and pedestrian traffic, creating a visual alert that communicates an ongoing security concern, necessitating heightened caution in the vicinity. Figure 2.3 illustrates a vehicle approaching a traffic signal. It shows the vehicle transmitting a LoRa signal using a LoRa module and Text labels indicate the traffic light is receiving a signal at the traffic signal post by the receiver module.

Simultaneously, a signal is transmitted from the traffic management system to alert nearby law enforcement authorities. This signal serves as a rapid notification to

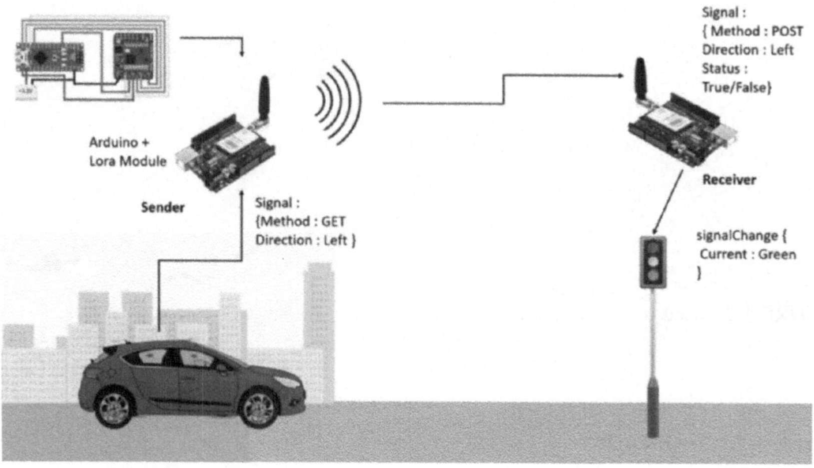

FIGURE 2.3 Proposed architecture design.

the local police or security personnel, prompting them to attend to the security concern immediately. The integration of this signalling system ensures a coordinated response to security incidents, enhancing the overall effectiveness of the security alert system and enabling swift on-the-ground intervention to address and resolve the distress situation.

Once the distress situation is resolved and the sender Arduino ceases transmission, the receiver Arduino seamlessly transitions back to the default traffic light scenario, where the lights alternate between the first red light and the green lights every 5 seconds. This innovative, security-focused adaptation to traffic management not only leverages cutting-edge communication technologies but also integrates Arduino control to provide a robust and responsive solution. The system's ability to quickly address and communicate security concerns on the road reflects a forward-thinking approach to public safety, emphasising the importance of integrating smart technologies into traditional infrastructure for enhanced security and efficiency.

2.5. RESULTS AND DISCUSSION

In the implemented LoRa-based traffic light control system with the provided sender and receiver, the functionality showcases a responsive approach to security-related events on the road. When the emergency signal is triggered due to security constraints associated with a particular vehicle suspected of criminal activities, the sender emits a singular "RED" signal, simulating a security alert system on a public transportation vehicle by activating its LoRa module. The receiver promptly executes a prompt action, leading to the instantaneous transition of all traffic lights to red across the intersection. This creates a visual signalling system indicating a security incident and effectively halting vehicular movement.

FIGURE 2.4 Vehicle's signal triggering the RED-LIGHT to turn ON.

After resolving the security incident and the discontinuation of the "RED" signal, the system smoothly returns to its standard traffic light configuration. In this default mode, the lights alternate between the red and green lights at 5-second intervals, providing an organised and controlled mechanism to maintain normal modes of transport.

The integration of LoRa communication and Arduino control in this security-responsive system enhances its ability to quickly communicate and manage road safety issues, ensuring a rapid response to unexpected events. Figure 2.4 illustrates the safe mode scenario, depicting the immediate transition of all traffic lights to red at the intersection in response to a security incident. Conversely, Figure 2.5 shows the default mode, representing the system's rotation of lights between the first red and green lights every 5 seconds to resume regular traffic patterns. This innovative system demonstrates a balance between security responsiveness and the seamless restoration of normal traffic flow, emphasising the effectiveness of modern technology in enhancing road safety.

2.6. CONCLUSION

In conclusion, the lack of safety for women on roads isn't just a statistic—it's a societal failing with far-reaching consequences. It limits women's mobility, stifles their opportunities, and casts a shadow of fear over their daily lives. This not only impacts their individual well-being but hinders the economic and social progress. Prioritising women's safety on the roads isn't just about individual rights; it's about unlocking the full potential of everyone. By working towards safer roads, we pave the way for a brighter future where all people, regardless of gender, can navigate with freedom and confidence.

FIGURE 2.5 Default mode of traffic light.

REFERENCES

1. Saxena, S., Mishra, S., Baljon, M., Mishra, S., Sharma, S. K., Goel, P., . . . & Kishore, V. (2023). IoT-Based Women Safety Gadgets (WSG): Vision, Architecture, and Design Trends. *Computers, Materials & Continua*, *76*(1).
2. Telagam, N., Kandasamy, N., & Naidu, U. S. (2023). Smart Device for Women's Safety Designed Using IoT and Virtual Instrumentation Browser. *iJIM*, *17*(2), 167.
3. Paknikar, R., Shah, S., & Gharpure, P. (2019, July). Wireless IoT Based Solution for Women Safety in Rural Areas. In *2019 International Conference on Communication and Electronics Systems (ICCES)* (pp. 232–237). IEEE.
4. Vahini, S. (2017). Efficient Tracking for Women Safety and Security Using IoT. *International Journal of Advanced Research in Computer Science*, *8*(9).
5. Harikiran, G. C., Menasinkai, K., & Shirol, S. (2016, March). Smart Security Solution for Women Based on Internet of Things (IOT). In *2016 International Conference on Electrical, Electronics, and Optimization Techniques (ICEEOT)* (pp. 3551–3554). IEEE.
6. Sogi, N. R., Chatterjee, P., Nethra, U., & Suma, V. (2018, July). SMARISA: A Raspberry PI Based Smart Ring for Women Safety Using IoT. In *2018 International Conference on Inventive Research in Computing Applications (ICIRCA)* (pp. 451–454). IEEE.
7. Venkatesh, K., Parthiban, S., Kumar, P. S., & Kumar, C. V. (2021, February). IoT Based Unified Approach for Women Safety Alert Using GSM. In *2021 Third International Conference on Intelligent Communication Technologies and Virtual Mobile Networks (ICICV)* (pp. 388–392). IEEE.
8. Anitha, G., Mohanavel, V., Tamilselvi, M., Ramkumar, G., & Prabu, R. T. (2022, November). An Intelligent LoRa Based Women Protection and Safety Enhancement Using Internet of Things. In *2022 Sixth International Conference on I-SMAC (IoT in Social, Mobile, Analytics and Cloud) (I-SMAC)* (pp. 43–48). IEEE.

9. Sen, T., Dutta, A., Singh, S., & Kumar, V. N. (2019, June). ProTecht–Implementation of an IoT Based 3–Way Women Safety Device. In *2019 3rd International Conference on Electronics, Communication and Aerospace Technology (ICECA)* (pp. 1377–1384). IEEE.
10. Nono, R., Alsudais, R., Alshmrani, R., Alamoudi, S., & Aljahdali, A. O. (2020). Intelligent Traffic Light for Ambulance Clearance. *Advances in Distributed Computing and Artificial Intelligence Journal*, *9*(3).
11. Long, S., & Miao, F. (2019, December). Research on ZigBee Wireless Communication Technology and Its Application. In *2019 IEEE 4th Advanced Information Technology, Electronic and Automation Control Conference (IAEAC)* (pp. 1830–1834). IEEE.
12. Pahlavan, K., & Krishnamurthy, P. (2021). Evolution and Impact of Wi-Fi Technology and Applications: A Historical Perspective. *International Journal of Wireless Information Networks*, *28*, 3–19.
13. Sharmitha, D. (2022, August). Automatic Traffic Clearance for Emergency Vehicles. In *2022 3rd International Conference on Electronics and Sustainable Communication Systems (ICESC)* (pp. 1132–1138). IEEE.
14. Agarwal, S., Anurag, K., Taluja, R., Dewangan, P. K., & Dr. Manoj, H. M. (2022). IoT Based Traffic Management System Prioritizing Emergency Vehicles. *International Journal of Engineering Research & Technology (IJERT)*, *11*(6), 1–7.
15. Patel, D., & Rohilla, Y. (2020, September). Infrared Sensor Based Self–Adaptive Traffic Signal System Using Arduino Board. In *2020 12th International Conference on Computational Intelligence and Communication Networks (CICN)* (pp. 175–181). IEEE.
16. Thangam, S., Tejaswi, M., & Supritha, V. (2023). Low Cost Precision Farming and Remote Monitoring Using Cloud. In *2023 14th International Conference on Computing Communication and Networking Technologies*. ICCCNT.
17. Sharma, D. R., Raghuwanshi, R. R., Chandak, T., & Ramdasi, D. (2023). LoRa-Based IoT System for Emergency Assistance and Safety in Mountaineering. *International Journal of Safety & Security Engineering*, *13*(3).
18. Dandu, R., & Thangam, S. (2023). IoT Based Single Axis Solar Tracker. In *2023 14th International Conference on Computing Communication and Networking Technologies*. ICCCNT.

3 A Comprehensive Review of Addressing Women's Safety Concerns Through an Integrated AI, IoT, and Cloud Computing Approach

Pratibha Singh and Alok Kumar Singh Kushwaha

3.1. INTRODUCTION

Women's safety is a critical and multifaceted issue that demands urgent attention in contemporary society. Despite significant advancements in technology, the challenges surrounding women's safety persist, ranging from the inadequate detection of threats to concerns regarding privacy infringement (Agrawal et al., 2021). In response to these pressing issues, this paper adopts a proactive stance by exploring the potential of integrating artificial intelligence (AI), the Internet of Things (IoT), and cloud computing to enhance women's safety.

The significance of this topic cannot be overstated. Ensuring the safety and security of women is not only a fundamental human right but also a cornerstone of building inclusive and equitable societies (Bento, 2021). However, traditional approaches to addressing safety concerns often fall short in providing real-time monitoring and effective threat detection. Moreover, the pervasiveness of digital technologies has introduced new dimensions to safety challenges, necessitating innovative solutions that leverage the power of AI, IoT, and cloud computing.

Our approach in this paper is twofold: first, to conduct a comprehensive review of existing research and case studies to elucidate the complexities surrounding women's safety; and second, to propose an integrated model that harnesses the synergies of AI, IoT, and cloud computing to overcome these challenges (Ruman et al., 2019). By critically examining the strengths and limitations of this proposed model, we aim to provide actionable insights that can inform the development of robust and efficient security solutions tailored to the specific needs of women. Through our meticulous review, we seek to contribute to the collective knowledge base, fostering a proactive and responsive approach to addressing women's safety concerns in an evolving technological landscape (Venkatesh et al., 2021). By synthesising transformative

 DOI: 10.1201/9781003538172-3

technologies, we not only aspire to address current safety issues but also pave the way for future advancements in women's safety initiatives. Ultimately, our endeavour is to empower women with the tools and resources necessary to navigate their environments safely and confidently.

3.2. RELATED WORK

Efforts to address women's safety have been the subject of extensive research and development across various disciplines. In the realm of technology, researchers have explored innovative approaches to enhance safety measures and mitigate risks faced by women in different contexts. This section provides a synopsis of key studies and initiatives in this domain.

One notable area of research focuses on the application of AI algorithms for threat detection and risk assessment. Studies such as (Kaur et al., 2020) have demonstrated the efficacy of machine learning techniques in analysing patterns of harassment and predicting potential safety threats in public spaces. These AI-driven systems leverage data from diverse sources, including social media, surveillance cameras, and sensor networks to identify and respond to safety concerns in real-time (Das et al., 2021).

In parallel, advancements in IoT technology have enabled the development of smart safety devices and infrastructure. Projects like (Gomathy and Geetha, 2021) have explored the integration of IoT sensors into wearable accessories and urban environments to provide women with discreet means of signalling distress and accessing emergency assistance. These IoT-enabled solutions offer enhanced monitoring capabilities and facilitate rapid response mechanisms, thereby augmenting women's sense of security in various settings.

Furthermore, the emergence of cloud computing has revolutionised the storage and processing of vast amounts of data generated by AI and IoT systems. Cloud-based platforms offer scalability, flexibility, and accessibility, enabling seamless integration and analysis of disparate data sources for improved safety outcomes. Research endeavours such as Sunehra et al., (2020) have leveraged cloud computing infrastructure to deploy AI models for predictive analytics and proactive risk management, demonstrating the potential for scalable and cost-effective safety solutions.

Despite these advancements, challenges remain in achieving comprehensive and inclusive women's safety initiatives. Issues such as privacy concerns, algorithmic bias, and unequal access to technology continue to pose barriers to effective implementation and adoption. Moreover, the intersectionality of gender with other social identities necessitates nuanced approaches that address the diverse safety needs of women from marginalized communities.

While existing research has made significant strides in leveraging technology to enhance women's safety, several gaps and limitations persist, which our approach aims to address comprehensively.

One notable gap in the current state-of-the-art methods is the insufficient integration of multiple technologies to provide holistic safety solutions. While individual studies have explored the application of AI, IoT, and cloud computing in isolation, there remains a dearth of comprehensive models that leverage the synergies of these technologies. Our approach fills this gap by proposing an integrated framework that harnesses the strengths of AI for accurate threat detection, IoT for enhanced data collection and monitoring, and cloud computing for optimised data processing and storage (Cardoso and Landers, 2019).

Furthermore, existing approaches (Chowdhuri, 2023) often overlook the intersectional nature of safety concerns, failing to adequately address the diverse needs of women from marginalised communities. Our approach recognises the importance of intersectionality and aims to develop inclusive solutions that consider the unique experiences and vulnerabilities of women based on factors such as race, ethnicity, socioeconomic status, and sexual orientation.

Another limitation of current methods is the lack of emphasis on privacy preservation and user autonomy. While technology-driven safety solutions offer unprecedented capabilities for monitoring and surveillance, they also raise concerns about data privacy and potential misuse of personal information. Our approach prioritises privacy by design principles, incorporating robust encryption mechanisms and user-centric controls to ensure that women feel empowered and secure in their use of safety technologies.

Moreover, there is a need for empirical validation and real-world deployment of proposed safety solutions to assess their effectiveness in diverse contexts. While many studies have demonstrated the feasibility of AI, IoT, and cloud computing in controlled environments, their scalability and adaptability in real-world settings remain uncertain. Our approach emphasises rigorous testing and validation through pilot implementations and field trials, allowing for iterative refinement and optimisation based on user feedback and performance metrics.

In summary, our approach builds upon the existing state-of-the-art methods by addressing gaps related to technology integration, intersectionality, privacy preservation, and empirical validation. By proposing a comprehensive framework that combines AI, IoT, and cloud computing, we aim to develop inclusive and effective safety solutions that empower women to navigate their environments safely and confidently.

3.3. APPROACHES

This review utilised a systematic literature review methodology, chosen for its organised approach in searching, classifying, and synthesising literature to achieve predefined objectives, thereby identifying areas for future research. The research methodology, involved three main stages. Initially, research objectives were defined, leading to the elaboration of research questions. Subsequently, a search scheme was established to identify relevant literature, followed by the development of inclusion/exclusion and quality scoring criteria. Following the establishment of criteria, studies were shortlisted based on inclusion/exclusion criteria, and then ranked according to quality scoring criteria.

The assessment of focuses on the technologies employed in IoT-based women's safety devices is outlined in Figure 3.1. These devices play a crucial role in alerting guardians when a woman is in danger. Main technologies utilised include GPS (Global Positioning System), GSM (Global System for Mobile Communication), and Raspberry Pi. GPS tracks and locates the victim's position, while GSM sends danger alerts to guardians. Raspberry Pi, a small computer chip-based technology, activates

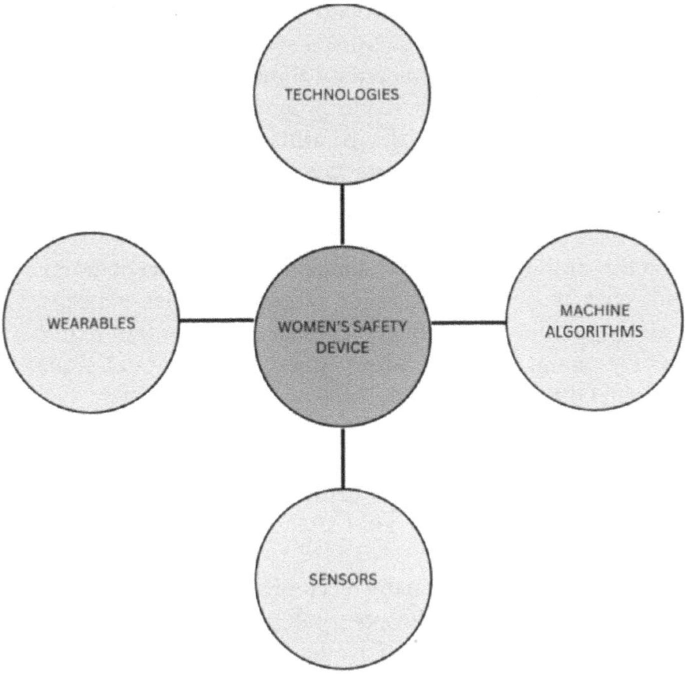

FIGURE 3.1 Classification of women's safety devices utilising Internet of Things (IoT) technology.

various features in safety devices (Jude et al., 2021). While Bluetooth is also used, its limited range makes it less effective in cases like kidnapping where the perpetrator can quickly move out of reach. GPS and GSM are predominant due to their tracking and communication capabilities, essential in women's safety systems. Modernisation has led to innovative devices like smart ring, integrating Raspberry Pi Zero and Raspberry Pi Camera, which automatically alerts guardians when activated.

However, some devices rely on manual activation, which poses limitations. For instance, in a device proposed by Kshirsagar (2020), the victim must press a button, delaying the alert. Similarly, another device described by the author requires multiple triggers and lacks automatic activation, rendering it less effective during emergencies (Bhate, 2019).

In summary, while various technologies like GPS, GSM, and Raspberry Pi enhance women's safety devices, automatic activation mechanisms are crucial to ensure timely responses in emergencies. This assessment underscores the importance of technological advancements in addressing women's safety concerns effectively. Ghosh and Hasan (2021) developed a sophisticated device integrating GPS, GSM, and Bluetooth modules, but its estimated cost may be prohibitive for lower-income women. However, ensuring the safety of all women, regardless of economic status, is imperative. Another study employed Raspberry Pi 3 along with GPS and GSM modules, automatically connecting to the internet upon activation to send location URLs to guardians (Seth et al., 2018). Nonetheless, this device's reliance on internet connectivity limits its effectiveness in areas with poor network coverage, unlike the model proposed in this paper, which functions offline. (Bento, 2021) proposed a device utilising machine learning algorithms, albeit with the drawback of high cost due to the inclusion of a GSM module. This paper aims to replicate the functionality of (Bhardwaj and Aggarwal, 2014) but at a more affordable price point accessible to all women in society. Agrima in Zhang (2009) presented a device activated by voice recognition to eliminate the need for physical interaction. If the recognised voice matches, GSM automatically alerts guardians and police via GPS. However, failure to recognise the voice leaves the victim unable to inform guardians. Ahir et al. (2018) designed a smart band with GPS and GSM, requiring manual activation by the victim, highlighting the need for automatic operation. Conversely, Syafrudin et al. (2018) proposed a comprehensive women's security system with GPS and GSM modules, a built-in camera, and audio recorder for police investigation. However, the audible activation buzzer may alert attackers, necessitating a more discreet design.

IoT-based evidence collection and women protection devices in (Sunehra et al., 2020) integrated GPS, GSM, and Raspberry Pi but required manual activation, posing challenges in emergencies. Similarly, the Guardian device in Das et al. (2021) utilised GPS, GSM, and IoT modules but relied on manual activation, contrasting with the autonomous operation advocated here. The BEACON device introduced in Kian (2019) incorporated GPS, GSM, and Bluetooth, assessing the woman's posture to predict danger. While innovative, devices employing these technologies often require constant internet connectivity, increasing costs, a streamlined and cost-effective system is essential to facilitate effective communication between women and their guardians.

The main features of women's safety devices are (Srinivasan et al., 2022) introduced a jacket equipped with GPS tracking and a temperature sensor, alongside a buzzer and electric shock feature for self-defence. However, the audible buzzer activation may alert attackers. Similarly, Ghosh and Hasan (2021) developed a device incorporating a panic button with GPS tracking and GSM modules. This device utilises an accelerometer to trigger an alarm if the woman falls, but its jacket-based design may not be suitable for constant wear.

Additionally, a smart ring designed in (Manikumar, 2021) includes a buzzer for activation, sending the current location via GPS and capturing the attacker's image through a Raspberry Pi camera. Despite its self-defence features, this device requires human interaction. Cardoso and Landers (2019) introduced a low-cost smart footwear device activated by foot tapping, utilising GPS and GSM. However, its motion sensor may lead to false activations. Another example is a smart band or watch that collects location, posture, and pulse-rate data, transmitting it via GSM through Raspberry Pi. Yet, changes in pulse-rate may affect accuracy. Chaware and Nimbarte (2020) automated a device to collect pulse-rate and pressure, sending messages to relatives without physical interaction, though health issues may influence readings.

Similarly, a smart, wearable band tracks location, sending alerts to the police via Wi-Fi module in Raspberry Pi 3. Machine learning is employed to monitor pulse-rate and temperature, but real-time training data may be necessary. Reddy et al. (2021) proposed a smart, wearable device activating email alerts and image capture via GSM/GPRS and GPS, respectively. However, manual activation and lack of sensor integration limit its functionality.

Finally, an advanced smart protection system (Shivani et al., 2018) not only collects data and tracks location but also streams live video and activates a loud buzzer for alerts. Despite its comprehensive features, sensor combinations may vary across devices.

Assessment of focuses on the machine learning algorithms utilised to identify threats to women's safety in IoT devices. These algorithms are tailored to learn individual patterns in women's body states, such as heartbeat and temperature fluctuations. For instance, logistic regression is employed for classification tasks, effectively predicting danger indicators based on pulse-rate and body temperature readings. Additionally, a smart wristband in Roy et al. (2015) utilises logistic regression to determine if a woman is in danger, requiring a substantial amount of real-time training data for accurate predictions.

Furthermore, Samantha developed a device (Ramesh Reddy et al., 2023) using logistic regression to detect abnormal heartbeat and temperature patterns, automatically alerting guardians when danger is predicted. However, reliance on an online portal for accurate predictions poses limitations in areas with limited internet connectivity.

Another approach involves Hidden Markov Models (HMM), offering enhanced prediction capabilities and sensitivity to suspicious activities. In women's safety applications, HMM analyses facial recognition and verbal conversations, achieving high accuracy rates. However, the device activation is contingent on after-shock events, potentially limiting its effectiveness in immediate threats.

Similarly, another HMM-based device in Reddy et al. (2021) utilises IoT and voice recognition to collect data but may fail to protect women in dire situations if attackers recognise and silence the victim. Overall, while these machine learning algorithms offer promising capabilities for threat identification in women's safety devices, considerations such as real-time data availability and device vulnerabilities must be addressed for optimal effectiveness.

Pressure and temperature sensors are integral components of women's safety systems, employed for outlier detection. When either sensor detects abnormal readings, indicating potential danger, the system identifies the threat. For example, the temperature sensor may trigger if someone suddenly approaches the woman, causing a rise in ambient temperature (Hyndavi, 2020). However, a limitation of outlier detection is that temperature fluctuations can occur for various reasons, including health issues.

IoT-based wearable devices incorporate embedded sensors to gather readings, which are then transmitted via internet connection if specific thresholds are surpassed (Pandey, 2018). These wearables, designed for women's safety, come in various forms such as smart clothing, bands, and accessories. However, an examination of the literature reveals that technological advancements in the field of women's safety devices remain limited.

A proposed innovative wearable device, as suggested in Pandey (2018), offers discreet protection by integrating heartbeat and temperature sensors with a logistic regression model. This smart band presents an intelligent safety solution for women. However, reliance on an online portal for connectivity may pose a risk if internet speed is slow, potentially compromising the device's effectiveness in safeguarding women.

3.4. DISCUSSIONS AND ANALYSIS

In this section, we engage in a thorough discussion and analysis of the review's outcomes and discoveries. Through an in-depth examination of the findings, we put forward a taxonomy for IoT-based women's safety devices, pinpoint the gaps and challenges evident in current devices, propose a model for practitioners and researchers to serve as a blueprint for constructing such devices, and outline implications for future directions within this domain.

Within our designed taxonomy, we delineate four fundamental attributes crucial to understanding IoT-based women's safety devices: IoT-based safety sensors, dominant features, machine learning algorithms, and the integration of IoT-based wearables with embedded sensors. These attributes encapsulate the essence of our analysis, which focuses on monitoring, controlling, and tracking precision attacks and victim locations through advanced IoT technologies.

The sensors employed in women's safety devices play a pivotal role, capturing and relaying invaluable data that is essential for threat detection and response. Additionally, we highlight the dominant features of IoT-based devices, which enhance their efficiency and usability in diverse situations, empowering victims to respond effectively to potential threats without explicit interactions.

Moreover, our taxonomy underscores the pivotal role of machine learning algorithms, which are trained to interpret sensor data and discreetly alert guardians when women may be in danger. This automated alert generation feature is a crucial aspect of ensuring swift and covert communication in critical situations.

Furthermore, we discuss the integration of IoT-based wearables with embedded sensors, emphasising their role in sensing danger and activating machine learning algorithms for threat identification. These wearables leverage hidden sensors to seamlessly collect user data, facilitating automated device operation without human intervention.

Our exploration reveals the importance of multiple sensors within wearable devices for optimal functionality. While some devices, like the smart ring proposed by Nanekar et al. (2021) may lack sensors initially, their potential for enhancement through sensor integration is evident. By incorporating multiple sensors with diverse functionalities into a single wearable device, our proposed architecture aims to provide comprehensive protection to women in various challenging scenarios.

3.4.1. CHALLENGES

In the 21st century, the focus on women empowerment extends beyond financial security to encompass social safety (Kaur et al., 2020). Despite the prevalence of

CCTV cameras, women still require protection, especially when guardians cannot accompany them at all times due to modern lifestyle demands. Consequently, technological solutions are essential for ensuring women's safety in the absence of direct supervision.

- In existing IoT-based women's safety devices is the reliance on only one or two sensors, which may lead to inaccuracies and suboptimal results. Devices equipped with multiple sensors offer enhanced accuracy and resilience, as they can compensate for sensor failures and provide comprehensive threat detection capabilities.
- Given the diverse age groups of women and their varying physiological norms, IoT-based wearable devices must adapt their threat detection algorithms based on sensor readings relative to age-specific ranges. Utilising multiple sensors and integrating their input values can improve the accuracy of threat detection by considering a broader spectrum of factors (Kumar et al., 2021).
- Challenges such as waterproofing and battery life affect the reliability of wearable devices. Ensuring water resistance and optimising battery longevity are crucial for uninterrupted operation, particularly in emergency situations where device failure is not an option.
- A significant gap identified in current research is the reliance on human interaction with devices. To address this, efforts should focus on developing automated systems that operate independently of human intervention. While some studies have proposed human interaction-free solutions, achieving full automation remains a priority to ensure prompt response in critical situations.
- The accuracy of existing devices, although improved by machine learning algorithms, still requires enhancement. Despite notable progress, none of the devices exhibit 100% accuracy, indicating the need for further refinement in prediction models and data sets.

In summary, while numerous devices have been designed, each has its shortcomings. The primary challenge lies in minimising human interaction with devices and ensuring seamless operation in emergency scenarios. As women may not be in a state of consciousness to operate devices during an attack, there is a pressing need for automatic rescue mechanisms to safeguard victims effectively (Farooq et al., 2023).

3.5. CONCLUSION

This study presents a comprehensive systematic literature review focused on IoT-based devices designed to enhance women's safety, addressing threats such as molestation, harassment, rape, and abuse. By meticulously analysing 34 research articles sourced from reputable publications, this review aims to provide insights into the landscape of women's safety technology. To gather relevant literature, a robust search strategy was employed, incorporating various keywords and their synonyms. Careful consideration was given to potential variations in terminology used across studies, ensuring comprehensive coverage of the topic. Classification of keywords into primary, secondary, and tertiary categories, coupled with the application of Boolean operators, helped refine the search string and minimise the risk of overlooking relevant studies. Additionally, the classification of studies was independently reviewed by two experts, with any discrepancies resolved through thorough discussion. Through detailed analysis, it was revealed that IoT-based women's safety devices leverage diverse technologies, features, sensors, and machine learning algorithms. These aspects were systematically categorised to create taxonomy, providing a structured framework for understanding the functionalities of these devices (Farooq et al., 2015). Despite the varied features offered by these systems, certain shortcomings hinder their efficacy in addressing safety threats effectively. This review also highlights the gaps and challenges associated with existing devices, shedding light on areas where improvements are needed to enhance functionality and effectiveness. Furthermore, an architectural model for IoT-based women's safety devices is proposed as a forward-looking recommendation, aiming to guide future research and development efforts in this domain. Overall, this study serves as a valuable resource for researchers seeking to gain insights into the current state-of-the-art in IoT-based women's safety devices. It also offers practical guidance for practitioners involved in the design and implementation of effective safety solutions tailored to the needs of women in various contexts.

REFERENCES

Agrawal, A.; Ankita Maurya; Amruta Patil, "Voice controlled tool for anytime safety of women," *Journal of Emerging Technology and Innovative Tool*, vol. 8, no. 5, 2021.

Ahir, Shivani; Smit Kapadia; Jigar Chauhan; Nidhi Sanghavi. "The personal stun-a smart device for women's safety," in *International Conference on Smart City and Emerging Technology (ICSCET)*, 2018. https://doi.org/10.1109/ICSCET.2018.8537376.

Bento, Carolina, "Decision tree classifier explained in real-life: Picking a vacation destination," 2021. https://towardsdatascience.com/decision-tree-classifier-explained-in-real-life-picking-a-vacation-destination-6226b2b60575.

Bhardwaj, N.; Nitish Aggarwal. "Design and development of 'Suraksha': A women safety device," *International Journal of Information & Computational Technology*, vol. 4, no. 8 spl., pp. 793–796, 2014.

Bhate, A.; Parveen Sultana H. "Smart wrist band for women security using logistic regression technique," *Blue Eyes Intelligence Engineering and Sciences Publication*, 2019. https://www.ijrte.org/wp-content/uploads/papers/v8i1/A2161058119.pdf.

Cardoso, Lauren F.; Sara Landers. "Recent and emerging technologies: Implications for women's safety," *Technology in Society*, vol. 58, 2019. https://doi.org/10.1016/j.techsoc.2019.01.001.

Chaware, Mona; Mrudula Nimbarte. "Smart safety gadgets for women: A survey," *Journal of University of Shanghai for Science and Technology*, vol. 22, no. 12, 2020.

Chowdhuri, A.N. "Suraksha: The ultimate self-defense kit for women," *International Journal of Engineering Research & Technology (IJERT)*, vol. 12, no. 2, 2023. https://doi.org/10.17577/IJERTV12IS020039.

Das, Sagarika; Baswakiran; Shweta Dasar; Jagadeesha; Shrinivas Rao. "Women's security system," *International Journal of Engineering Research & Technology (IJERT)*, pp. 121–126, 2021.

Farooq, M.S.; A. Masooma; U. Omer; R. Tehseen; S.A.M. Gilani; Z. Atal. "The role of IoT in woman's safety: A systematic literature review," *IEEE Access*, vol. 11, pp. 1234–1250, 2023. https://doi.org/10.1109/ACCESS.2023.3252903.

Farooq, M.U.; Muhammad Waseem; Sadia Mazhar; Anjum Khairi; Talha Kamal. "A review on Internet of Things (IoT)," *International Journal of Computer Applications*, pp. 174–179, 2015.

Ghosh, Prottasha; Emran Hasan. "Smart security device for women based on IoT using raspberry Pi," in *2nd International Conference on Robotics, Electrical and Signal Processing Techniques (ICREST)*. Dhaka, Bangladesh, 2021.

Gomathy, Dr. C.K.; S. Geetha. "Women safety device using IoT," *International Journal of Scientific Research in Engineering and Management (IJSREM)*, vol. 5, no. 10, 2021.

Hyndavi, Rakesh. "Smart wearable device for women safety using IoT," in *5th International Conference on Communication and Electronics Systems (ICCES)*, pp. 459–463, 2020. https://doi.org/10.1109/ICCES48766.2020.9138047.

Jude, A.B.; D. Singh; S. Islam, et al. "An artificial intelligence based predictive approach for smart waste management." *Wireless Personal Communications*, 2021. https://doi.org/10.1007/s11277-021-08803-7.

Kaur, Deepinder; Ravita Chahar; Jatinder Ashta. "IOT based women security: A contemplation," in *International Conference on Emerging Smart Computing and Informatics (ESCI)*, pp. 257–262, 2020. https://doi.org/10.1109/ESCI48226.2020.9167584.

Kian, F.R. "Patterns of intimate partner violence: A study of female victims in urban versus rural areas of Southeast Iran," *Shiraz E-Medical Journal*, vol.20, no. 10, 2019.

Kshirsagar, P. "Brain tumor classification and detection using neural network," in *Proceedings of the 2013 Fourth International Conference on Computing, Communications and Networking Technologies (ICCCNT)*, pp. 83–88, IEEE, Tiruchengode, India, January, 2020.

Kumar, K. Venkatesh; S. Parthiban; P.S. Kumar; C.V. Kumar. "IoT based unified approach for women safety alert using GSM," in *Third International Conference on Intelligent Communication Technologies and Virtual Mobile Networks (ICICV)*, pp. 388–392, 2021. https://doi.org/10.1109/ICICV50876.2021.9388415.

Manikumar, M. Murugan. "Guardian device for women—a survey and comparison study," in *Second International Conference on Robotics, Intelligent Automation and Control Technologies (RIACT 2021)*. Chennai, India, 2021.

Nanekar, Nikhil Balu; Omkar Subhash More; Gangaram Kauthale. "Woman safety device," *International Advanced Research Journal in Science, Engineering and Technology*, vol. 8, no. 5, 2021. https://doi.org/10.17148/IARJSET.2021.8596.

Pandey, Muskan. "Women safety device designed using IoT and machine learning," in *2018 IEEE Smart World, Ubiquitous Intelligence & Computing, Advanced & Trusted Computing, Scalable Computing & Communications, Cloud & Big Data Computing, Internet of People and Smart City Innovation*, pp. 1204–1210, 2018. https://doi.org/10.1109/SmartWorld.2018.00210.

Ramesh Reddy, B.; T. Sowjanya; N. Bala Subrahmanayam; G. Mahantesh; S. Prudhvi. "IOT based smart protective equipment for women," *Materials Today: Proceedings*, vol. 80, no. 3, pp. 2895–2900, 2023. https://doi.org/10.1016/j.matpr.2021.07.058.

Reddy, Kakanuru Manikanteswara; Sri Raksha S.; Yerrapadu Raghavendra Reddy; Ediga Indu Meghana; Prabhat Kumar Panda. "Design of a smart women safety band using IOT and machine learning," *International Journal of Contemporary Architecture*, vol. 8, no. 1s, 2021.

Roy, Sohini; Abhijit Sharma; Uma Bhattacharya. "MoveFree: A ubiquitous system to provide women safety," in *Third International Symposium on Women in Computing and Informatics WCI '15At*. Kochi, India, 2015. https://doi.org/10.1145/2791405.2791415.

Ruman, Md. Raseduzzaman; Joybrota Kumar Badhon; Saikat Saha. "Safety assistant and harassment prevention for women," pp. 346–350, 2019. https://doi.org/10.1109/ICAEE48663.2019.8975648.

Seth, Debojyoti; Ahana Chowdhury; Shreya Ghosh. "A hidden Markov model and Internet of Things hybrid based smart women safety device," in *2nd International Conference on Power, Energy and Environment: Towards Smart Technology (ICEPE)*, 2018. https://doi.org/10.1109/EPETSG.2018.8658848.

Srinivasan, S.; P. Muthu Kannan; R. Kumar. "A machine learning approach to design and develop a BEACON device for women's safety," pp. 111–115, 2022. https://doi.org/10.1007/978-3-030-90119-6_9.

Sunehra, Dhiraj; V. Sai Sreshta; V. Shashank; B. Uday Kumar Goud. "Raspberry Pi based smart wearable device for women safety using GPS and GSM technology," in *2020 IEEE International Conference for Innovation in Technology (INOCON)*, 2020. https://doi.org/10.1109/INOCON50539.2020.9298449.

Syafrudin, Muhammad; Ganjar Alfian; Norma Latif Fitriyani; Jongtae Rhee. "Performance analysis of IoT-based sensor, big data processing, and machine learning model for real-time monitoring system in automotive manufacturing," *Sensors*, 2018. https://doi.org/10.3390/s18092946.

Venkatesh, K.; S. Parthiban; P.S. Kumar; C.V. Kumar. "IoT based unified approach for women safety alert using GSM," in *Third International Conference on Intelligent Communication Technologies and Virtual Mobile Networks (ICICV)*, 2021. https://doi.org/10.1109/ICICV50876.2021.9388415.

Zhang, Sun. "Study of ZigBee wireless Mesh networks," in *2009 Ninth International Conference on Hybrid Intelligent Systems*, 2009. https://doi.org/10.1109/HIS.2009.164.

4 Secure Women's Safety Platform Using Ethereum Blockchain

Shinu M. Rajagopal, Supriya M., and Rajkumar Buyya

4.1. INTRODUCTION

In today's dynamic technological landscape, the convergence of Artificial Intelligence (AI), Internet of Things (IoT), and blockchain has opened up unprecedented avenues to tackle pressing societal issues. This chapter introduces a visionary project aimed at leveraging these cutting-edge technologies to address the crucial challenge of women's safety. The development of a decentralised application, rooted in the Ethereum blockchain, promotes a secure and immutable environment for the deployment of innovative safety solutions. By utilising the power of AI, IoT, and cloud computing, the proposed platform proposes to establish a robust system that not only responds to emergencies but also proactively identifies potential threats through AI-driven anomaly detection. The idea of this approach lies in the concept of decentralised identity management, facilitated by Ethereum's blockchain technology. Through the implementation of smart contracts, users gain control over their personal information, ensuring tamper-proof storage and fostering a sense of empowerment (Henry et al., 2018)

Central to the project is the integration of IoT wearable devices equipped with advanced sensors such as GPS, accelerometers, and panic buttons, enabling real-time location tracking and swift response to emergency situations. The AI-powered anomaly detection system analyses user behaviour patterns, enabling the platform to detect deviations and trigger timely alerts, thereby enhancing user safety. A standout feature of the project is its emergency alert system, allowing users to activate a panic button on their wearable devices, initiating an immediate broadcast on the Ethereum network. This prompts the notification of predefined contacts and relevant authorities, expediting response times and ensuring the safety of users (Zhou & Paffenroth, 2017; Chen et al., 2018; Akram et al., 2019).

Moreover, the project underscores user-centric data management, emphasising the retention of data ownership and privacy through Ethereum's blockchain capabilities. Users can manage access permissions through smart contracts, ensuring

DOI: 10.1201/9781003538172-4

the security of their personal information. The immutability of blockchain technology guarantees the integrity of personal data, laying a trustworthy foundation for informed decision-making (Zyskind & Nathan, 2015). In essence, the Secure Women Safety Platform epitomises the integration of state-of-the-art technologies to create a comprehensive solution for women's safety. By deploying Ethereum's blockchain, the project supports decentralisation, security, and user empowerment, signalling a significant stride towards building safer and more secure communities. This initiative not only addresses immediate safety concerns but also sets a precedent for future innovations in personal security.

4.1.1. Technological Transformation in Society

In today's ever-evolving landscape, technology plays an increasingly pivotal role in shaping our society. From the proliferation of smartphones to the integration of artificial intelligence into everyday devices, the impact of technological advancements is undeniable. This transformation extends beyond mere convenience, touching upon fundamental aspects of our lives, including safety and security. As we navigate the complexities of modern living, the intersection of AI, IoT, and blockchain technologies emerges as a solution, offering innovative answers to address pressing societal challenges.

The combination of AI, IoT, and blockchain presents an unprecedented opportunity to revolutionise safety measures and empower individuals. By leveraging AI's analytical abilities, IoT's real-time data collection capabilities, and blockchain's decentralised nature, novel approaches to enhancing safety and security are within reach. This transformative journey is exemplified by initiatives like the Secure Women Safety Platform, which harnesses the collective power of these technologies to create a comprehensive safety solution. As we embark on this technological revolution, we pave the way for a future where safety is not just a concept but a tangible reality, underpinned by the seamless integration of cutting-edge innovations.

4.1.2. Intersection of AI, IoT, and Blockchain

The convergence of Artificial Intelligence (AI), Internet of Things (IoT), and blockchain technologies represent a transformative force in addressing societal challenges, particularly in the domain of safety and security. AI, with its ability to analyse vast datasets and extract meaningful insights, enables proactive threat detection and response. When integrated with IoT devices, which encompass a myriad of sensors capable of collecting real-time data, AI becomes empowered to monitor user activities, detect anomalies, and respond swiftly to emergent situations (Khandelwal et al., 2018). Furthermore, blockchain technology, renowned for its decentralised and tamper-proof nature, provide a secure and transparent platform for managing data and transactions.

In the context of the Secure Women Safety Platform, the intersection of these technologies forms the cornerstone of its innovative approach to women's safety.

By leveraging AI-powered anomaly detection, the platform can analyse user behaviour patterns in real-time, identifying deviations that may indicate potential threats. This proactive approach enhances user safety by enabling timely intervention and response. Additionally, the integration of IoT wearable devices equipped with GPS, accelerometers, and panic buttons facilitates continuous monitoring of user activities, ensuring fast assistance in emergency situations. The utilisation of Ethereum's blockchain ensures decentralised identity management, tamper-proof storage of user data, and user-centric control over personal information through smart contracts (Gaetani et al., 2017). This integration of AI, IoT, and blockchain not only addresses immediate safety concerns but also lays the groundwork for future innovations in personal security, marking a significant advancement towards building safer and more secure communities.

4.2. LITERATURE SURVEY

In the realm of women's safety, the integration of blockchain technology and anomaly detection techniques has garnered attention from researchers aiming to enhance security and prevent incidents of violence. The following discussion explores the literature relevant to this field. Cai et al. suggests that the evolution of blockchain systems is essential for comprehending the significance of decentralised applications and forecasting the future value of blockchain (Cai et al., 2018). Through a comprehensive survey of the current landscape, the authors highlight the critical role of dApps and engage in discussions regarding the trajectory of blockchain development. In addressing the escalating concerns surrounding surveillance and privacy breaches, Zyskind and Nathan propose a paradigm shift away from the prevailing model of centralised data collection and control. It concludes by exploring potential extensions to blockchain technology, envisioning its broader application as a comprehensive solution to address trust and security challenges in society's computing landscape (Zyskind & Nathan, 2015).

In response to the growing significance of Medical IoT devices in revolutionising healthcare, Pawar et al. propose a novel approach to Personal Health Information Management Systems which encompasses four integral layers: a blockchain layer for hosting a secure and immutable database, an IoT device layer for collecting patient bio-signals, an application layer for facilitating health data sharing, and an adapter layer bridging the blockchain with the application layer (Pawar et al., 2022). Recognising the inconveniences and vulnerabilities inherent in traditional document-based registration processes, Jamal et al. propose a novel approach that empowers registered individuals to access and control their personal records securely. The envisioned system caters to three key stakeholders: users, authorities, and third-party requesters, offering a decentralised framework that mitigates the risks of data breaches and identity theft (Jamal et al., 2019). Aliyu et al. present a pioneering research endeavour that aims to revolutionise child safety through the integration of anomaly detection techniques in wearable location trackers. Focusing on the untapped potential of these trackers to identify outlying incidents, the study underscores the critical need for advanced technological solutions in combating child loss and kidnapping cases. Central to their approach is the incorporation of machine learning, particularly unsupervised outlier detection techniques, into low-powered gyroscope-enabled electronic trackers (Aliyu et al., 2022).

In our exploration of user identity saving mechanisms and anomaly detection systems for women's safety, a notable void emerges in the utilisation of blockchain technology coupled with advanced anomaly detection techniques. While blockchain has demonstrated its efficacy in enhancing security and decentralisation in identity management, its fusion with anomaly detection specifically tailored for women's safety still remains new. We propose a novel framework that integrates blockchain-based user identity saving mechanisms with anomaly detection systems, offering a comprehensive solution to empower women in managing their identities securely while proactively identifying and addressing potential threats. By harnessing the immutable and transparent nature of blockchain alongside advanced anomaly detection algorithms, our approach seeks to fill a critical gap in existing safety technologies, promising enhanced effectiveness and reliability in safeguarding the well-being and autonomy of women. This initiative underscores the urgency of leveraging cutting-edge technology to combat gender-based violence and harassment, calling for further research and development to realize its full potential in promoting women's safety and empowerment globally.

4.3. DEVELOPMENT OF DECENTRALISED APPLICATION

The vision for the Secure Women Safety Platform involves the development of a decentralised application utilising the Ethereum blockchain. This approach ensures a secure and tamper-proof environment for deploying innovative safety solutions. The integration of AI, IoT, and cloud computing technologies forms the backbone of the platform, enabling a comprehensive and reliable system capable of proactively identifying potential threats through AI-powered anomaly detection. Central to the platform's architecture is decentralised identity management, facilitated by Ethereum's blockchain (Baucas et al., 2023; Dorri et al., 2017; Taş & Tanrıöver, 2019). Through the use of smart contracts, users maintain control over their personal information, ensuring tamper-proof storage and safeguarding their privacy. The core of the platform's AI-powered anomaly detection system lies in its ability to analyse user behaviour patterns in real-time. By processing data from IoT devices, the system can identify deviations such as unusual travel routes or activity patterns, triggering real-time alerts in response to potential threats.

Furthermore, the platform incorporates an emergency alert system, allowing users to activate a panic button on their wearable devices. This action initiates an emergency signal broadcasted on the Ethereum network, notifying predefined contacts and relevant authorities promptly. Emphasising user-centric data management, the platform ensures that users retain ownership of their data and can manage access permissions through smart contracts. Overall, the Secure Women Safety Platform represents a cutting-edge integration of state-of-the-art technologies, paving the way for safer and more secure communities while setting a blueprint for future innovations in personal security.

4.3.1. Utilisation of Ganache Ethereum Blockchain

The Secure Women Safety Platform leverages the Ethereum blockchain, utilising the Ganache tool for local blockchain development and testing. This decision ensures the creation of a secure and tamper-proof environment for deploying innovative safety solutions. Ganache, a personal blockchain for Ethereum development, allows for rapid prototyping and testing of smart contracts and decentralised applications in a controlled environment.

By utilising Ganache, developers can simulate Ethereum blockchain networks locally, enabling seamless integration and testing of smart contracts responsible for decentralised identity management and tamper-proof storage of user identities. Moreover, Ganache provides robust testing capabilities, allowing developers to verify the functionality and security of the platform's smart contracts before deployment to the main Ethereum network (Taş & Tanrıöver, 2019). Through the utilisation of Ganache Ethereum blockchain, the Secure Women Safety Platform ensures the reliability and scalability of its decentralised application. By leveraging this tool, developers can accelerate the development process while maintaining the integrity and security of the platform's underlying blockchain infrastructure. This strategic utilisation of Ganache underscores the platform's commitment to providing a comprehensive and reliable system for enhancing women's safety.

4.4. FOUNDATION IN DECENTRALISED IDENTITY MANAGEMENT USING GANACHE ETHEREUM BLOCKCHAIN

The Secure Women Safety Platform is grounded in decentralised identity management, leveraging Ethereum's blockchain technology and Ganache for local blockchain development and testing. This foundational aspect ensures a secure and tamper-proof environment for deploying innovative safety solutions while prioritising user control over personal information.

Through the utilisation of smart contracts deployed on the Ethereum blockchain, the platform guarantees tamper-proof storage of user identities. Smart contracts enable transparent and immutable management of user data, granting individuals autonomy, and ensuring privacy and security. Ganache, as a tool for local blockchain development and testing, allows for the rapid prototyping and verification of smart contracts responsible for decentralised identity management in a controlled environment.

The integration of IoT wearable devices, equipped with anomaly detection abilities strengthens the platform's decentralised identity management capabilities. These devices facilitate real-time location tracking and continuous monitoring of user activities, enabling fast responses to emergency situations while upholding user privacy. By integrating Ethereum's blockchain technology using Ganache for decentralised identity management, the Secure Women Safety Platform establishes a robust and user-centric approach to personal security. Empowering users with control over their personal information and leveraging blockchain's immutable ledger, the platform lays a solid foundation for building safer and more secure communities.

4.4.1. Role of Smart Contracts

Smart contracts play a pivotal role in the foundation of the Secure Women Safety Platform, ensuring decentralised identity management and tamper-proof storage of user identities. These self-executing contracts, deployed on the Ethereum blockchain, enable transparent and immutable management of user data, granting individuals control over their personal information. Through the utilisation of smart contracts, the platform guarantees tamper-proof storage of user identities, enhancing security and privacy. These contracts facilitate user-centric data management, empowering users to retain ownership of their data and manage access permissions. By encoding the rules and logic governing interactions within the platform, smart contracts ensure that personal information remains secure and private, while also facilitating seamless communication and coordination between various components of the system.

A fundamental aspect of the Secure Women Safety Platform is the assurance of tamper-proof storage for user identities, facilitated by Ethereum's blockchain technology. Through the utilisation of smart contracts, the platform establishes a robust mechanism for securely storing and managing user identities, ensuring transparency, immutability, and user control over personal information. Smart contracts, deployed on the Ethereum blockchain, act as self-executing digital agreements that enforce predefined rules and logic. In the context of the Secure Women Safety Platform, these smart contracts are responsible for managing user identities in a tamper-proof manner. By encoding the rules governing user data access and ownership, smart contracts ensure that user identities remain secure and private.

When a user interacts with the platform, such as registering their identity or updating personal information, smart contracts execute the necessary operations to record and validate these actions on the blockchain. This process guarantees that user identities are securely stored and cannot be altered or manipulated without proper authorisation. Furthermore, the decentralised nature of the Ethereum blockchain ensures that user identities are not controlled by any single entity, reducing the risk of data breaches or unauthorized access. Users retain ownership of their data and have the ability to manage access permissions through smart contracts, empowering them with control over their personal information.

The proposed IdentityContract smart contract provides two main functionalities: storeIdentity and userMappings. The storeIdentity function allows users to store their identity information by providing a string, which is then associated with their address within the contract's storage. This enables users to securely link their identity data to their blockchain address. On the other hand, the userMappings function retrieves the identity string associated with a given address from the contract's mapping. By inputting an address, users can retrieve their stored identity information, enhancing transparency and accountability within decentralised applications that utilise the IdentityContract. The algorithm steps for the proposed smart contract are presented in Algorithm 1. Together, these functionalities empower users to manage and access their identity data securely on the blockchain. In summary, smart contracts form the backbone of the Secure Women Safety Platform, ensuring decentralised identity management, tamper-proof storage of user data, and the seamless execution of key platform features. By leveraging the capabilities of Ethereum's blockchain, smart contracts contribute to the platform's mission of providing a holistic and reliable solution for women's safety, while also laying the groundwork for future innovations in the realm of personal security.

ALGORITHM 1. IDENTITYCONTRACT SMART CONTRACT

Algorithm: IdentityContract
Functions:
storeIdentity(string _name):
Stores the provided identity string (_name) for the caller's address.
userMappings(address):
Retrieves the identity string associated with the given address from the userMappings mapping.

4.5. IMPLEMENTATION OF IOT WEARABLE DEVICES

The Secure Women Safety Platform integrates IoT wearable devices equipped with advanced sensors and capabilities to enhance user safety and security. These devices play a crucial role in the continuous monitoring of user activities and swift response to emergency situations.

4.5.1. Sensors and Capabilities

The IoT wearable devices are equipped with a range of sensors including GPS, accelerometers, and panic buttons. These sensors provide valuable data that is essential for ensuring the safety and well-being of users:

GPS: The GPS sensor enables accurate real-time location tracking of users. This functionality allows the platform to pinpoint the exact whereabouts of individuals in case of emergencies, facilitating rapid response and assistance.

Accelerometers: Accelerometers measure changes in acceleration, providing insights into user movement and activity levels. By analysing accelerometer data, the platform can detect sudden falls or unusual movements, triggering alerts and ensuring prompt intervention when necessary.

Panic Buttons: Panic buttons serve as an immediate means for users to signal distress or emergency situations. When activated, these buttons initiate an emergency signal broadcasted on the Ethereum network, notifying predefined contacts, and relevant authorities for swift response and assistance.

4.5.2. Real-Time Location Tracking

Real-time location tracking is a core feature enabled by the integration of GPS sensors in the IoT wearable devices. This functionality ensures that the platform can continuously monitor the movements and whereabouts of users, providing a proactive layer of security. Continuous Monitoring constantly tracks the real-time location of users, allowing it to detect any deviations from regular travel routes or unexpected movements that may indicate potential threats or emergencies. In the event of suspicious or concerning activities, the platform triggers real-time alerts to notify users, predefined contacts, and relevant authorities. These alerts facilitate rapid response and intervention, enhancing user safety and security. In times of distress or emergency situations, users can activate the panic button on their wearable devices (Harikiran et al., 2016).

In summary, the implementation of IoT wearable devices with advanced sensors and capabilities, including GPS, accelerometers, and panic buttons, enhances the Secure Women Safety Platform's ability to monitor user activities and provide fast response to emergencies. Real-time location tracking enables proactive security measures, ensuring the safety and well-being of users in various situations.

4.6. AI-POWERED ANOMALY DETECTION SYSTEM USING AUTOENCODER

The Secure Women Safety Platform incorporates an AI-powered anomaly detection system utilising autoencoder method. This innovative approach enables the platform to analyse user behaviour patterns and trigger real-time alerts in response to potential threats or emergencies.

4.6.1. Analysis of User Behaviour Patterns

The AI-powered anomaly detection system analyses user behaviour patterns by processing data collected from IoT wearable devices. Using autoencoder technology, the system learns and identifies typical user activities and behaviours (Bhatia & Sangwan, 2021; Sakurada & Yairi, 2014). It then compares real-time data against these learned patterns to detect deviations that may indicate potential threats or abnormal activities.

Autoencoder Functions as follows:

Learning User Behaviour: The autoencoder algorithm learns and encodes typical user behaviour patterns based on historical data collected from IoT wearable devices. This includes factors such as regular travel routes, activity levels, and typical behaviour patterns during different times of the day.

Detection of Anomalies: In real-time, the system compares incoming data from wearable devices to the learned behaviour patterns. Deviations from these patterns are flagged as anomalies, signalling potential threats or emergency situations.

Adaptability: The AI-powered anomaly detection system continuously adapts and updates its understanding of user behaviour based on new data inputs. This ensures that the system remains effective in detecting both known and emerging threats.

4.6.2. Triggering Real-Time Alerts

Upon detecting anomalies in user behaviour patterns, the AI-powered system triggers real-time alerts to notify users, predefined contacts, and relevant authorities. These alerts serve as proactive measures to ensure swift response and intervention in potential emergency situations. Immediate Alert Generation will happen when anomalies are detected, the system generates real-time alerts, signalling potential threats or emergencies (An & Cho, 2015; Garg et al., 2019). These alerts are transmitted through various communication channels, including mobile notifications and email, to ensure prompt awareness.

Predefined response protocols that specify the appropriate actions to be taken in different emergency scenarios. These protocols outline the steps for notifying emergency contacts, dispatching assistance, and providing support to affected users. As a future work, the platform seamlessly integrates with emergency services, enabling rapid dispatch of assistance to the user's location. This integration ensures that help is quickly mobilised to address the emergency and ensure the safety of the user.

4.7. PROPOSED METHOD

The proposed method for enhancing women's safety entails a sophisticated integration of Ganache blockchain technology and AI-powered anomaly detection mechanisms. In this innovative approach, user login details are securely stored within the Ganache blockchain, ensuring tamper-proof management of identities. Whenever a user accesses the application, transactions are recorded on the blockchain, establishing a transparent and immutable record of user activities. Concurrently, wearable devices worn by users continuously collect location data and timestamps, which are transmitted for analysis. This data stream is fed into an autoencoder-based anomaly detection machine learning model, meticulously designed to identify deviations in user behaviour patterns. By scrutinising variations in travel routes or activity timings, the AI model discerns potential threats or emergencies with remarkable accuracy.

Upon detecting anomalies in user behaviour, the system swiftly triggers emergency alerts to designated SOS mobile numbers, facilitating rapid responses to potential threats. This proactive approach to safety ensures that users are promptly notified and assisted in times of distress. Furthermore, the integration of Ganache blockchain technology guarantees the security and privacy of user data. Through smart contracts, users retain ownership of their information and have granular control over access permissions, reinforcing the system's commitment to user empowerment and data sovereignty. By synergistically harnessing the power of blockchain and AI technologies, the proposed method establishes a robust and comprehensive framework for enhancing women's safety, marking a significant stride towards building safer and more secure communities. The proposed method data flow diagram is depicted in Figure 4.1

The sequence diagram in Figure 4.2 illustrates the process flow of a user logging into the application. Initially, the user interacts with the application by logging in.

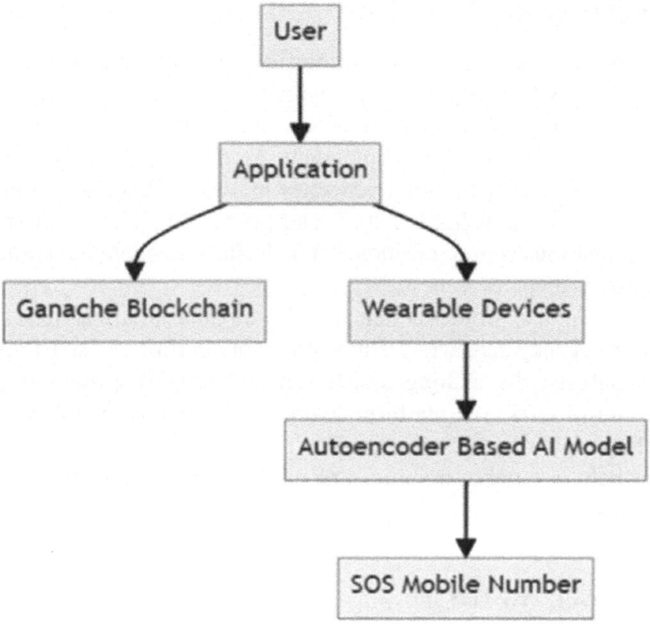

FIGURE 4.1 Women Safety Decentralized Application data flow diagram.

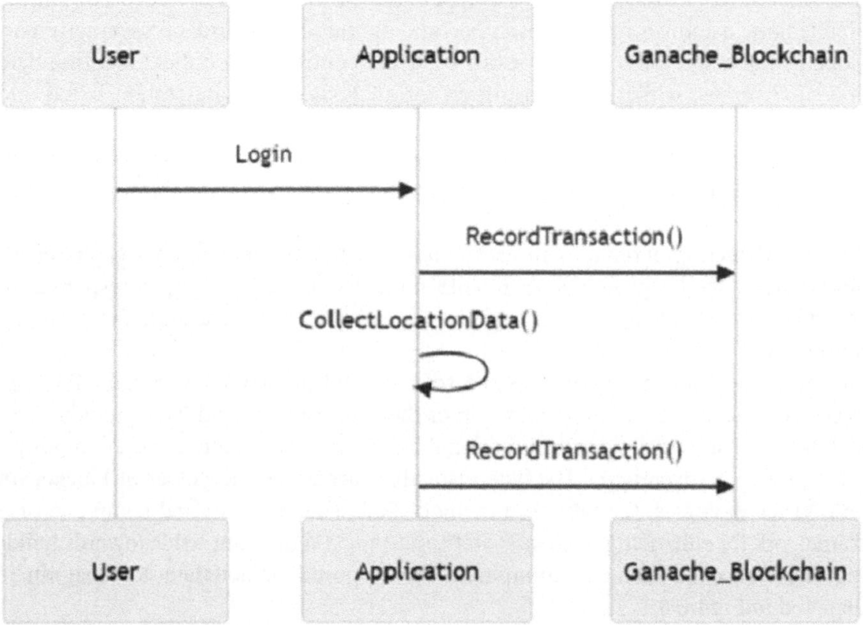

FIGURE 4.2 Ganache blockchain.

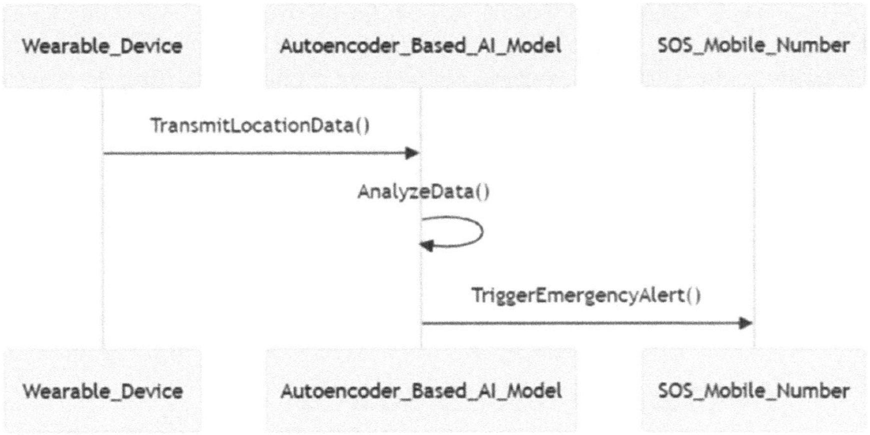

FIGURE 4.3 Location based anomaly detection.

Subsequently, the application records this login transaction in the Ganache blockchain, ensuring the integrity and immutability of the data. Concurrently, the application collects location data from wearable devices associated with the user. Once the location data is collected, another transaction is recorded in the Ganache blockchain, documenting the timestamped location information. This systematic approach ensures that login activities and location data are securely stored in the blockchain, facilitating transparency and accountability.

The sequence diagram in Figure 4.3 outlines the process of transmitting location data from the wearable device to the Autoencoder-based AI Model for analysis, followed by triggering an emergency alert to the SOS mobile number if any anomalies are detected. Initially, the wearable device transmits location data to the Autoencoder-based AI Model. Upon receiving the data, the AI model conducts an analysis using its anomaly detection capabilities to identify any irregular patterns or deviations. If anomalies are detected, indicating potential threats or emergency situations, the AI model initiates the transmission of an emergency alert to the designated SOS mobile number. This seamless interaction between the wearable device and the AI model ensures swift and proactive responses to any abnormal events, enhancing user safety and security.

4.8. RESULTS AND DISCUSSION

The developed application successfully integrates data extraction from wearable devices, with all login details securely stored in the Ganache blockchain. Upon login from the application, transactions are automatically recorded in the Ganache blockchain, ensuring a transparent and immutable record of user activities. Furthermore, the application retrieves location data and timestamps from wearable devices, transmitting this information to an autoencoder-based anomaly detection machine learning model.

The anomaly detection AI module analyses the received location and timestamp data for any deviations from regular patterns. In the event of an anomaly detected in the location or time data, an emergency alert is promptly dispatched to the designated SOS mobile number. This seamless integration of Ganache blockchain for transaction logging and the anomaly detection AI module for proactive anomaly identification enhances the application's security and responsiveness. Thus, the application effectively utilises Ganache blockchain as one module and anomaly detection AI as another, ensuring robustness and reliability in enhancing user safety. Result showcasing the implemented modules are depicted in Figure 4.4, 4.5 and 4.6. For the proposed method, a synthetic data set is used for development and testing purposes.

FIGURE 4.4 Interface of the Women Safety Decentralised Application when login is successful.

FIGURE 4.5 Interface of the Women Safety Decentralised Application when no anomaly.

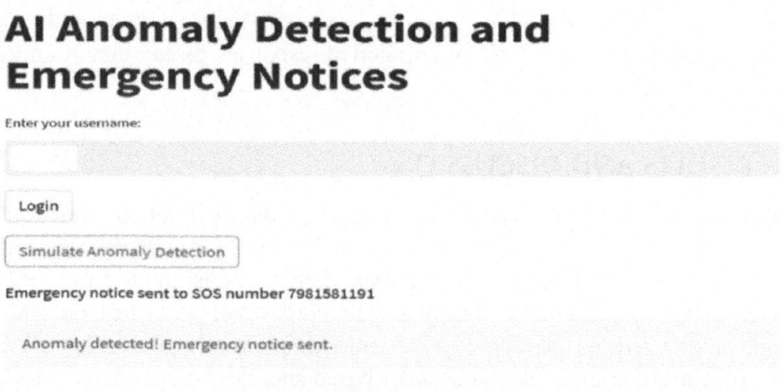

FIGURE 4.6 Interface of the Women Safety Decentralised Application when anomaly detected.

4.9. CONCLUSION

In conclusion, the integration of Ganache blockchain and an anomaly detection AI module within the developed application has demonstrated its effectiveness in enhancing user safety and security. By securely storing login details and recording transactions on the blockchain, coupled with real-time anomaly detection based on location and timestamp data from wearable devices, the application provides a robust framework for proactive threat identification and response. Moving forward, future work could focus on refining the anomaly detection algorithms, exploring additional data sources for enhanced accuracy, and expanding the application's capabilities to address a wider range of safety concerns and scenarios.

REFERENCES

Akram, W., Jain, M., & Hemalatha, C. S. (2019). Design of a smart safety device for women using IoT. *Procedia Computer Science*, 165, 656–662.

Aliyu, M. B., Amr, A., & Ahmad, I. S. (2022). Anomaly detection in wearable location trackers for child safety. *Microprocessors and Microsystems*, 91, 104545.

An, J., & Cho, S. (2015). Variational autoencoder based anomaly detection using reconstruction probability. *Special Lecture on IE*, 2(1), 1–18.

Baucas, M. J., Spachos, P., & Plataniotis, K. N. (2023). Federated learning and blockchain-enabled fog-IoT platform for wearables in predictive healthcare. *IEEE Transactions on Computational Social Systems*, 10(4), 1732–1741.

Bhatia, M. P. S., & Sangwan, S. R. (2021). Soft computing for anomaly detection and prediction to mitigate IoT-based real-time abuse. *Personal and Ubiquitous Computing*, 1–11.

Cai, W., Wang, Z., Ernst, J. B., Hong, Z., Feng, C., & Leung, V. C. (2018). Decentralized applications: The blockchain-empowered software system. *IEEE Access*, 6, 53019–53033.

Chen, Zhaomin, et al. (2018). Autoencoder-based network anomaly detection. *2018 Wireless Telecommunications Symposium (WTS)*. IEEE.

Dorri, A., Kanhere, S. S., & Jurdak, R. (2017, April). Towards an optimized blockchain for IoT. In *Proceedings of the Second International Conference on Internet-of-Things Design and Implementation* (pp. 173–178). IEEE.

Gaetani, E., Aniello, L., Baldoni, R., Lombardi, F., Margheri, A., & Sassone, V. (2017). Blockchain-based database to ensure data integrity in cloud computing environments. *ELETTRONICO – 1816:(2017)* (pp. 146–155) https://eprints.soton.ac.uk/411996/.

Garg, S., Kaur, K., Kumar, N., Kaddoum, G., Zomaya, A. Y., & Ranjan, R. (2019). A hybrid deep learning-based model for anomaly detection in cloud datacenter networks. *IEEE Transactions on Network and Service Management*, 16(3), 924–935.

Harikiran, G. C., Menasinkai, K., & Shirol, S. (2016, March). Smart security solution for women based on Internet of Things (IoT). In *2016 International Conference on Electrical, Electronics, and Optimization Techniques (ICEEOT)* (pp. 3551–3554). IEEE.

Henry, R., Herzberg, A., & Kate, A. (2018). Blockchain access privacy: Challenges and directions. *IEEE Security & Privacy*, 16(4), 38–45.

Jamal, A., Helmi, R. A. A., Syahirah, A. S. N., & Fatima, M. A. (2019, October). Blockchain-based identity verification system. In *2019 IEEE 9th International Conference on System Engineering and Technology (ICSET)* (pp. 253–257). IEEE.

Khandelwal, T., Khandelwal, M., & Pandey, P. S. (2018, October). Women safety device designed using IOT and machine learning. In *2018 IEEE SmartWorld, Ubiquitous Intelligence & Computing, Advanced & Trusted Computing, Scalable Computing & Communications, Cloud & Big Data Computing, Internet of People and Smart City Innovation (SmartWorld/SCALCOM/UIC/ATC/CBDCom/IOP/SCI)* (pp. 1204–1210). IEEE.

Pawar, P., Parolia, N., Shinde, S., Edoh, T. O., & Singh, M. (2022). eHealthChain—a blockchain-based personal health information management system. *Annals of Telecommunications*, 1–13.

Sakurada, M., & Yairi, T. (2014, December). Anomaly detection using autoencoders with non-linear dimensionality reduction. In *Proceedings of the MLSDA 2014 2nd Workshop on Machine Learning for Sensory Data Analysis* (pp. 4–11). ACM.

Taş, R., & Tanrıöver, Ö. Ö. (2019, October). Building a decentralized application on the ethereum blockchain. In *2019 3rd International Symposium on Multidisciplinary Studies and Innovative Technologies (ISMSIT)* (pp. 1–4). IEEE.

Zhou, C., & Paffenroth, R. C. (2017, August). Anomaly detection with robust deep autoencoders. In *Proceedings of the 23rd ACM SIGKDD International Conference on Knowledge Discovery and Data Mining* (pp. 665–674). ACM.

Zyskind, G., & Nathan, O. (2015, May). Decentralizing privacy: Using blockchain to protect personal data. In *2015 IEEE Security and Privacy Workshops* (pp. 180–184). IEEE.

5 Personal Security Through Wearable Technology

Mamta

5.1. INTRODUCTION

5.1.1. Overview of Personal Security Challenges for Women

In the complex tapestry of contemporary life, personal security stands as a critical concern, and for women, it often involves confronting unique challenges. This chapter embarks on a journey to understand and address the distinctive safety hurdles that women encounter daily. From navigating public spaces to dealing with situational vulnerabilities, women's safety encompasses a spectrum of concerns that demand nuanced solutions (Dey et al., 2016). This introduction illuminates the multidimensional nature of personal security for women in various contexts and provides a foundation for an examination of these challenges. We facilitate a thorough analysis of inventive resolutions by recognising these obstacles. Gaining a comprehension of the complexities surrounding women's safety concerns (Harikiran et al., 2016) initiates the exploration of how technological advancements—specifically, wearable devices—can significantly improve personal security. The primary objective of this study is to make a positive contribution towards a global environment in which women feel more confident and empowered when navigating their surroundings.

5.1.2. Evolution of Wearable Technology in Addressing Safety Concerns

Technological developments, a focus on user-friendliness, and a dedication to bolstering individual protection influence the complex progression of wearable technology in relation to safety issues. Initially conceived primarily for fitness tracking and health monitoring, wearables have transformed into sophisticated devices with the capacity to enhance personal safety (Hyndavi et al., 2020).

Here are some important aspects of the evolution of wearable technology in addressing safety concerns:

- **Advanced Sensors:** Wearables now use a variety of sensors like accelerometers, GPS, and heart rate monitors for detailed data collection.

DOI: 10.1201/9781003538172-5

FIGURE 5.1 Evolution of wearable technology in addressing safety concerns.

- **Real-Time Location Monitoring:** GPS integration allows wearables to share users' locations discreetly, improving personal safety, and emergency response.
- **AI Integration:** Artificial intelligence in wearables enables real-time data analysis, helping detect anomalies, assess threats, and provide timely alerts or assistance.
- **Communication and Emergency Features:** Wearables have voice recognition, messaging, and emergency response functions, initiating protocols and contacting help in critical situations.
- **User-Friendly Interfaces:** Wearables prioritise easy-to-use designs to ensure quick access to safety features, encouraging widespread adoption.
- **Privacy and Security Measures:** There's an increased focus on strong encryption, secure data storage, and transparent privacy policies to build user trust.
- **Ecosystem Integration:** Wearables seamlessly integrate with larger ecosystems, enhancing user experience, and safety through multiple technologies.
- **Adaptive Learning:** AI-driven wearables adapt over time, improving threat detection accuracy, and personalising safety features based on individual preferences.
- **Health Monitoring:** Wearables go beyond fitness tracking, monitoring health indicators and providing data to medical professionals in emergencies.

- **Fall Detection and Injury Prevention:** Accelerometers in wearables can detect falls, automatically sending alerts or calling for help, particularly beneficial for the elderly or those with medical conditions.

5.2. ROLE OF AI, IOT, AND CLOUD COMPUTING IN REVOLUTIONARY SOLUTIONS

The role of Artificial Intelligence (AI), Internet of Things (IoT), and Cloud Computing in revolutionary solutions, particularly in the context of wearable technology for personal security, is transformative (Sowmya et al., 2020). By collaborating, these technologies generate interconnected, intelligent solutions that not only identify and address hazards but also advance the overarching objective of establishing more secure and protected environments for individuals.

i) **Artificial Intelligence (AI)**
   - **Real-time Threat Detection:** AI algorithms facilitate the analysis of extensive volumes of data by sensors in real-time, thereby enabling real-time threat detection. The ability to detect potential hazards or anomalous patterns in the user's environment is of the utmost importance, as it significantly contributes to the improvement of safety.
   - **Adaptive Learning:** AI enables wearables to acquire knowledge and adjust in response to evolving user behaviour. By enhancing the precision of threat detection, this adaptive learning mechanism renders the system more individualised and proactive in addressing the safety requirements of each user.
   - **Predictive Analytics:** One potential application of AI-powered wearables is predictive analytics, which leverages historical data, user

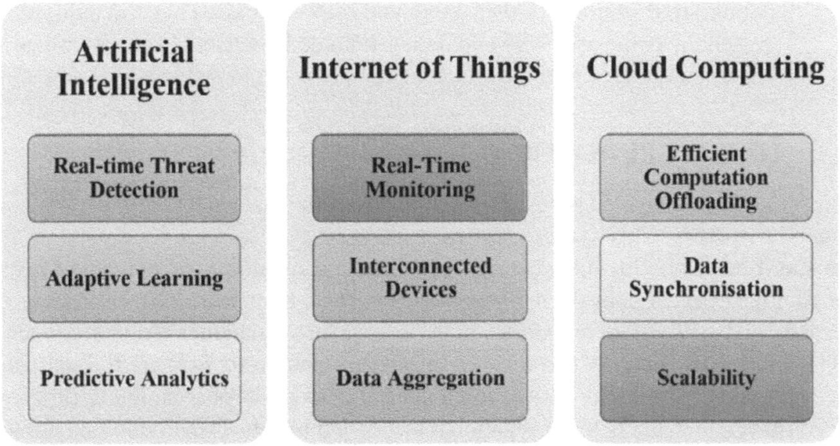

FIGURE 5.2 Role of AI, IoT, and Cloud Computing in revolutionary solutions.

behaviour, and environmental variables to forecast potential hazards. Implementing this preventative measure enhances the level of security on an individual level.

ii) **Internet of Things (IoT)**
- **Real-Time Monitoring:** IoT Integrating IoT sensors into devices provides real-time monitoring capabilities. The integration of GPS tracking, accelerometers, and physiological sensors provides a holistic comprehension of the user's surroundings, thereby facilitating safer evaluations with greater precision.
- **Interconnected Devices:** Through IoT, wearables and other intelligent devices are able to communicate and connect without interruption. The interconnectivity between wearables and other IoT-enabled systems improves the overall efficacy of personal security solutions by enabling the exchange of vital data.
- **Data Aggregation:** The IoT can consolidate data from numerous wearables. The analysis of this dataset as a whole has the potential to detect safety patterns, thereby facilitating the creation of safety protocols and applications that are better informed.

iii) **Cloud Computing**
- **Efficient Computation Offloading:** By transferring computationally demanding duties from wearables to remote servers, cloud computing optimises the utilisation of device resources and extends the capacity of the battery. Ensuring the ongoing operation of safety features is of the utmost importance.
- **Data Synchronisation:** Cloud-based platforms facilitate the seamless synchronisation of data across multiple devices. This ensures that information, such as user preferences, emergency contacts, and historical safety data, is readily available and consistent across the wearable ecosystem.
- **Scalability:** Cloud computing provides the scalability required for handling large volumes of data generated by wearables. This scalability is essential as the user base and data generated by personal security wearables continue to grow.

5.3. LITERATURE REVIEW

Teizer (2015) investigated a wearable technology called SmartHat, designed for construction workers. This system can warn workers of hazardous conditions on the job site. Lee et al. (2017) studied the usability and reliability of wearable sensors for roofing workers both during work and off-duty. Kim et al. (2017) proposed a hazard avoidance system for construction sites that uses computer vision and Google Glass to identify dangers and display safety information to workers through augmented reality. Choi et al. (2017) researched the adoption of wearable technology by construction workers for occupational safety and health. They found that providing important information to workers can encourage them to use wearable devices.

Awolusi et al. (2018) reviewed applications of wearable devices for personalised construction safety, suggesting that technologies from other industries could also benefit construction safety. Schall et al. (2018) explored the benefits and barriers of using wearable sensors in occupational health and safety. Hwang et al. (2016) studied using activity trackers to monitor construction workers' health, finding that heart rate sensors can effectively monitor workers' heart rates. Sandoval and Kwon (2019) analysed the use of wearable devices to improve construction safety, highlighting their potential to monitor processes and create safer workplaces. Jacobs et al. (2019) identified factors influencing employees' acceptance of wearable devices, emphasising the importance of user adoption for realising the benefits of wearable technology. Xie and Chang (2019) developed a wearable safety system to predict personal safety risks in real-time work environments. Kiehl et al. (2020) proposed a system for remote monitoring of confined spaces in aircraft maintenance to reduce risks associated with confined spaces. Haikio et al. (2020) surveyed construction workers about their perceptions of using IoT technology for occupational safety, noting concerns about privacy and security. Niknejad et al. (2020) reviewed developments and challenges of smart wearable devices, observing a significant increase in studies in recent years. Marra et al. (2021) developed a strain sensor for fabric-based wearable devices using graphene nanoplatelets. Bangaru et al. (2021) proposed an automatic activity recognition method for construction workers based on artificial neural networks, aiming to improve safety on construction sites.

5.4. PURPOSE AND SCOPE OF THE CHAPTER

i) **Purpose**

This chapter explores how smart devices, like watches and other wearables, are getting super smart with technologies like AI, IoT, and Cloud Computing (Chaudhari et al., 2020). We want to show how these technologies make these devices not just cool gadgets but also really good at keeping people safe, especially women.

ii) **Scope**

The scope of this chapter encompasses unravelling the technological evolution of wearable devices, spotlighting the smart functionalities that make them powerful tools for personal security (Paradkar and Sharma, 2015). We explore how AI, IoT, and Cloud Computing synergise within wearables, shaping a safer and more connected future.

- **How Wearables Got Smarter:** We'll talk about how these smart devices have changed from just counting steps to being super smart gadgets that can keep us safe.
- **Smart Detectives with AI:** Find out how AI, which is like a smart detective, helps these devices quickly spot if something unusual or risky is happening.
- **Wearable Sensors Checking Everything:** Learn about the cool sensors in these gadgets that check where we are, how our bodies are doing, and even what's happening around us.

- **Loud Magic Making Devices Talk:** Understand how cloud computing helps these gadgets share information with each other, making them work together like a team.
- **Helpful Buttons and Quick Responses:** See how these gadgets have buttons and features that can quickly call for help or tell someone we trust if we're in trouble.
- **Keeping Secrets Safe:** We'll talk about how these gadgets keep our personal information safe and why it's important.
- **Challenges and What's Next:** Find out about the problems these gadgets still have to solve, like being fair to everyone, and what cool things might come next.
- **Wrapping It Up:** We'll sum up all the cool stuff we learned and talk about why these super-smart gadgets can make the world a safer place for everyone, especially women (Strauss et al., 2005).

5.5. WEARABLES AS GUARDIANS: A TECHNOLOGICAL EVOLUTION

5.5.1. Historical Perspective on Wearable Devices

Let's take a trip down memory lane to the early days of wearables. Back then, we had simple gadgets like step counters and watches that did more than just tell time—they woke us up and even helped with math problems! These early devices may not have been focused on keeping us safe, but they laid the groundwork for the incredible wearables we have today (Lee and Mase, 2002).

In the 2000s, fitness trackers came into the scene. They were like our personal coaches, keeping tabs on our exercises, and telling us how active we were. But that was just the beginning of something even more fantastic. In recent years, wearables have evolved into our personal guardians (Tejonidhi et al., 2019). They're not just tracking our steps; they're like our superhero companions. How did they become so smart? Well, it's because of amazing technologies like Artificial Intelligence (AI), Internet of Things (IoT), and Cloud Computing. Imagine your wearable being more than just a fitness buddy—it's your super helper, always looking out for you. That's what we're exploring in this chapter. To understand the journey of wearables, we'll look back at their history—how they started small and became the incredible helpers we rely on today (Aqilah Arshad et al., 2022).

5.5.2. Evolution From Fitness Trackers to Personal Safety Devices

Certainly, here are some important points summarising the evolution from fitness trackers to personal safety devices:

- **Starting Point:** Wearables began as devices focused on fitness, mainly tracking steps and calories for health-conscious users (Saxena et al., 2023).

- **Health-Centric Focus:** Initially, wearables were all about promoting a healthy lifestyle, providing insights into exercise routines and overall well-being.
- **Expansion to Safety:** Over time, wearables evolved beyond fitness tracking, expanding their role to include personal safety features.
- **Well-Being beyond Health:** The shift represents a broader understanding of well-being, now covering not just physical health but also safety and security (Gopalakrishnan et al., 2023).
- **New Safety Features:** Modern wearables offer features like real-time location tracking and emergency response, enhancing personal safety.
- **Communication:** They now enable discreet communication, adding an extra layer of security for users.
- **AI Integration:** The inclusion of Artificial Intelligence (AI) makes wearables smarter, allowing them to analyse data and enhance safety features.
- **Blurred Categories:** The distinction between fitness trackers and personal safety devices is fading, emphasising a holistic approach to well-being.
- **Sensor Advancements:** Wearables benefit from improved sensor technologies, ensuring more accurate and diverse data collection.

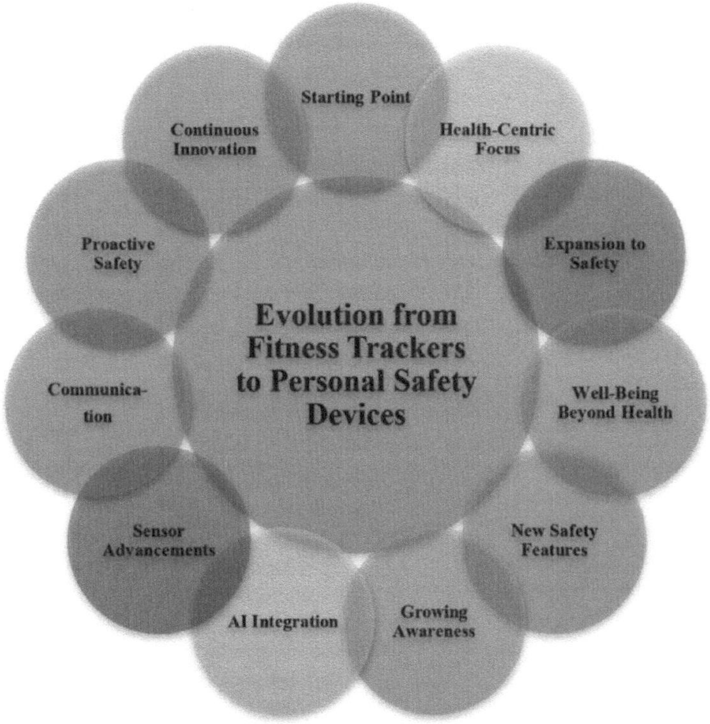

FIGURE 5.3 Evolution from fitness trackers to personal safety devices.

- **Growing Awareness:** People are becoming more aware of the need for technology that addresses not only physical health but also safety concerns (Jatti et al., 2016).
- **Proactive Safety:** Wearables are now proactive in ensuring safety, offering features that go beyond traditional health tracking.
- **Continuous Innovation:** The evolution of wearables is an ongoing process, with constant technological innovation shaping them into versatile tools for health and safety (Sharma and Kapoor, 2014).

5.6. IOT SENSORS FOR REAL-TIME AWARENESS

5.6.1. Role of IoT Sensors in Wearable Devices

- **Real-Time Monitoring:** IoT sensors make wearables able to check and share information instantly.
- **Comprehensive Health Tracking:** These sensors help wearables give detailed info about your health, going beyond just basic stuff.
- **Location Awareness:** Thanks to IoT, wearables can accurately track where you are in real-time, making safety features better.
- **Environmental Sensing:** Wearables with IoT sensors can notice changes in your surroundings, like the air quality or temperature.
- **Interconnected Devices:** IoT helps wearables talk to other smart devices easily, making them work together better.
- **Data Aggregation:** IoT lets wearables collect info from different places, helping us understand our health and safety better.
- **Energy-Efficient Operation:** IoT sensors help wearables use less energy, so they can work for a long time without any problems (Filios et al., 2015).
- **Enhanced Context Awareness:** Because of IoT, wearables can understand more about what you're doing, helping them give you better, and more personalised responses.

5.6.2. Utilising GPS Tracking for Precise Location Data

When it comes to wearable, GPS tracking stands out as a crucial feature, providing accurate and precise location information.

Here are key points highlighting the utilisation of GPS tracking in wearables:

- **Pinpoint Accuracy:** GPS in wearables gives super accurate location info.
- **Real-Time Tracking:** It lets you track locations instantly, helpful for you and others to know where you are.
- **Safety Boost:** GPS makes safety features better, especially in emergencies, ensuring quick responses.
- **Geofencing Magic:** Wearables use GPS to create virtual boundaries, triggering alerts when you enter or leave specific areas (Baksi et al., 2022).

- **Guided Navigation:** GPS helps wearables guide you with turn-by-turn directions, handy for activities like running or exploring new places.
- **Location History:** Wearables with GPS store where you've been, useful for personal records, fitness tracking, or revisiting favourite spots (Harikiran et al., 2016).
- **Mapping Integration:** GPS in wearable's works with maps, making your experience richer by providing insights into your surroundings.
- **Outdoor Adventure Tool:** For outdoor activities, GPS in wearables is a powerful tool, ensuring you stay on the right path during adventures.
- **Environmental Sensors and Their Contribution to Contextual Awareness**
- Environmental sensors in wearable devices play a crucial role in making these gadgets more aware of the user's surroundings (Thierer, 2015). Here are key points highlighting the contribution of environmental sensors to contextual awareness:
- **Detecting Changes:** Sensors in wearable's notice shifts in things like temperature and air quality.
- **Understanding Everything:** These sensors help wearables understand more about where you are and what's happening around you.
- **Air Quality Check:** They can tell you about the air quality, helping you stay aware of potential health issues.
- **Feeling the Temperature:** Wearable's can sense temperature changes, useful for outdoor activities and keeping you comfortable.
- **Smart Responses:** Using data from sensors, wearable's can adapt to your surroundings, like adjusting activities during extreme weather.
- **Personal Tips:** Thanks to these sensors, wearables can give you personalised tips, such as reminding you to drink more water in hot weather (Punait and Askhedkar, 2017).
- **Boosting Safety:** Wearables alert you to potential risks, like extreme temperatures or bad air quality, making sure you stay safe.
- **Health Insights:** Environmental data blends with health tracking, giving you a more complete picture of how your surroundings affect your well-being.

5.7. CENTRAL ROLE OF CLOUD COMPUTING IN WEARABLE TECHNOLOGY

Cloud computing plays a central role in making wearable technology more powerful and connected (Tanwar et al., 2021).

Here are the key points highlighting its significance:

- **Data Storage and Access:** Cloud stores wearable data remotely, making it easy to access from anywhere.
- **Connected Experience:** Cloud helps wearables stay connected to other devices, creating a smoother and integrated user experience.

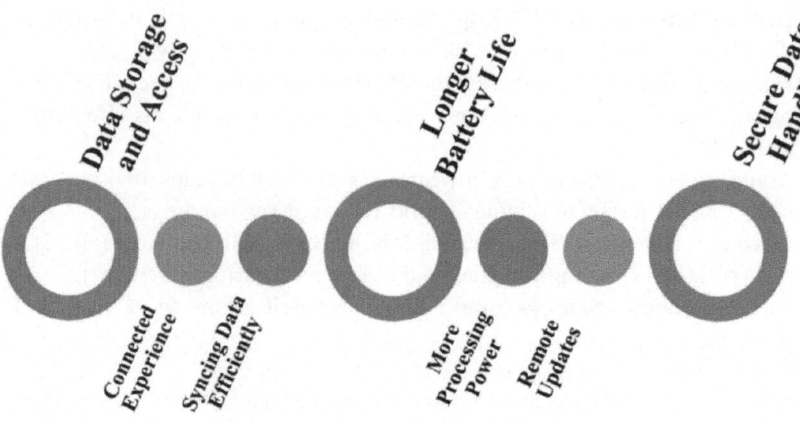

FIGURE 5.4 Role of cloud computing in wearable technology.

- **Syncing Data Efficiently:** Wearables use the cloud to update data across devices in real-time, keeping information consistently current.
- **Longer Battery Life:** Cloud computing reduces the workload on wearable batteries, leading to longer battery life for user convenience.
- **More Processing Power:** Cloud provides wearables access to advanced processing power for running complex tasks or algorithms.
- **Remote Updates:** Wearables receive updates and maintenance through the cloud, ensuring they stay current without manual intervention.
- **Secure Data Handling:** Cloud services offer strong security measures, keeping wearable user information safe.
- **Scalability:** Cloud allows wearables to grow as needed. If data or service requirements increase, the cloud can easily adapt to these changes.

5.8. EMERGENCY RESPONSE AND COMMUNICATION

5.8.1. Initiating Emergency Protocols Through Wearable Technology

When things get tough, wearables are like your emergency superheroes. Here's how they help:

- **Quick Help:** Wearables are super quick to activate emergency plans when you really need them.
- **Fast Alerts:** They can send fast alerts to your friends, family, or even emergency services, telling them exactly where you are.
- **SOS Button:** Many wearables have a special SOS button. Press it, and help is on the way, even if your device is locked.
- **Smart Alerts**: Some wearables are really smart. They can sense when something's wrong and send alerts automatically—no need to press any buttons.

- **Location Tracker:** If you're lost or in trouble, wearables with GPS can share your exact location. This helps rescuers find you super fast.
- **Talk Anytime:** You can talk directly to emergency services or your loved ones through your wearable. It's like having a phone right on your wrist.
- **Medical Info Help:** In emergencies, wearables can share important info about your health with the heroes coming to help. This helps them make the best decisions.
- **Teamwork with Emergency Services:** Some wearables are great teammates for emergency services. They make communication smooth and help everyone work together to keep you safe.

5.8.2. Contacting Emergency Services and Trusted Contacts

In case of urgency, wearables make it easy to reach out for help. Here's how they do it:

- **Quick Emergency Call:** Wearables have an easy way to call emergency services when you need urgent help.
- **SOS Alerts:** Some wearables send alerts to chosen contacts or emergency services when you activate the SOS feature.
- **Automatic Alerts:** Certain wearables can automatically send alerts based on detected emergencies, without you doing anything.
- **Precise Location Sharing:** Wearables with GPS can share your exact location with trusted contacts or emergency services for faster assistance.
- **Direct Communication:** You can talk in real-time with emergency services or trusted contacts directly through your wearable.
- **Medical Information Help:** Wearables can share important medical details with first responders for better assistance.
- **Custom SOS Messages:** Some wearables let you set up personalized SOS messages to communicate specific details about the situation.
- **Sync with Phones:** Wearables often connect with your mobile phone, making communication with emergency services or trusted contacts seamless through the paired device (Jain et al., 2023).

5.8.3. Discreet Communication Features for Seeking Help

When you need help without drawing attention, wearables offer discreet communication features. Here are the key points:

- **Quiet Alerts:** Wearables can silently alert trusted contacts or emergency services, ensuring help without noise.
- **Vibration Notifications:** Some wearables use gentle vibrations instead of loud sounds for notifications, keeping communication discreet.
- **Hidden SOS Buttons:** Certain wearables have secret SOS buttons, letting you call for help without anyone noticing.

- **Voice Commands:** Wearables with voice commands allow you to ask for assistance without physically interacting with the device.
- **Text Messaging:** You can send quiet text messages for help directly from your wearable.
- **Subtle Designs:** Wearables are made to look like regular accessories, helping you seek help without making it obvious that you're using a safety device.
- **Customisable Alerts:** Some wearables let you choose the type of alert you send, ensuring it fits the situation and remains discreet.
- **Gesture Recognition:** Wearables with gesture recognition can detect specific movements as emergency signals, ensuring help is on the way without speaking.

5.9. PRIVACY AND ETHICAL CONSIDERATIONS

i) **Addressing Privacy Concerns in Wearable Technologies**
   - **Clear User Consent:** Get permission from users before collecting their personal data.
   - **Limited Data Collection:** Only gather data that's necessary, avoiding unnecessary intrusion.
   - **Anonymous Data Options:** Allow users to contribute data anonymously for privacy.

ii) **Implementing Robust Security Measures**
   - **Data Encryption:** Keep user data safe by using strong encryption methods.

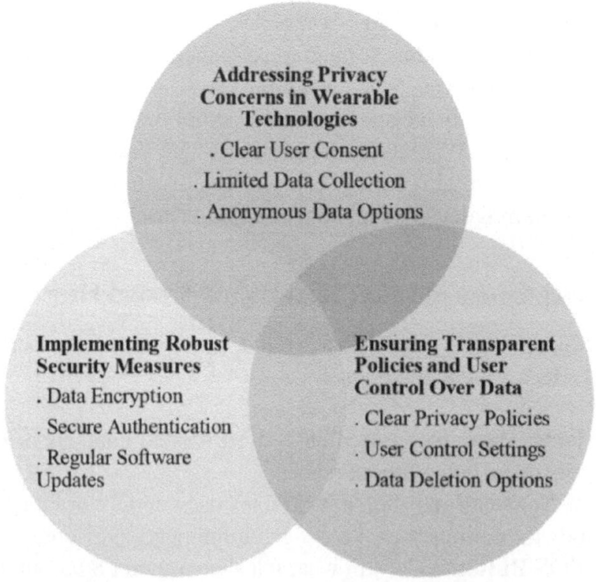

FIGURE 5.5 Privacy and ethical considerations in wearable technologies.

- **Secure Authentication:** Use secure methods like biometrics or strong passwords for user access.
- **Regular Software Updates:** Keep the wearable's software updated to fix security issues.

iii) **Ensuring Transparent Policies and User Control Over Data**

- **Clear Privacy Policies:** Have clear policies on how user data is collected, used, and shared.
- **User Control Settings:** Let users manage and customize their privacy settings.
- **Data Deletion Options:** Allow users to delete their data from the device when they want.

5.10. CHALLENGES AND FUTURE DIRECTIONS

i) **Persistent Challenges in the Field**

- **Battery Life:** Making wearables last longer without needing frequent charging.
- **Data Security:** Ensuring that user data is safe from unauthorized access and breaches.
- **Interoperability:** Making different wearables and platforms work together seamlessly.

ii) **Ensuring Accessibility to Diverse Populations**

- **Inclusive Design:** Designing wearables to meet the needs of diverse users, including those with disabilities.
- **Affordability:** Making wearable technology affordable for more people.

iii) **Navigating Bias in AI Algorithms**

- **Algorithmic Bias:** Dealing with biases in AI algorithms to ensure fairness, especially in health-related applications.
- **Ethical AI Use:** Making sure AI in wearables is used ethically, considering privacy and avoiding discrimination.

iv) **Future Developments and Applications in Wearable Technology**

- **Health Monitoring Advancements:** Expecting better sensors and diagnostic features for improved health monitoring.
- **Integration with Smart Environments:** Wearables becoming part of smart homes and cities for more functionality.
- **Advanced AI Applications:** Wearables using more sophisticated AI for personalised and context-aware experiences.
- **Fashion-Tech Integration:** Exploring ways to make wearables not just functional but also stylish by integrating them with fashion.

5.11. CONCLUSION

In conclusion, the fusion of wearable technology with Artificial Intelligence (AI), Internet of Things (IoT), and Cloud Computing marks a transformative shift from mere accessories to powerful tools for enhancing women's safety. This evolution is rooted in the recognition of challenges faced by women in personal security. The development of wearables as sophisticated guardians, employing advanced AI algorithms for threat detection and risk assessment, showcases a commitment to addressing these challenges innovatively. Real-time monitoring, facilitated by IoT sensors, provides a nuanced understanding of users' surroundings, while Cloud Computing ensures seamless connectivity for effective communication and information sharing. The discreet initiation of emergency response protocols demonstrates the practical application of AI in critical situations. Privacy and ethical considerations are at the forefront, emphasising the importance of robust security measures and user control over information. Looking ahead, ongoing developments promise even more sophisticated applications, demanding a collective focus on universal accessibility, addressing biases in AI, and maintaining ethical standards. As we navigate this path, it is essential to remain vigilant, innovative, and ethically grounded, ensuring that wearable technology continues to contribute to a world where every woman feels secure, empowered, and confident in her daily life.

REFERENCES

Aqilah Arshad, S. R., Mansor, Z., Maharum, S. M. M., & Ahmad, I. (2022). Women safety device with real-time monitoring. In *Advanced Materials and Engineering Technologies* (pp. 273–282). Springer International Publishing.

Awolusi, I., Marks, E., & Hallowell, M. (2018). Wearable technology for personalized construction safety monitoring and trending: Review of applicable devices. *Automation in Construction*, 85, 96–106.

Baksi, K., Ghosh, G., Banik, D., Das, S., Saha, A., & Alam, M. Y. (2022, December). RESPECTO: Now we may go alone, safety is in our hand. In *International Conference on Frontiers in Computing and Systems* (pp. 183–197). Springer Nature Singapore.

Bangaru, S. S., Wang, C., Busam, S. A., & Aghazadeh, F. (2021). ANN-based automated scaffold builder activity recognition through wearable EMG and IMU sensors. *Automation in Construction*, 126, 103653.

Callejas Sandoval, S., & Kwon, S. (2019). Smart wearable technologies to promote safety in aging construction labor. In *Creative Construction Conference 2019* (pp. 733–738). Budapest University of Technology and Economics.

Chaudhari, A., Patel, J., Savla, K., Shetty, A., & Shah, V. (2020). Women's safety band using IoT. In *Proceedings of International Conference on Wireless Communication: ICWiCOM 2019* (pp. 493–501). Springer.

Choi, B., Hwang, S., & Lee, S. (2017). What drives construction workers' acceptance of wearable technologies in the workplace?: Indoor localization and wearable health devices for occupational safety and health. *Automation in Construction*, 84, 31–41.

Dey, T., Paul, T., Mukherjee, S., & Ghoshhajra, R. (2016). 'WeRSafe': An Android apps for society. *International Journal of Computer Trends and Technology (IJCTT)*, 42(1), 47–50.

Filios, G., Nikoletseas, S., Pavlopoulou, C., Rapti, M., & Ziegler, S. (2015, December). Hierarchical algorithm for daily activity recognition via smartphone sensors. In *2015 IEEE 2nd World Forum on Internet of Things (Wf-IoT)* (pp. 381–386). IEEE.

Gopalakrishnan, M. A., Arugadoss, J., Vijayan, S., Sadi, S. R., Murali, S., Ansari, M. T. T., & Prasad, S. G. V. (2023, August). AI based smart wearable safety system for women to fight against sexual assault and harassment with IoT connectivity. In *AIP Conference Proceedings* (Vol. 2790, No. 1). AIP Publishing.

Häikiö, J., Kallio, J., Mäkelä, S. M., & Keränen, J. (2020). IoT-based safety monitoring from the perspective of construction site workers. *International Journal of Occupational and Environmental Safety*, 4(1), 1–14.

Harikiran, G. C., Menasinkai, K., & Shirol, S. (2016, March). Smart security solution for women based on Internet of Things (IOT). In *2016 International Conference on Electrical, Electronics, and Optimization Techniques (ICEEOT)* (pp. 3551–3554). IEEE.

Hwang, S., Seo, J., Jebelli, H., & Lee, S. (2016). Feasibility analysis of heart rate monitoring of construction workers using a photoplethysmography (PPG) sensor embedded in a wristband-type activity tracker. *Automation in Construction*, 71, 372–381.

Hyndavi, V., Nikhita, N. S., & Rakesh, S. (2020). Smart wearable device for women safety using IoT. In *2020 5th International Conference on Communication and Electronics Systems (ICCES)* (pp. 459–463). Coimbatore, India. http://doi.org/10.1109/ICCES48766.2020.9138047.

Jacobs, J. V., Hettinger, L. J., Huang, Y. H., Jeffries, S., Lesch, M. F., Simmons, L. A., . . . & Willetts, J. L. (2019). Employee acceptance of wearable technology in the workplace. *Applied Ergonomics*, 78, 148–156.

Jain, A., Thomas, S., Tejasvi, S., Shreenidhi, T. L., Anbalagan, R., & Kantanavar, P. (2023, January). Self-defence gadget for women: Design and development. In *International Conference on Research into Design* (pp. 29–41). Springer Nature Singapore.

Jatti, A., Kannan, M., Alisha, R. M., Vijayalakshmi, P., & Sinha, S. (2016). Design and development of an IOT based wearable device for the safety and security of women and girl children. In *2016 IEEE International Conference on Recent Trends in Electronics, Information & Communication Technology (RTEICT)* (pp. 1108–1112). Bangalore, India. http://doi.org/10.1109/RTEICT.2016.7808003.

Kiehl, Z. A., Durkee, K. T., Halverson, K. C., Christensen, J. C., & Hellstern, G. F. (2020). Transforming work through human sensing: A confined space monitoring application. *Structural Health Monitoring*, 19(1), 186–201.

Kim, K., Kim, H., & Kim, H. (2017). Image-based construction hazard avoidance system using augmented reality in wearable device. *Automation in Construction*, 83, 390–403.

Lee, S. W., Lin, K. Y., Seto, E., & Migliaccio, G. C. (2017). Wearable sensors for monitoring on-duty and off-duty worker physiological status and activities in construction. *Automation in Construction*, 83, 341–353.

Lee, S. W., & Mase, K. (2002). Activity and location recognition using wearable sensors. *IEEE Pervasive Computing*, 1(3), 24–32.

Marra, F., Minutillo, S., Tamburrano, A., & Sarto, M. S. (2021). Production and characterization of Graphene Nanoplatelet-based ink for smart textile strain sensors via screen printing technique. *Materials & Design*, 198, 109306.

Niknejad, N., Ismail, W. B., Mardani, A., Liao, H., & Ghani, I. (2020). A comprehensive overview of smart wearables: The state of the art literature, recent advances, and future challenges. *Engineering Applications of Artificial Intelligence*, 90, 103529.

Paradkar, A., & Sharma, D. (2015). All in one intelligent safety system for women security. *International Journal of Computer Applications*, 130(11), 33–40.

Punait, S., & Askhedkar, A. R. (2017). An improved personal security system. *International Journal of Engineering Research and Application*, 7(6), 102–105.

Saxena, S., Mishra, S., Baljon, M., Mishra, S., Sharma, S. K., Goel, P., . . . & Kishore, V. (2023). IoT-Based Women Safety Gadgets (WSG): Vision, architecture, and design trends. *Computers, Materials & Continua*, 76(1).

Schall Jr, M. C., Sesek, R. F., & Cavuoto, L. A. (2018). Barriers to the adoption of wearable sensors in the workplace: A survey of occupational safety and health professionals. *Human Factors*, 60(3), 351–362.

Sharma, T., & Kapoor, B. (2014, February). Intelligent data analysis algorithms on biofeedback signals for estimating emotions. In *2014 International Conference on Reliability Optimization and Information Technology (ICROIT)* (pp. 335–340). IEEE.

Sowmya, T., Triveni, D., Keerthana, D., Lakshmi, A. V., Priya, K. P., & Kavya, G. (2020). Women's safety system using IoT. *International Journal of Science and Technology*, 7(3), e-ISSN: 2395-0056.

Strauss, M. D., Reynolds, C., Hughes, S., Park, K., McDarby, G., & Picard, R. W. (2005). HandWave: Design and manufacture of a wearable wireless skin conductance sensor and housing. In *Affective Computing and Intelligent Interaction* (pp. 699–706). https://doi.org/10.1007/11573548_90

Tanwar, D., Nijhawan, V., Sinha, P., & Gupta, R. (2021, March). Design of low-cost women safety system using GPS and GSM. In *2021 8th International Conference on Computing for Sustainable Global Development (INDIACom)* (pp. 827–831). IEEE.

Teizer, J. (2015). Wearable, wireless identification sensing platform: Self-monitoring alert and reporting technology for hazard avoidance and training (SmartHat). *Journal of Information Technology in Construction (ITcon)*, 20(19), 295–312.

Tejonidhi, M. R., Aishwarya, C. K., Dayana, M. K., & Nagamma, H. (2019, July). IoT based smart security gadget for women's safety. In *International Conference on Advances in Information Technology* (pp. 348–352). https://doi.org/10.1109/ICAIT47043.2019.8987242

Thierer, Adam D. (2015). The Internet of Things and wearable technology: Addressing privacy and security concerns without derailing innovation. *Richmond Journal of Law and Technology*, 21(6). https://ssrn.com/abstract=2494382 or http://doi.org/10.2139/ssrn.2494382

Xie, X., & Chang, Z. (2019). Intelligent wearable occupational health safety assurance system of power operation. *Journal of Medical Systems*, 43, 1–7.

6 Emergency Response Mobile Apps

Parul Dubey, Pushpa Birha, and Rahul Vinayak Bambodkar

6.1. INTRODUCTION

The significance of effective and quick emergency response systems in today's highly-connected society, particularly for protecting people, cannot be emphasised enough. In this setting, emergency response mobile apps are crucial because they provide users with cutting-edge, tech-driven solutions that allow them to get assistance quickly when they need it. This chapter explores the complexities of these applications, which are leading the way in improving emergency responses by using advances in cloud computing, the Internet of Things (IoT), and Artificial Intelligence (AI).

A wide variety of emergencies, from those involving our own health to those involving our physical safety, are always a possibility as we negotiate the intricacies of contemporary life. In such situations, the response's swiftness and efficacy often determine whether the result is favourable or bad. Apps that streamline communication in times of crisis and make use of state-of-the-art technology to provide immediate aid have been developed by inventors and developers in response to this realisation.

In this chapter, we will go over the basics of emergency response mobile apps, including how they use AI to interpret data and foretell possible dangers to safety, how they use IoT devices for tracking and notifications in real-time, and how they depend on cloud computing for data management and scalability. These applications take a multipronged approach to user safety by providing one-touch warnings for emergency contacts and by sharing users' real-time whereabouts with first responders.

In addition, we will take a look at the design difficulties and factors that went into making these life-saving technologies, such as making sure they are accessible, addressing privacy issues, and working across many platforms. Our goal is to provide a thorough review of emergency response mobile apps by examining case studies and real-world implementations. We will focus on how these apps affect community safety and the safety of women.

In this section, we'll take a look at a few of the most well-known applications aimed at protecting women from harm. For the benefit of the reader, they will be thoroughly examined.

DOI: 10.1201/9781003538172-6

6.2. LITERATURE REVIEW

Based on an examination of relevant current contributions and researchers own hands-on expertise in building and analysing emergency management solutions, they aimed to present different conclusions about the design of efficient and successful mobile emergency notification apps (Romano et al., 2016). They used mobile devices' basic sensors and users' expertise to attain this aim. In practise, they generated a genuine traffic accident scenario with a motionless person next to a driving car. On the theoretical side, they interviewed several emergency doctors about the remedy's feasibility. Operators and people benefit from EN implementation, as shown by the evaluation phase. The final redesign of the proposed application yielded various conclusions that may be applied to future design difficulties in the same sector.

In another article (Kavitha et al., 2021), authors discussed the RESCUER App, a mobile application that enables citizens to take part in emergency response efforts by communicating with a command centre and receiving orders within. The ability of humans to engage with computers in times of crisis prompted us to create a human response model for such scenarios. On the basis of this concept, they established three distinct ways of interaction: one-click, guided, and chat. Authors put these types of engagement into an interactive prototype and tested it in an experiment that mimicked the stress of an emergency by inducing a high cognitive load. The RESCUER App's three preset interaction modes allowed users to engage with it in stressful conditions, according to the study's findings.

By using Mobile Cloud Computing, smart devices with limited resources may enhance their computational behaviour by outsourcing tasks like storage, virtual servers, and web services (MCC). In another study (Nanda et al., 2020), authors have compiled a comprehensive literature review of Emergency Management System (EMS) and MCC applications as well as a list of the design issues addressed by each. For the purpose of developing an EMS employing MCC, they have outlined the design issues and potential solutions. To construct an MCC-based automated EMS, we provide a specific design. We wrap off the article with some concrete recommendations for the future.

With a focus on how sensors and IoT devices provide real-time data to first responders, another study (Damaševičius et al., 2023) seeks to investigate the role of IoES in disaster management and emergency response. In addition to discussing the possible effects of IoES on public safety and crisis management, authors analysed the difficulties and possibilities of implementing this technology. A more rapid and effective response to emergencies, along with better citizen safety and security in general, are all possible outcomes of incorporating IoES into emergency management. To make sure this technology is used effectively and responsibly, however, it's crucial to know what the restrictions are and what the hazards are.

6.3. POPULAR EMERGENCY APPS

It is very crucial to have an emergency plan in place in today's uncertain and fast-paced environment. Numerous emergency applications have emerged with the proliferation of smartphones, with the goal of equipping users with vital information and resources in the event of unforeseen emergencies. Apps in this category include a wide variety of uses, from providing weather and catastrophe alerts in real time to helping with first aid, sending out SOS signals in an emergency, and letting loved ones know where user is. For those who want to be better prepared for any catastrophe, popular emergency applications are a must-have. Medical crises, natural catastrophes, and personal safety issues are just a few examples of the many types of situations that these apps may help with. In what follows, we will go into more depth on these topics.

6.4. LIFE360: FAMILY LOCATOR AND GPS TRACKER FOR SAFETY

Instead of using advanced communication and location sharing features, the all-inclusive Life360 software for mobile devices seeks to enhance the safety and connection of loved ones (Aagaard et al., 2023). Its main function is to allow users to monitor the whereabouts of connected family members in real-time on a private map, which may be useful for both routine and emergency situational monitoring. Detailed in the following subsection are Life360's characteristics, functions, and ways in which it stands out in the market:

6.4.1. Key Features

i Real-time Location Sharing: People may choose to keep their loved ones up-to-date on their current location in real-time. This feature will be quite useful for parents who are worried about their children's safety.
ii Place Alerts (Geofencing): Anyone may set up geofences around their house, office, or school using Life360. Users will get information whenever a family member visits or leaves these particular places. They may rest easy knowing that their loved ones are safe because of this.
iii Crash Detection and Roadside Assistance: One of the app's innovative driver safety features is accident detection, which can identify when a car has collided and, if necessary, summon help from nearby emergency services. For emergencies like dead batteries or flat tyres, it also offers roadside help.
iv SOS Alert: Users may tell their loved ones of their precise position and the fact that they need assistance in the event of an emergency by sending an SOS alert. In life-threatening emergencies, this function is essential for providing prompt aid.
v History Log: Every location a user has been to is recorded by Life360. If user need to go back a few steps or see patterns in our day-to-day activities, this could help.
vi Battery Monitoring: The programme also monitors and reports on the battery levels of all linked devices, allowing users to be notified if a family member's phone battery is going low, possibly affecting their ability to interact.

6.4.2. Privacy and Security

Life360 prioritises privacy and security, ensuring that location sharing and conversation inside the app are encrypted and only accessible to invited family members (Mavoa et al., 2023). Users have control over their location sharing options, and they may disable sharing or become "invisible" at any moment. Figure 6.1 shows the User Interface (UI) for Life360.

6.4.3. Use Cases

- Family Safety: Parents use Life360 to keep their children safe when they are away from home, travelling to and from school, or on social excursions.
- Coordination: Families may use the app to organise meets or see whether someone has arrived safely at their location without having to make repeated calls or messages.
- Emergency Situations: The SOS function and accident detection capabilities allow a direct channel of communication in emergency circumstances.

6.4.4. Market Position and Reception

Life360 has established itself as a global leader in the family safety app category, with millions of users worldwide praising its dependability, extensive functionality, and user-friendly layout. Its approach to mixing safety and technology has made it a top option for families wishing to remain connected while protecting their loved ones.

The app's popularity stems from its ability to combine practical location-sharing capabilities with superior safety measures, serving a broad variety of user demands from everyday logistics to emergency response. Despite the privacy issues that are common with location-sharing apps, Life360's dedication to user control and data security helps to preserve user confidence.

6.5. NOONLIGHT: SAFE EVERYWHERE

With its many personal safety features and emergency services, Noonlight (previously SafeTrek) is a high-tech safety software that aims to give users a sense of calm (Pedrayes, 2022). Engineered to provide safety and help without the need to make a phone call, it acts as a silent bodyguard for people. What makes Noonlight such a useful instrument for personal safety may be shown here.

6.5.1. Key Features

i Silent Alarm: Silent alarms are Noonlight's bread and butter; all it takes to set one is a quick push and hold of an app button. The user may cancel the alarm by releasing the button and entering a pin if they feel insecure. The user will be notified to summon emergency services to their location by Noonlight's monitoring team if the pin is not entered.

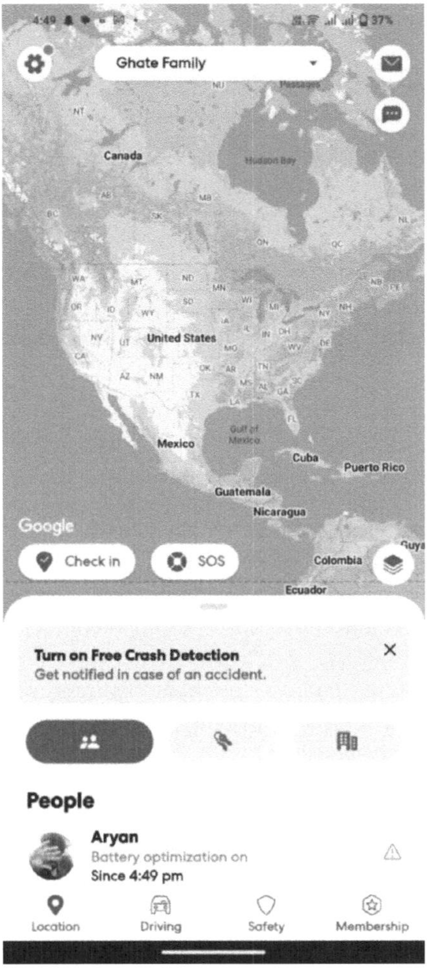

FIGURE 6.1 UI for Life360.

ii Precise Location Sharing: When an alert is activated, Noonlight shares exact location data with emergency responders by integrating with the device's GPS capability. This guarantees that assistance may be sent out without delay, regardless of whether the user can't verbalise their whereabouts.

iii Timeline: Noonlight users may customise their timelines with information like meeting times, locations, and projected return times. Should an alarm be activated, this data may prove to be quite useful to those sent to the scene.

iv Integration with Smart Devices and Apps: Noonlight distinguishes itself by connecting to a wide range of smart platforms and devices, such as health applications, home security systems, and wearables. Multiple alarm triggers and the ability to exchange vital health data with first responders are made possible by this connection, which improves user safety.

v Safety Button Widget: Users may set alarms without ever opening the Noonlight app thanks to the app's widget, which can be installed to the home screen.

6.5.2. Privacy and Security

When it comes to sharing location data and personal information with emergency services, Noonlight makes sure that user privacy and data security are top priorities (Koury, 2021). Protecting user data, the software employs strong encryption mechanisms.

6.5.3. Use Cases

- Personal Safety: People who travel alone, work late, or are in potentially dangerous circumstances where they need covert access to emergency services will find Noonlight to be excellent.
- Emergency Medical Assistance: Noonlight also helps provide medical help to people faster in health situations by letting them exchange health data via app connections.
- Home and Community Safety: Noonlight can improve home security systems by integrating with smart home devices, which adds an additional layer of emergency response.

6.5.4. Market Position and Reception

With its innovative combination of stealthy emergency activation, extensive device and app connections, and proactive safety planning features, Noonlight has established itself as a leading personal safety app. College student, working professionals, and families are all drawn to its approach to personal safety, which centres on quiet alerts and accurate location sharing.

One of the main reasons Noonlight has been so successful is its flexibility to work with different platforms and technologies. This makes it a strong and flexible tool for improving personal and community safety. Users who are concerned about protecting themselves and their loved ones in different scenarios will find it to be a reliable friend due to its dedication to data security and privacy.

6.6. bSAFE

With its many cutting-edge features, bSafe is an all-inclusive personal safety software that aims to increase users' sense of safety and tranquillity (Tan et al., 2020). In an effort to provide a comprehensive solution for personal safety, bSafe integrates features such as location sharing, real-time tracking, voice activation, and video recording to make it easy for users to summon assistance or ward off danger. Take a look at bSafe's features in depth:

6.6.1. Key Features

i SOS Button- An alert is sent to the user's selected emergency contacts when the SOS button is triggered, making it the most crucial function of bSafe. With the user's current position and the ability to stream audio and video from their phone, this alert gives them a bird's-eye view of the scenario right now.

ii Follow Me- This function enables chosen contacts to monitor the user's whereabouts in real time using GPS tracking. It's especially important for assuring safety when walking home or to a car late at night.

iii Voice Activation- Recognising that physically activating the app may not always be practical or safe, bSafe enables users to activate the SOS alert by voice command, making it simpler to ask for assistance discreetly or when physical connection with the phone is difficult.

iv Timer Alarm- Users may programme a timer to trigger an SOS warning if not deactivated in time. This is great for instances when there is a chance of danger, such as meeting a stranger or exploring new locations.

v Video Recording- When users activate the SOS function, the app instantly begins recording video and audio. This recording is transmitted to emergency contacts and may be useful evidence if a crime is committed.

vi Fake Call- bSafe's fake call capability may be used to avoid uncomfortable situations or to create an excuse to escape a potentially hazardous situation. Users may arrange a phone call to themselves for a certain time.

6.6.2. Privacy and Security

By limiting the sharing of location data and personal information to selected contacts only and as needed, bSafe prioritises user privacy and data security (Wang et al., 2020). To keep user information and conversations secure, the app uses strong encryption mechanisms.

6.6.3. Use Cases

- Personal Safety: Ideal for individuals who frequently travel alone, especially at night, providing a sense of security with real-time location sharing and emergency alerts.
- Emergency Situations: The SOS button and live streaming capabilities are crucial for quickly sharing distress signals and situational awareness with trusted contacts or authorities.
- Daily Commutes and Meetings: For those who need confidence on their regular journeys or while meeting new people, the Timer Alarm and Follow Me functions are great options.

6.6.4. Market Position and Reception

Because of its all-encompassing approach to personal safety and its portfolio of proactive and reactive safety measures, bSafe has been highly appreciated. What makes this security software unique is its intuitive design and cutting-edge features, such as voice activation, automated video recording, and live streaming. The bSafe software has established itself as a frontrunner in the personal safety space by giving users a powerful means of self-defence and emergency notification.

Positive feedback has been received from users worldwide on the app's efficacy in real-world settings, such as deterring prospective assailants and supplying evidence in criminal cases. Its emphasis on giving users agency for their own safety and the comfort it provides to loved ones highlight bSafe's significance in the modern app market.

6.7. MY SAFETIPIN

Providing users with information on the safety level of various places, My Safetipin is a unique mobile application that aims to increase personal and community safety. It uses computer analysis and crowdsourcing data to rank different places according to their safety. Users, particularly women and other vulnerable groups, will be able to utilise the app to weigh the pros and drawbacks of potential routes and destinations in light of safety concerns (Bhimanpallewar et al., 2024). Figure 6.2 shows the User Interface for Safetipin app. The features and functionality of My Safetipin are described in full below:

6.7.1. Key Features

- i Safety Score- The safety score, which may be anything from zero to ten, is the main element of My Safetipin. Several factors are taken into consideration while calculating these rankings; they include things like illumination, accessibility, crowd size, visibility, security, sidewalk condition, and the availability of public transportation. Greater safety is indicated by higher ratings.
- ii Safety Audits- By doing safety audits in their immediate environments, users may add to the app's database.
- iii To do this, we'll need to answer several questions about the criteria described before and, if user want to, submit some images. Location safety ratings are regularly reviewed and improved via these assessments.
- iv Safe Route Suggestions- After determining the level of danger in different areas, My Safetipin suggests those with the lowest risk to its customers. This feature is great for when we're exploring a new city or region.
- v Safety Pin- By "pinning" both safe and dangerous spots on a map, app users may alert others to potential dangers and share their own experiences. Using this function together is a better way to ensure everyone's safety.
- vi Night Mode- In order to provide more accurate safety ratings after dark, My Safetipin's night mode evaluates sites according to nighttime-specific parameters, such illumination and the presence of people.

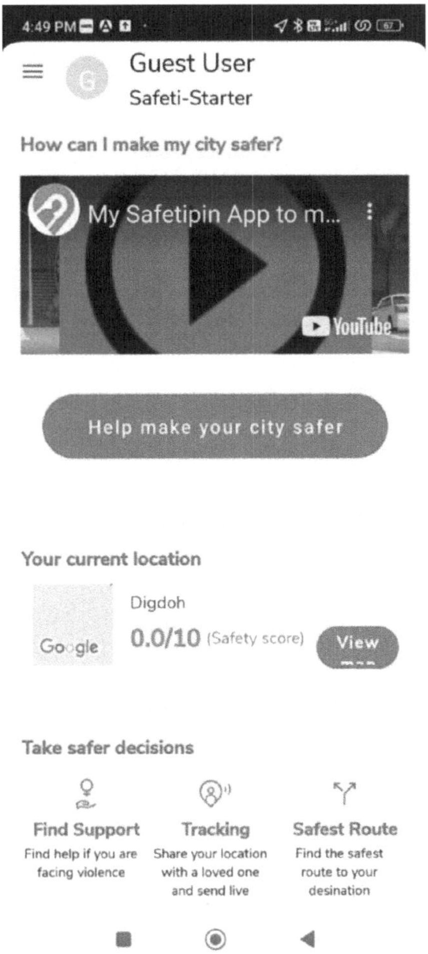

FIGURE 6.2 User interface for Safetipin app.

vii Emergency Contacts- Users can list emergency contacts within the app. In case of distress, My Safetipin facilitates quick communication with these contacts, providing an additional layer of safety.

6.7.2. Privacy and Security

By taking reasonable precautions with users' private information and geolocation data, My Safetipin guarantees their privacy and data security. For the most part, the app utilises this information to refine its safety score algorithm and provide customers more reliable safety ratings

6.7.3. Use Cases

- Urban Planning and Advocacy: In addition to helping individuals, the aggregated data from My Safetipin may be used by urban planners and lawmakers to pinpoint problem regions in terms of safety.
- Personal Safety: This app is great for everyone, but particularly for students and women, since it lets user know how secure certain regions are for things like evening commuting, visiting new cities, and more.
- Community Engagement: My Safetipin promotes a feeling of belonging and shared duty to improve safety by inviting users to do audits and report their findings.

6.7.4. Market Position and Reception

By fusing technology with community interaction to map out safety ratings across cities, My Safetipin has carved out a position for itself in the safety app industry (Shenoy et al., 2021). Differentiating it from conventional GPS or emergency alert applications is its emphasis on concrete elements influencing human safety, in addition to user engagement in content production.

Urban planners, safety advocates, and app users have all acknowledged and praised the app for its novel approach to safety, which places special focus on protecting vulnerable populations in cities and on women in particular. My Safetipin is an essential tool for creating safer cities all across the globe since it gives practical advice and encourages community participation.

6.8. SILENT BEACON

When combined with a physical device, the personal safety software Silent Beacon provides users with a flexible way to request assistance in an emergency without having to unlock their phone or go through other applications. The wearable panic button and the accompanying mobile app work together to notify predetermined contacts or emergency services in the event of the user's crisis, allowing for quick aid. Figure 6.3 shows the User Interface for Silent Beacon. Here, we take a close look at what makes Silent Beacon special in the personal safety industry as well as its features and functionalities:

6.8.1. Key Features

i Panic Button- Silent Beacon's physical panic button—a fastener for keys, garments, or even a pocket—is its foundation. When the user presses the button, an alarm will be sent via the linked smartphone app in the event of an emergency.

ii Customisable Alerts- In case of an emergency, users have the option to pre-configure the app to notify certain people by text, email, or phone call. In order to facilitate rapid reaction and help, these notifications provide the user's GPS position.

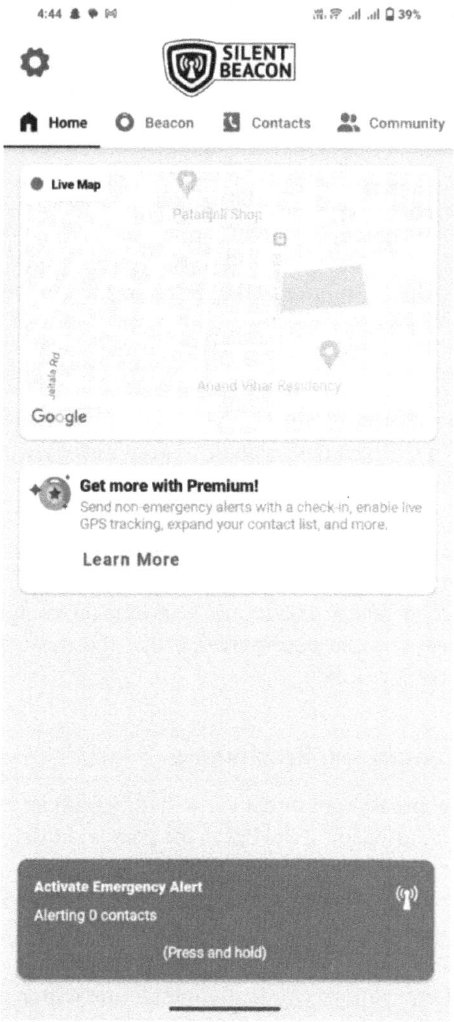

FIGURE 6.3 User interface for Silent Beacon app.

iii Emergency Services Integration- In addition to or instead of notifying personal contacts, Silent Beacon enables direct connection to emergency services (e.g., 911 in the US). When users need help from an expert right away, this tool is life-saving.

iv No Monthly Fees- The fundamental functions of Silent Beacon are available without a monthly cost, making it accessible to a larger audience than certain personal safety gadgets and services that need a membership.

v Two-Way Communication- The device's built-in speaker and microphone enable users to engage in two-way audio communication, enabling them to talk directly with their emergency contacts or responders.

- vi Location Tracking- Upon activation of an alert, Silent Beacon allows the user's designated emergency contacts to follow their whereabouts in real-time, enabling them to respond quickly.
- vii Water-Resistant and Durable- The water-resistant and ruggedly constructed Silent Beacon gadget is ideal for both regular usage and sudden crises.

6.8.2. Privacy and Security

To ensure the safety of its users' private information and location data sent during alerts, Silent Beacon uses encryption and secure connection methods.

6.8.3. Use Cases

- Personal Safety: Perfect for those who have a tendency to travel alone, work long hours, or partake in outdoor activities that might put them in danger.
- Elderly and Medical Emergencies: Users who are old or have medical issues and may need to rapidly notify caretakers or emergency services may find Silent Beacon's button-press design to be acceptable.
- Children and Students: Students and children on campus or en route to school might feel more at ease knowing that there is a hidden and easily accessible emergency button.

6.8.4. Market Position and Reception

The revolutionary combination of a real panic button with an extensive smartphone app is what makes Silent Beacon stand out in the personal safety industry. Compared to relying on apps or devices alone, this dual strategy covers a wider spectrum of emergency circumstances. Offering a cost-effective, one-time purchase solution, the no-monthly-fee concept adds to its attractiveness.

Users have a fast and covert method to summon assistance because of the device's capacity to trigger alerts without physically interacting with a phone. Silent Beacon is a multipurpose and efficient instrument for improving personal safety and peace of mind, especially when combined with personalised alarms and direct connectivity with emergency services.

6.9. RED PANIC BUTTON

In case of an emergency, users of the Red Panic Button app may elevate their level of personal safety by quickly and easily sending out a distress signal via the virtual button they click. This software fits into a larger trend of safety apps that use technology to provide people peace of mind and rapid help when they're in risky circumstances. An easy way to call for assistance, the Red Panic Button is both functional and eye-catching. Figure 6.4 shows the User Interface of Red Panic Button. The Red Panic Button's characteristics are described in full below:

FIGURE 6.4 User interface of Red Panic Button.

6.9.1. Key Features

- i Panic Button- The Red Panic Button, which, when hit, activates the app's alarm system, is its main feature. The user's designated emergency contacts will be notified by this system, who will also send them a message with the user's current GPS position.
- ii Customisable Messages- A user's emergency contacts may get a personalised alert message. The option to include particular instructions or information in the warning and make it more personalised is made possible by this.
- iii Multiple Alert Methods- Sending warnings via numerous channels increases the odds of a speedy response. The software supports SMS, email, and even social media platforms, so the distress signal reaches the contacts through many ways.

iv GPS Location Sharing- The software not only notifies emergency contacts of the user's locations, but it also provides them the user's current position, which may help them determine the user's whereabouts faster and perhaps expedite response times.
v Group Alerts- In critical, time-sensitive emergencies, the ability to transmit notifications to several people at once—as is possible with the red panic button—is invaluable.

6.9.2. Privacy and Security

When designing the Red Panic Button app, the developers took user privacy and safety very seriously. It makes sure that the user's selected contacts are the only ones to get location data and personal information in the event of a panic. Users' privacy is prioritised in the app's design, which also happens to be a crucial safety element.

6.9.3. Use Cases

- Personal Safety: Perfect for those who aren't comfortable wandering alone at night, exploring new places, or facing any other potentially dangerous circumstance.
- Elderly and Health-Related Emergencies: The software gives users a simple method to notify loved ones in the event of a medical emergency or fall, which is especially helpful for those who are older or have preexisting problems.
- Children and Teenagers: As a preventative measure, parents may put the app on their children's phones. This will allow them to quickly notify them if they feel threatened or need assistance.

6.9.4. Market Position and Reception

Users love the Red Panic Button app because it's easy to use and has a single, uncomplicated feature: a panic button. A great tool for personal safety, it may immediately notify a pre-defined set of contacts of the user's trouble and whereabouts. Users of all kinds, from parents concerned about their children's safety to lone travellers, find value in the app's adaptability.

With its exclusive emphasis on rapidly notifying contacts in the event of an emergency, the Red Panic Button stands out in a market crowded with complicated safety solutions (Menon et al., 2023). The Red Panic Button is a user-friendly and successful personal safety software because of its emphasis on simplicity, adaptable alarms, and several notification options.

6.10. TRENDS AND DEVELOPMENTS

Apps like this show how people are using technology in all sorts of ways to make communities and individuals safer. The use of Artificial Intelligence (AI) for predictive analytics, Internet of Things (IoT) devices to expand functionality, and advanced data encryption to safeguard privacy are all on the rise. Software engineers are always thinking of new ways to improve upon current emergency response systems by creating solutions that are easier to use, more accessible, and compatible with more platforms.

The capabilities and features of emergency response applications are constantly evolving along with technology. There is an increasing focus on user privacy, making them available across platforms, and making them accessible globally. In order to choose the most suitable app for their individual safety requirements, users should compare the features, privacy policies, and dependability of each.

6.11. CONCLUSION

Several smartphone applications for emergency response and personal safety have been covered in this chapter. Every app has its own special function that may aid people in trouble. For example, Life360 can watch families, Noonlight can set quiet alerts, and My Safetipin can rate public locations based on how safe they are. To protect users' privacy and security, these applications employ cutting-edge tech like Artificial Intelligence, the Internet of Things, and data encryption. The development of more user-friendly safety apps shows how vital it is to have easy access to tools that may help us stay safe. Making these tools accessible and inclusive to everyone will be a challenge as technology evolves. To optimise their effect, developers, law enforcement, and community groups must collaborate. Finally, people may feel more secure and in control of their own safety via emergency response applications. These applications have the potential to make our world a safer place via ongoing development and widespread use.

REFERENCES

Aagaard, P., Dinyarian, B., Abduljabbar, O., & Choo, K. K. R. (2023). Family locating sharing app forensics: Life360 as a case study. *Forensic Science International: Digital Investigation*, *44*, 301478.

Bhimanpallewar, R. N., Dedgaonkar, S., Bagade, J. V., Shelke, P., & Sable, N. P. (2024). The prediction of the critical condition for a weak entity using fuzzy system. *International Journal of Intelligent Systems and Applications in Engineering*, *12*(12s), 513–521.

Damaševičius, R., Bacanin, N., & Misra, S. (2023, May 16). From sensors to safety: Internet of Emergency Services (IoES) for emergency response and disaster management. *Journal of Sensor and Actuator Networks*, *12*(3), 41. https://doi.org/10.3390/jsan12030041

Kavitha, M., Gnaneswar, G., Dinesh, R., Sai, Y. R., & Suraj, R. S. (2021, January 20). Heart disease prediction using hybrid machine learning model. In *2021 6th International Conference on Inventive Computation Technologies (ICICT)*. https://doi.org/10.1109/icict50816.2021.9358597

Koury, R. (2021, May 10). *Places Lost and Found*. Syracuse University Press. http://books.google.ie/books?id=BhYwEAAAQBAJ&printsec=frontcover&dq=Places+Lost+and+Found:+Travel+Essays+from+the+Hudson+Review&hl=&cd=1&source=gbs_api

Mavoa, J., Coghlan, S., & Nansen, B. (2023). "It's about safety not snooping": Parental attitudes to child tracking technologies and geolocation data. *Surveillance & Society*, *21*(1), 45–60.

Menon, A. B., Devipriya, Jyothika, S., Ratheesh, K., Sudev, K. U., & Anjali, T. (2023, January). STING—A user governed crime alert app. In *International Conference on Smart Trends in Computing and Communications* (pp. 61–69). Springer Nature Singapore.

Nanda, S., Panigrahi, C. R., & Pati, B. (2020, November 3). Emergency management systems using mobile cloud computing: A survey. *International Journal of Communication Systems*, *36*(12). https://doi.org/10.1002/dac.4619

Pedrayes, C. (2022). *The Mom Friend Guide to Everyday Safety and Security: Tips from the Practical One in Your Squad.* Simon and Schuster.

Romano, M., Onorati, T., Aedo, I., & Diaz, P. (2016). Designing mobile applications for emergency response: Citizens acting as human sensors. *Sensors*, *16*(3), 406.

Shenoy, M. V., Sridhar, S., Salaka, G., Gupta, A., & Gupta, R. (2021). A holistic framework for crime prevention, response, and analysis with emphasis on women safety using technology and societal participation. *IEEE Access*, *9*, 66188–66207.

Tan, M. L., Prasanna, R., Stock, K., Doyle, E. E., Leonard, G., & Johnston, D. (2020, November). Usability factors influencing the continuance intention of disaster apps: A mixed-methods study. *International Journal of Disaster Risk Reduction*, *50*, 101874. https://doi.org/10.1016/j.ijdrr.2020.101874

Wang, Y., Li, J., Zhao, X., Feng, G., & Luo, X. (2020, September 16). Using mobile phone data for emergency management: A systematic literature review. *Information Systems Frontiers*, *22*(6), 1539–1559. https://doi.org/10.1007/s10796-020-10057-w

7 Boosting Emergency Management

Leveraging Mobile Apps for Rapid Response to Crises

Rajendra Kumar, Manas Rathore, Chandra Kumar Sahu, Praveen Kumar Yadaw, and Soma Rajwade

7.1. INTRODUCTION

Technology is causing a revolution in the field of crisis management at a time when events are occurring more frequently and with greater complexity. Emergency Response Mobile Applications (ERMAs) are among these developments that have shown great promise in changing how we approach and handle disasters. This introduction lays the groundwork for a thorough examination of the function, meaning, and influence of ERMAs in modern crisis management.

7.1.1. Context and Background

In the ever-changing field of crisis management and emergency response, technology integration has become critical to improving overall efficacy, coordination, and efficiency. There is a rising opportunity to use mobile devices and their increasing ubiquity to utilise these technologies for accessible and quick emergency response. It is necessary to comprehend the historical development and contextual elements that have contributed to the creation of mobile crisis management applications in order to investigate the importance of these tools in tackling modern issues. The contemporary landscape of crisis management is evolving in tandem with advancements in technology, presenting an unprecedented opportunity to revolutionise emergency response strategies. In times of calamity, rapid and effective communication plays a pivotal role in saving lives and mitigating the impact of disasters. Mobile applications have emerged as powerful tools in this context, offering a dynamic platform to streamline communication, coordination, and resource allocation during critical situations. Traditional emergency response systems have often grappled with limitations such as delayed information dissemination, lack of real-time data sharing, and challenges in coordinating efforts among various stakeholders. Recognising the potential of mobile applications, the focus has shifted towards harnessing the

DOI: 10.1201/9781003538172-7

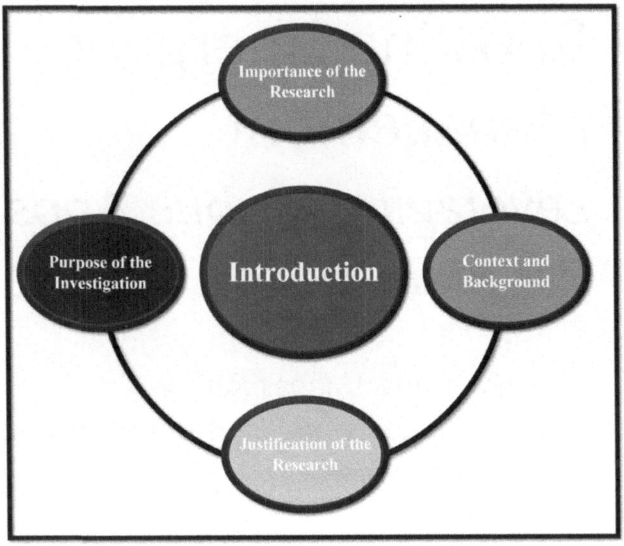

FIGURE 7.1 Introduction to crisis management.

ubiquitous presence of smartphones to create a responsive and interconnected framework for crisis management.

These applications empower both responders and the affected population by providing instant access to vital information, enabling real-time communication, and facilitating the efficient deployment of resources. From natural disasters like earthquakes and hurricanes to public health emergencies and man-made crises, mobile applications have demonstrated their capacity to enhance the speed and efficacy of emergency response efforts. The integration of features such as geo location services, push notifications, and multimedia sharing capabilities equips emergency responders with the tools to make informed decisions swiftly. Additionally, these applications empower citizens to actively participate in their safety by offering real-time alerts, evacuation routes, and guidance on emergency protocols.

This background sets the stage for a comprehensive exploration of the role that mobile applications play in revolutionising crisis management. By delving into the functionalities, successes, and challenges associated with these technologies, we can better understand how they contribute to creating a more resilient and responsive emergency response ecosystem. "Empowering Crisis Management: Harnessing Mobile Applications for Swift Emergency Response" seeks to unravel the transformative impact of these digital solutions in the pursuit of safeguarding lives and minimizing the impact of crises on communities worldwide.

New developments in technology, such as AI systems, drones, and state-of-the-art sensors, offer new opportunities to improve survival discovery in catastrophe situations. This article focuses on technology for detecting survivors in land-based disaster scenarios by conducting a systematic evaluation of 67 studies from 2009 to

2023. Following PRISMA principles, the review outlines the state of the literature, highlighting the use of Wi-Fi, smartphones, radars, unmanned vehicles, and wireless sensors as common modalities. Limited validation in the real world, logistics of on-site deployment, dependence on communication infrastructure, and power consumption are major obstacles. However, novel approaches like multimodal integration and on-site TinyML processing show promise in mitigating these drawbacks, indicating encouraging directions for further study. Given the abundance of investigations, the conclusions adopt a practical viewpoint, rejecting less developed technologies unfit for early physical world implementation.

7.1.2. Justification of the Research

The necessity of optimising and innovating crisis management systems in the face of changing situations and dangers is the driving force behind this study. Even if they work well, traditional approaches sometimes have issues with speed, accessibility, and real-time coordination. Through an analysis of the justification for implementing Emergency Response Mobile Applications (ERMAs), this study aims to identify the particular benefits and opportunities brought about by this technological change. Policymakers, first responders, and software developers can all benefit from knowing why ERMAs are deemed necessary in the modern emergency response environment.

7.1.3. Purpose of the Investigation

- This study's main goals are to: Examine the condition of emergency response mobile applications today, taking into account their features, used technologies, and current implementations.
- Assess how well ERMAs improve emergency response teams' coordination, incident reporting, and real-time communication. Analyse how ERMAs can be scaled and adjusted to different crisis situations.
- Evaluate the effect of ERMAs on the readiness and resilience of the community.
- The methodical investigation of ERMAs' potential and usefulness in crisis management is guided by these goals.

7.1.4. Importance of the Research

This study is significant in several ways. Initially, it adds to the scholarly conversation on how technology and emergency response intersect by offering a thorough examination of ERMAs. Second, the results of the study should educate decision-makers in government, emergency response teams, and IT companies on the advantages and disadvantages of using ERMAs. Finally, by highlighting the importance of ERMAs, this study hopes to highlight how they support a society that is more connected and resilient and is better equipped to handle a variety of emergencies and crises.

7.2. LITERATURE REVIEW

The body of research on Emergency Response Mobile Applications (ERMAs) and crisis management includes historical analyses, technical advancements, and empirical investigations.

7.2.1. Looking Back at Emergency Response in History

It is essential to trace the historical development of emergency response methodologies in order to understand the current state of Emergency Response Mobile Applications (ERMAs). This part offers a historical framework that paves the way for comprehending the changes in emergency response paradigms across time, from the early development of civil defence systems to the creation of centralized emergency services. Analysing the past highlights the need for modern solutions and provides insights into the difficulties experienced by conventional methods.

7.2.2. The Development of Mobile Technology for Crisis Intervention

This topic explores how mobile technology is revolutionising the field of crisis management. Beginning with the introduction of mobile communication devices and ending with the current day of smartphones and pervasive connection, the overview identifies significant turning points in the development of mobile technology. The foundation for investigating the formation of ERMAs as a cutting-edge and significant solution is an understanding of how these technical developments have impacted and altered emergency response techniques.

7.2.3. Current Studies on Mobile Applications for Emergency Response

A thorough review of the literature now available on ERMAs demonstrates the wide range of research projects, case studies, and technical frameworks that have been used to investigate the potential and constraints of these applications. The research on the features, practicality, and efficacy of ERMAs in actual emergency situations is summarised in this section. This segment seeks to identify common trends, best practices, and places where ERMAs have shown a significant influence by reviewing the literature.

7.2.4. Gaps in the Current Literature

Although research has made significant contributions to our understanding of ERMAs, a critical evaluation identifies areas that still need to be explored. The limits and undiscovered aspects of the current literature are described in this section. Gaps could include problems with user uptake, technological limitations, or the requirement for more thorough case studies involving various emergency scenarios.

Finding these gaps is essential to shaping the current study's objectives and focus, directing future investigations, and offering a comprehensive picture of the status of the field's knowledge at the moment.

The objective of this literature review is to integrate pertinent historical viewpoints, technological developments, and empirical research to create a thorough framework for the investigation of Emergency Response Mobile Applications in crisis management that follows.

7.3. APPROACH

The research approach used to examine the function and efficacy of Emergency Response Mobile Applications (ERMAs) in crisis management is described in this section. The research design, participant selection, data collection techniques, and data analysis strategies are all included in the methodology.

7.3.1. Design of the Research

The study uses a mixed-methods approach, integrating quantitative and qualitative techniques to develop a thorough grasp of ERMAs in crisis management. In-depth case studies and interviews are used in the qualitative component to investigate the subtleties of the context and user experiences. The quantitative component measures user perceptions, application usage trends, and overall impact through surveys and data analytics. (Omondiagbe, 2016)

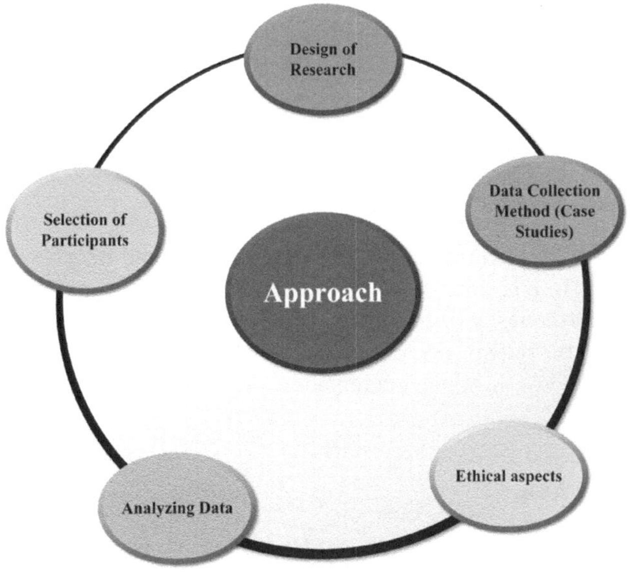

FIGURE 7.2 Various approaches to crisis management.

7.3.2. Data Collection Methods: Case Studies

Selected regions or organisations that have incorporated ERMAs into their crisis response plans will be the subject of in-depth case studies. In these case studies, system functionality, user experiences, and the results of employing ERMAs in actual emergency situations will all be thoroughly examined. (Zuefle, 1994)

7.3.2.1. Interviews

Key stakeholders involved in the deployment of ERMAs, such as emergency responders, application developers, and government officials, will be the subject of semi-structured interviews. The purpose of these interviews is to record qualitative observations, viewpoints, and difficulties related to ERMAs.

7.3.2.2. Surveys

To gather quantitative information on user satisfaction, perceived effectiveness, and improvement ideas, surveys will be given to a broad sample of ERMA customers. Likert scales and open-ended questions will be used in the surveys to collect data on both the quantitative and qualitative aspects.

7.3.2.3. Data Analytics

To find usage trends, response times, and opportunities for improvement, usage data from deployed ERMAs will be examined. This quantitative investigation will shed light on how ERMAs actually function in various emergency situations.

7.3.3. Selection of Participants

The emergency response ecosystem will be taken into consideration while choosing participants. Interviews and surveys will be conducted with emergency responders, application developers, government officials, and end-users of ERMAs. Diversity in terms of demographics, emergency categories, and geographic regions will be prioritised during the selection process (Zhang et al., 2017)

7.3.4. Analysing Data

Thematic analysis of qualitative data from case studies and interviews will reveal recurrent themes, trends, and difficulties related to ERMAs. To provide quantitative insights, such as frequency distributions, correlations, and user satisfaction scores, survey data will be statistically evaluated. Triangulation is made possible by the mixed-methods approach, which guarantees a solid and thorough grasp of the study concerns.

7.3.5. Ethical Aspects

Getting participants' informed consent, protecting the privacy of their data, and abiding by moral standards for study involving human beings are all examples of ethical aspects. Additionally, sensitive data and privacy will be respected throughout the research, especially when it comes to real-world emergency response circumstances.

Through the use of a mixed-methods approach, this study seeks to bridge the gap between qualitative insights and quantitative data for a more comprehensive understanding by offering a nuanced and thorough review of ERMAs in crisis management.

7.4. EMERGENCY RESPONSE MOBILE APPLICATION LANDSCAPE

This section explores the ever-changing field of Emergency Response Mobile uses (ERMAs) and offers a thorough examination of the state-of-the-art, features, and practical uses of these apps.

7.4.1. Synopsis of Upcoming Applications

An extensive summary of the state of Emergency Response Mobile Applications (ERMAs) is given in this section. It entails a methodical analysis of current crisis management solutions, emphasising their range, reach, and uptake in many industries and geographical areas (Rueß, 2018).

7.4.2. Features and Functionalities

Understanding the capabilities and characteristics that ERMAs offer is essential to appreciating their value in emergency response. The main components of these applications—real-time communication, incident reporting, geographic mapping, sensor integration, and artificial intelligence—are broken down in this subsection. Gaining knowledge of these characteristics helps one better understand the skills necessary for crisis management success.

7.4.3. Case Studies: Effective Applications

The aim of this analysis is to examine situations in which ERMAs have proven to be beneficial and effective.

7.4.3.1. Method

Carefully reviewing case studies that demonstrate effective ERMA deployments. This includes a thorough examination of the situations in which these apps were used, the particular features that were made use of, and the ways in which they improved emergency response.

7.4.3.2. Obstacles and Setbacks

The goal is to pinpoint the situations in which ERMAs had difficulties or fell short of expectations.

7.4.3.3. Method

Careful examination of case studies illustrating difficulties and shortcomings related to ERMAs. This entails looking into things like user acceptance problems,

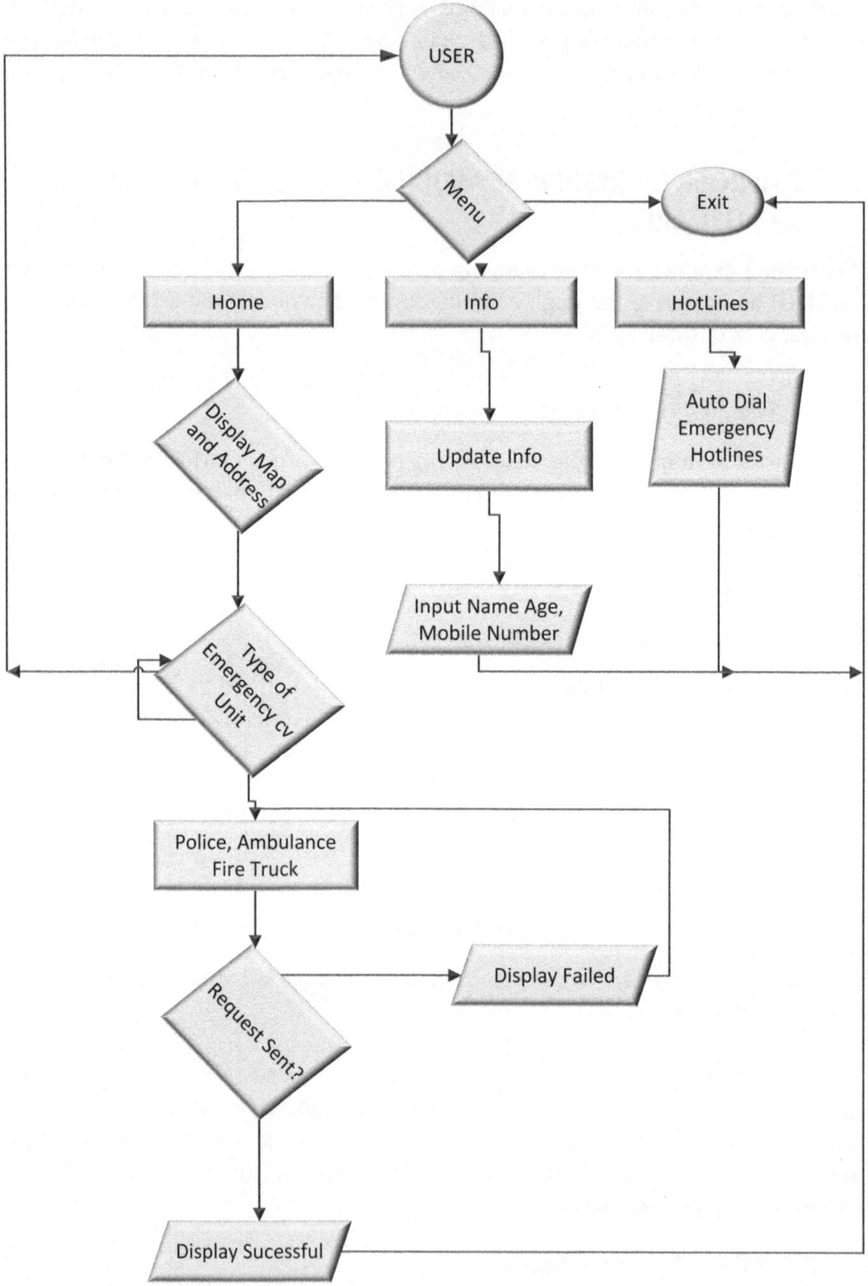

FIGURE 7.3 Systematic architecture of a mobile application.

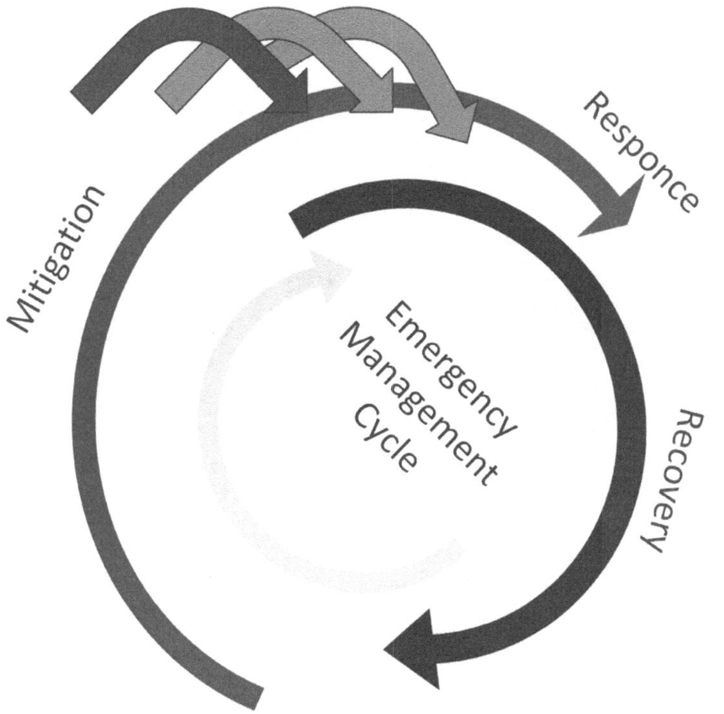

FIGURE 7.4 Key points for emergency response mobile application landscape.

technology constraints, and unanticipated difficulties during crisis situations. (Frerk et al., 2015)

In order to provide a clear picture of the current state of ERMAs, this section will explain their features, successful implementations, and places where difficulties or failures have occurred. A comprehensive grasp of the real-world applications and constraints of ERMAs in various settings will be investigated via case studies. (Brunton & Coll, 2005).

7.4.4. Real-Time Communication

Emergency response mobile applications facilitate instant communication among responders, enabling swift exchange of critical information (Yılankıran & Guney, 2021). Real-time updates on the evolving situation, alerts, and advisories are disseminated efficiently through these platforms.

7.4.5. Geolocation Services

Integration of GPS technology enables precise location tracking of both responders and affected individuals. Geospatial data aids in resource allocation, evacuation planning, and mapping the extent of the crisis.

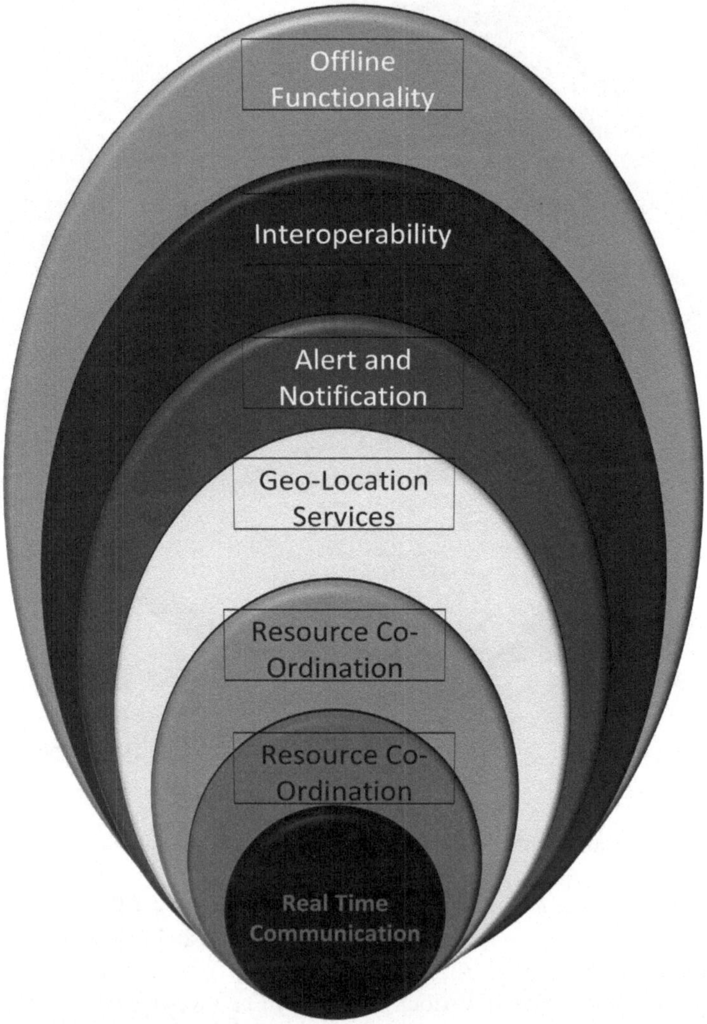

FIGURE 7.5 Various layers of mobile applications and their functions.

7.4.6. Resource Coordination

Mobile applications streamline the allocation and deployment of resources by providing a centralised platform for managing assets (Dittakavi, 2022). Efficient coordination among different response teams, agencies, and organisations enhances overall effectiveness.

7.4.7. Alerts and Notifications

Push notifications and alert systems ensure that users receive timely and crucial information, including evacuation orders, weather updates, and safety instructions.

Customisable alert settings cater to the specific needs of users based on their location and preferences.

7.4.8. Multimedia Sharing

Mobile applications allow the sharing of multimedia content, such as images and videos, providing real-time visual insights into the crisis. Multimedia sharing aids in situation assessment, decision-making, and public awareness.

7.4.9. Community Engagement

Empowering citizens to actively participate in their safety through features like reporting incidents, marking safe locations, and requesting assistance. Social media integration enhances community engagement and information dissemination.

7.4.10. Offline Functionality

Some applications offer offline functionality, ensuring that users can access critical information even in areas with limited connectivity. Offline maps, emergency contact lists, and basic functionalities enhance the application's reliability during network disruptions.

7.4.11. Data Security and Privacy

Robust security measures safeguard sensitive information, recognising the importance of protecting user data in emergency situations. Adherence to privacy standards and regulations builds trust among users and stakeholders.

7.4.12. Interoperability

Seamless integration with existing emergency response systems and communication channels enhances collaboration between different agencies and organisations. Compatibility with various devices and platforms ensures broader accessibility.

7.4.13. Training and Simulation

Some applications offer training modules and simulation exercises to prepare responders and the community for potential emergencies. Virtual drills and educational content contribute to increased preparedness and effective response.

7.4.14. Post-Event Analysis

Analytics and reporting features allow for post-event analysis, aiding in the evaluation of response strategies, identification of areas for improvement, and lessons learned. Understanding the landscape of emergency response mobile applications involves recognising the synergy of these key points, which collectively contribute to a more resilient and responsive crisis management ecosystem.

7.5. EFFECT ON COMMUNICATION DURING CRISIS

The diverse effects of Emergency Response Mobile Applications (ERMAs) on crisis communication are examined in this section. (Corbin et al., 2021). We may learn more about the revolutionary impacts of these applications in emergency settings by looking at their roles in community participation, responder coordination, real-time information distribution, and user experience.

7.5.1. Instantaneous Information Sharing

Goal: Assess how ERMAs aid in the prompt distribution of vital information in times of emergency.

Methods: Examine user reviews and case studies to gauge how quickly and effectively information is disseminated using ERMAs. Analyse how often features like geographical alerts, live updates, and push notifications are used.

7.5.2. Respondent Coordination

Goal: Examine how ERMAs help emergency responders coordinate and communicate more easily.

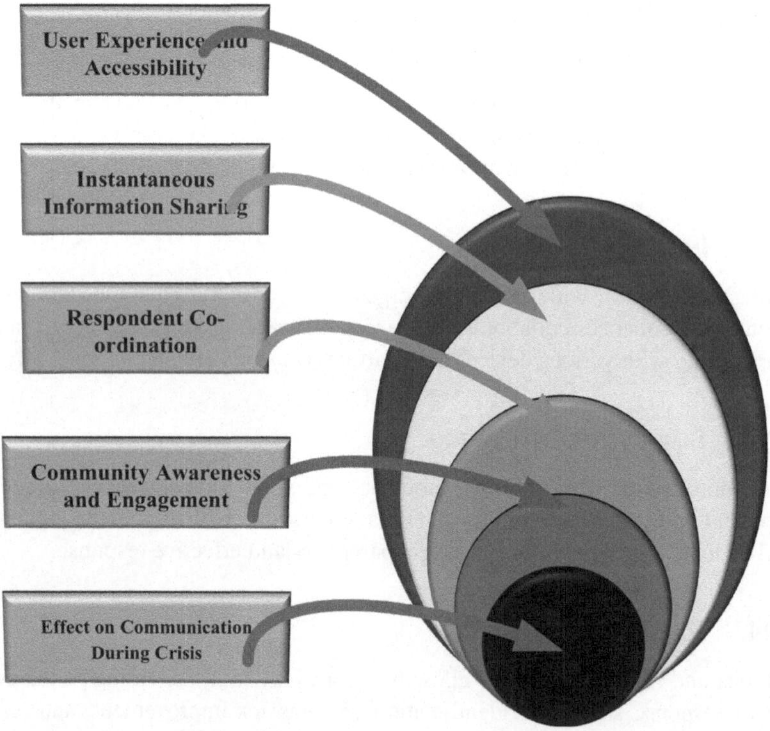

FIGURE 7.6 The mobile application layers for various crisis management applications.

Methods: Analyse case studies of successful deployments, emphasising situations in which ERMAs have improved teamwork. Examine aspects that help with efficient coordination, such as group messaging, real-time mapping, and resource allocation.

7.5.3. Community Awareness and Engagement

Goal: Evaluate how well ERMAs have worked to involve communities and increase public knowledge of emergency circumstances.

Methods: Examine community participation tools and user reviews in ERMAs. Examine case studies where these apps have effectively encouraged community members to report events, exchange information, and take part in readiness exercises.

7.5.4. User Experience and Accessibility

Goal: Assess ERMAs' general usability and accessibility in emergency scenarios.

Techniques: Assess the usability, efficacy, and accessibility of ERMAs using survey results, interviews, and user feedback. Examine the ways in which applications' functionality and impact during emergencies are enhanced by user-centric design.

This section tries to provide a nuanced knowledge of how ERMAs affect crisis communication by a thorough investigation of various effect elements. Through an analysis of their contributions to the broadcast of information in real-time, response coordination, community participation, and user experience, we may extract important lessons about the efficacy and possible areas for development for these applications in the context of crisis management.

7.6. STRENGTHENING PEOPLE AND ORGANIZATIONS

This section explores the ways in which Emergency Response Mobile Applications (ERMAs) provide businesses and individuals with enhanced crisis management capabilities (Laverack, 2017). Through an analysis of their effects on readiness, response effectiveness, fostering resilience, and resolving obstacles, we can reveal the revolutionary possibilities of these applications.

A. Improving readiness: Goal: Assess how ERMAs help to improve community and individual readiness.

7.6.1. Methods

Examine elements of ERMAs that support preparedness, such as training modules, educational materials, and pre-incident planning tools, by analysing user comments and case studies.

7.6.2. Increasing Response Efficiency

Goal: Examine how ERMAs enhance emergency response operations' effectiveness.

Methods: Study case studies of successful implementations, with an emphasis on situations in which ERMAs have shortened reaction times, improved resource allocation, and streamlined response procedures.

7.6.3. Building Resilience

Goal: Evaluate how ERMAs contribute to building resilience in communities and individuals.

Methods: To understand how ERMAs help to create resilience by providing people with knowledge and tools for efficient reaction and recovery, analyse community participation.

7.6.4. Getting Past Obstacles and Restraints

Goal: Determine the tactics used by ERMAs to get over obstacles and constraints while putting them into practice.

Methods: Examine case studies that illustrate the difficulties ERMAs encounter, such as technological limitations, problems with user acceptance, or contextual restrictions. Examine the ways in which these difficulties are resolved and lessened in successful implementations. (Darke et al., 1998)

This section attempts to clarify the ways in which ERMAs help people and organisations during emergencies by thoroughly examining these dimensions. Through evaluating their effects on readiness, response effectiveness, resilience development, and problem-solving skills, we may extract important information on the comprehensive empowerment that these crisis management technologies enable.

7.7. ANALYSES AND CASE STUDIES

In-depth analyses of certain emergency situations involving the deployment of Emergency Response Mobile Applications (ERMAs) are the main objective of this section (Pereira, 2013). This analysis intends to contribute to a thorough knowledge of the impact and prospective improvements in the use of ERMAs in crisis management by assessing their efficacy, identifying best practices, and drawing lessons from real-world scenarios.

7.7.1. Analysing Particular Emergency Situations

Goal: Look into and evaluate particular emergency situations when ERMAs were used.

Methods: Choose a variety of emergency situations where ERMAs were used, such as accidents, natural catastrophes, or risks to public safety. (Wulandari et al., 2023). Analyse in detail how ERMAs contributed to these incidents, taking into account the type of emergency, the features used, and the results obtained.

7.7.2. Assessing the Mobile Applications' Effectiveness

Goal: Evaluate how well ERMAs perform overall in handling various emergency situations.

Techniques: Use a mix of quantitative and qualitative metrics, such as impact evaluations, response times, and user feedback. Examine how successfully ERMAs functioned in various situations and how well they handled the particular difficulties that each emergency event brought.

7.7.3. Takeaways and Optimal Methodologies

Goal: Determine best practices for ERMA deployment in crisis management by distilling learning from the case studies.

Methods: Highlight important conclusions and takeaways from the case studies, highlighting achievements, difficulties, and potential areas of development (Ibraeva et al., 2020). Determine the most important takeaways and condense the best practices that will direct ERMA initiatives in the future.

The objective of this case study research is to offer a comprehensive grasp of the usefulness and practical applicability of ERMAs in diverse emergency situations. Through an analysis of particular situations, a judgement call, and lessons learned from actual events, this section offers insightful information to guide and enhance the usage of mobile applications in crisis management.

7.8. VIEWS FROM USERS

Examining user viewpoints after interacting with Emergency Response Mobile Applications (ERMAs) is the main goal of this section (Abdelouhab et al., 2018). In order to make sure that the applications meet the requirements and expectations of the intended users, surveys and interviews are used to assess user satisfaction, obtain feedback, and pinpoint areas that require development.

7.8.1. Interviews and Surveys With Users of Applications

Goal: Obtain firsthand knowledge from people who have used ERMAs in emergency situations.

7.8.1.1. Techniques

Surveys: Give structured questionnaires to a cross-section of ERMA users. Find information about their preferences, experiences, and general level of satisfaction with the apps.

Interviews: To gain a more nuanced insight of users' experiences, conduct in-depth interviews with a selection of users to go further into their opinions.

7.8.1.2. User Input and Contentment

Goal: Assess user satisfaction levels and collect qualitative input regarding their ERMA experiences.

Techniques: Examine survey results to determine the general level of user satisfaction.

Analyse interview transcripts thematically to find reoccurring themes, obstacles encountered, and good experiences that users have shared.

7.8.1.3. Determining What Has to Be Improved

Goal: Based on user feedback, pinpoint particular places where ERMAs might be enhanced.

Methods: Highlight areas for improvement by summarising prevalent themes from user comments.

Perform a comparison analysis of various ERMAs to find aspects or functionalities that are frequently recommended for improvement.

This section attempts to offer useful insights into the usability, efficacy, and user satisfaction levels related to ERMAs by focusing on user viewpoints. In order to better meet the requirements of people and communities in times of emergency, the findings will help to optimise and refine these applications. (Du et al., 2019).

7.9. UPCOMING DEVELOPMENTS AND TRENDS

This section explores the future trends and breakthroughs that are expected to occur in the field of Emergency Response Mobile Applications (ERMAs). This analysis attempts to provide insight into how the emergency response landscape may change in the future by looking at possible technical developments, how they might integrate with other technologies, and what opportunities and challenges they might present.

7.9.1. Developments in Technology for Emergency Response

Goal: Investigate cutting-edge technologies that may influence ERMAs in the future.

Methods: Examine existing studies and publications to find technology developments that are pertinent to emergency response.

Examine advancements in fields including sensor technology, artificial intelligence, and communication protocols to see how they can improve ERMA capabilities.

7.9.2. Possible Integrations With Other Technologies

Goal: Look into ways that ERMAs and other technical solutions could work together to create possible synergies.

Methods: Examine the most recent developments in the ecosystem for emergency response technology integration. (Guzman de et al., 2014)

Determine potential areas of cooperation between ERMAs and cutting-edge technologies, like block chain, augmented reality, and the Internet of Things (IoT), to improve their functions.

7.9.3. Expected Challenges and Opportunities

Goal: Foresee potential obstacles and chances in the future as ERMAs are developed and implemented.
Methods: Perform a detailed examination of the difficulties that ERMAs are currently facing and extrapolate future difficulties.

Determine areas that could utilize innovation and enhancement while taking into account user behaviour shifts, technological improvements, and changing emergency response plans.

This section seeks to offer a forward-looking viewpoint on the development of ERMAs by examining prospective technological integrations, future trends, and obstacles and opportunities. Policymakers, developers, and other stakeholders interested in determining the direction of emergency response technologies will find great value in this knowledge.

7.10. SUGGESTIONS FOR CONCERNED PARTIES

Specialised advice for important parties operating in the field of Emergency Response Mobile Applications (ERMAs) is given in this area. The purpose of these guidelines is to maximise the impact and efficacy of emergency response management applications (ERMAs) for the benefit of emergency responders, developers, policymakers, and the general public.

7.10.1. Government Agencies and Policymakers

7.10.1.1. Invest in Infrastructure

Set aside funds to improve the communication infrastructure necessary to ensure that ERMAs operate without a hitch in an emergency.

7.10.1.2. Standardisation and Interoperability

To make it easier to integrate various ERMAs and guarantee compatibility between systems and areas, work towards the establishment of standardised frameworks and interoperability standards.

7.10.1.3. Regulatory Support

To foster public confidence and guarantee appropriate data handling procedures, create and implement regulations that place a high priority on data security and privacy inside ERMAs.

7.10.2. The Tech Industry and Developers

7.10.2.1. User-Centric Design

To make sure that ERMAs are intuitive and easy to use, especially in stressful emergency situations, give priority to the user experience and accessibility while designing and developing these apps.

Encourage the creation of open Application Programming Interfaces (APIs) and collaboration in order to facilitate seamless interaction with various systems and technologies and create a more linked emergency response ecosystem.

7.10.2.2. Constant Innovation

Keep up with new developments in fields like artificial intelligence, geographic mapping, and communication protocols. Also, keep your ERMAs up to date by consistently innovating them.

7.10.2.3. Organisations and Emergency Responders

Instruction and Acquaintance: It is imperative to guarantee that emergency responders possess enough training and familiarity with ERMA features in order to maximise their effectiveness during crisis scenarios.

7.10.2.4. Integration With Current Systems

To establish a unified and interconnected infrastructure that improves overall coordination and efficacy, integrate ERMAs with current emergency response systems.

7.10.2.5. Feedback Mechanisms

Set up procedures for gathering emergency responders' opinions on the functionality and effectiveness of ERMAs. This will enable incremental changes based on practical experience.

7.10.2.6. Awareness and Adoption among the General Public

Learn about the various ERMAs that are available and their features. Engage in initiatives to raise community awareness in order to encourage the use of these applications for individual and group safety.

7.10.2.7. Participate in Reporting Incidents

Urge the public to actively participate in incident reporting via ERMAs, offering up-to-date information that might support first responders in their work.

7.10.2.8. Regular Changes

Keep up with ERMA changes and new features. Update the apps frequently to guarantee access to the newest features and enhancements. These suggestions are meant to establish an educated and cooperative environment so that ERMAs can reach their full potential as useful instruments for crisis management. The effective creation, implementation, and use of these applications depend on the active participation of stakeholders at all levels.

7.11. FINAL THOUGHTS

In this final section, the main conclusions are summarized, the contributions made to the field are highlighted, and the implications for future study in the field of crisis management and Emergency Response Mobile Applications (ERMAs) are discussed.

7.11.1. Synopsis of Results

7.11.1.1. Technological Impact

ERMAs are essential for increasing response coordination, real-time information transmission, and crisis communication.

7.11.1.2. User Viewpoints

It is evident from user viewpoints that well-designed ERMAs can lead to high levels of user engagement and satisfaction. Users value features that improve community resilience overall, readiness, and response effectiveness.

7.11.1.3. Case Studies

Comprehensive case studies highlight situations when ERMAs have been successfully implemented, highlighting their efficacy in a range of emergency incidents. Obstacles and setbacks offer priceless insights for improvement.

7.11.1.4. Empowering People and Organisations

By increasing readiness, boosting response effectiveness, and building community resilience, ERMAs have a big impact on empowering people and organisations.

7.11.1.5. Future Innovations and Trends

A variety of opportunities and challenges will influence how ERMAs evolve in the future, including possible integrations with developing technologies and technical developments.

7.11.2. Input Into the Domain

This study offers a thorough overview of ERMAs, covering user viewpoints, future trends, and their current environment and impact on crisis communication.

User-focused suggestions: Customised recommendations are intended to improve the usability and efficacy of ERMAs for various stakeholders, such as policymakers, developers, emergency responders, and the general public.

7.11.3. Implications for Future Research

Advanced Technological Integration: To create more reliable crisis management solutions, future research may examine how to incorporate cutting-edge technology like block chain, augmented reality, and artificial intelligence into ERMAs.

Cross-Border Cooperation: Examine the possibility of standardising ERMAs and conducting cross-border cooperation to establish an emergency response network that is connected worldwide.

Long-Term User Engagement: Investigate methods to guarantee ERMA adoption and long-term user engagement while taking changing user requirements and technology preferences into account.

To sum up, this study adds insightful knowledge to the field of emergency response and ERMAs and lays the groundwork for further investigation and improvement of these vital instruments. The dynamic nature of emergencies and the constant advancement of technology highlight the significance of continuing study to improve the effectiveness of ERMAs in crisis management.

REFERENCE

Abdelouhab, K. A., Idoughi, D., & Kolski, C. (2018). "A framework combining agile, user-centred design and service-oriented architecture approaches for collaborative disaster management system design." *International Journal of Information and Communication Technology*, 12(3–4), 364–392.

Brunton, M., & Coll, R. K. (2005). "Enhancing technology education by forming links with industry: A New Zealand case study." *International Journal of Science and Mathematics Education*, 3, 141–166.

Corbin, J. H., Oyene, U. E., Manoncourt, E., Onya, H., Kwamboka, M., Amuyunzu-Nyamongo, M., . . . & Van den Broucke, S. (2021). "A health promotion approach to emergency management: Effective community engagement strategies from five cases." *Health Promotion International*, 36(Supplement_1), i24–i38.

Darke, P., Shanks, G., & Broadbent, M. (1998). "Successfully completing case study research: Combining rigour, relevance and pragmatism." *Information Systems Journal*, 8(4), 273–289.

Dittakavi, R. S. S. (2022). "Evaluating the efficiency and limitations of configuration strategies in hybrid cloud environments." *International Journal of Intelligent Automation and Computing*, 5(2), 29–45.

Du, G., Zheng, L., & Ouyang, X. (2019). "Real-time scheduling optimization considering the unexpected events in home health care." *Journal of Combinatorial Optimization*, 37, 196–220.

Frerk, C., Mitchell, V. S., McNarry, A. F., Mendonca, C., Bhagrath, R., Patel, A., . . . & Ahmad, I. (2015). "Difficult airway society 2015 guidelines for management of unanticipated difficult intubation in adults." *BJA: British Journal of Anaesthesia*, 115(6), 827–848.

Guzman, Jethro B. de et al. (2014). "Mobile emergency response application using geolocation for command centers." *International Journal of Computer and Communication Engineering*, 3, 235–238.

Ibraeva, A., de Almeida Correia, G. H., Silva, C., & Antunes, A. P. (2020). "Transit-oriented development: A review of research achievements and challenges." *Transportation Research Part A: Policy and Practice*, 132, 110–130.

Laverack, G. (2017). *Health promotion in disease outbreaks and health emergencies*. CRC Press.

Munawar, H. S., Qayyum, S., Ullah, F., & Sepasgozar, S. (2020). "Big data and its applications in smart real estate and the disaster management life cycle: A systematic analysis." *Big Data and Cognitive Computing*, 4(2), 4.

Omondiagbe, H. (2016). "How can engaging communities aid in developing new conservation initiatives?" Diss., Auckland University of Technology.

Pereira, E. B. J. F. (2013). "An oil spill surveillance program for Lake Pontchartrain." *Journal of Emergency Management*, 11(6), 447.
Rueß, A. K. (2018). "An exploration of critical junctures for public participation in multinational final nuclear waste disposal." Diss., Publication Year.
Wulandari, F., Budijanto, B., Bachri, S., & Utomo, D. H. (2023). "The relationship between knowledge and disaster preparedness of undergraduates responding to forest fires." *Jàmbá-Journal of Disaster Risk Studies*, 15(1), 1408.
Yılankıran, F. Ç., & Guney, C. (2021). "Emergency response with mobile geosocial sensing in the post-app era." *Transactions in GIS*, 25(2), 897–922.
Zhang, H., Mittal, N., Leamy, L. J., Barazani, O., & Song, B. H. (2017). "Back into the wild—Apply untapped genetic diversity of wild relatives for crop improvement." *Evolutionary Applications*, 10(1), 5–24.
Zuefle, D. M. (1994). "The interface of religious beliefs and environmental values within the interpretive profession: A multimethodological exploratory study." Diss., Texas A&M University.

8 Artificial Intelligence, IoT, and Cloud in Transportation Safety

Minakshi Ramteke, Shashank Borikar, Shivraj Guduri, and Sujal Raut

8.1. INTRODUCTION

In the rapidly evolving landscape of transportation, the integration of cutting-edge technologies has become pivotal in addressing safety challenges, optimising operations, and enhancing overall efficiency. This study delves into the synergistic application of Artificial Intelligence (AI), Internet of Things (IoT), and Cloud technologies to revolutionise transportation safety. As the world witnesses an increasing reliance on interconnected systems and smart infrastructure, the amalgamation of AI, IoT, and Cloud solutions offers a transformative paradigm for ensuring safer and more resilient transportation ecosystems (Qi et al., 2010). Artificial Intelligence, with its predictive modelling capabilities, machine learning algorithms, and sophisticated computer vision techniques, has emerged as a powerful tool for analysing diverse data sources. AI helps with proactive risk identification in the context of transportation safety, allowing for real-time decision-making and traffic flow optimisation. The ability of AI to forecast outcomes leads to a more efficient emergency response system that takes into account important safety issues with different kinds of transportation (Azgomi and Jamshidi, 2018).

In order to provide real-time communication within the transportation network, the Internet of Things is essential. IoT makes seamless data interchange possible by integrating smart sensors into wearables, infrastructure, and cars. The foundation of Intelligent Transportation Systems (ITS) is this connectedness, which promotes dynamic decision-making processes and enhances communication between various components of the transportation ecosystem (Iqbal et al., 2018). Data-driven insights and real-time monitoring enable stakeholders to react quickly to changing circumstances and possible safety risks.

8.2. LITERATURE REVIEW

The Internet of Things (IoT), Cloud Computing, and Artificial Intelligence (AI) have come together to arose as a revolutionary force in resolving transportation-related safety issues. A paradigm change is brought about by this synergy, which introduces intelligent and linked systems that rethink the way that the transportation industry

 DOI: 10.1201/9781003538172-8

handles safety. Predictive analytics and machine learning algorithms, combined with AI applications, make them particularly useful for spotting possible risks and strengthening decision-making procedures (Torbaghan et al., 2022). Specifically, computer vision technologies are essential to the advancement of automated cars and advanced driver assistance systems (ADAS), greatly reducing the hazards associated with human mistake.

Concurrently, the deployment of sensors and cameras throughout transportation networks demonstrates the integration of IoT, facilitating gathering data in real time about weather patterns, traffic patterns, and vehicle performance. The study (Javaid et al., 2018) on IoT-based smart traffic management might have neglected socioeconomic ramifications and real-world implementation difficulties, which could have limited its application. The resultant network of linked cars and gadgets creates a vast ecosystem that makes data sharing and analysis easy. Mahor et al.'s research from 2023 examines how IoT and artificial intelligence might improve public safety and security, and Nanda et al.'s study from 2018 presents an IoT-based smart system that can be used to prevent and detect accidents, which advances safety technology.

These developments are enhanced by cloud computing, which offers flexible and scalable infrastructure for processing and storing enormous volumes of transportation data. Cloud platforms facilitate real-time analysis and improve safety measures' ability to adapt to changing circumstances. As presented at the International Conference on Smart Technologies For Smart Nation (SmartTechCon), the study (Saarika et al., 2017) explores the implementation of a Smart Transportation System leveraging IoT, offering insights into IoT applications for transportation optimisation. Notwithstanding these developments, issues like privacy (Chavhan et al., 2020) and standards remain, necessitating careful thought. The effective integration of these technologies into automated emergency response systems, intelligent vehicle-to-everything (V2X) communication, and smart traffic management systems is demonstrated by a number of case studies. In the future, this field's research trajectory should concentrate on tackling current issues, investigating novel applications, and assessing the long-term effects of these technologies. In order to provide comprehensive solutions that take into consideration technological, regulatory, and societal factors, interdisciplinary collaboration is prioritised. This will ultimately promote a safer and more effective transportation environment.

8.3. INTRODUCTION TO ARTIFICIAL INTELLIGENCE IN TRANSPORTATION SAFETY

In a block diagram, "Introduction to Artificial Intelligence in Transportation Safety" is shown in Figure 8.1.

1 **Contextual Challenge**: Traffic accidents, traffic jams, and infrastructural issues make transportation safety a global priority that calls for creative solutions.
2 **Artificial Intelligence's (AI)** Transformative **Potential**: AI is a game-changer, providing sophisticated capabilities including processing power, machine learning algorithms, and predictive analytics.

3 **Proactive Risk Mitigation:** Artificial Intelligence (AI) makes it possible to create prediction models that examine large datasets and identify possible risks in real time on roads, trains, and aircraft.
4 **Real-time Traffic Management:** By processing a variety of data sources, such as weather and traffic patterns, machine learning algorithms make it possible to adopt real-time traffic management methods that aim to prevent accidents.
5 **Route Optimization**: AI-driven algorithms that optimize travel routes help to improve the overall efficiency of transportation networks by lowering traffic.
6 **Human mistake Reduction:** AI technologies, including self-driving cars and sophisticated driver aid systems, address how often human mistake causes transportation accidents.
7 **Computer Vision Technologies:** By combining AI with these technologies, cars can sense and react to their surroundings, which helps to reduce the number of accidents.

8.3.1. Artificial Intelligence (AI) and Its Relevance in Transportation Safety, IoT, and Cloud

Artificial Intelligence (AI) and its relevance in transportation safety, IoT, and Cloud is explained together with its constituent parts in Figure 8.1.

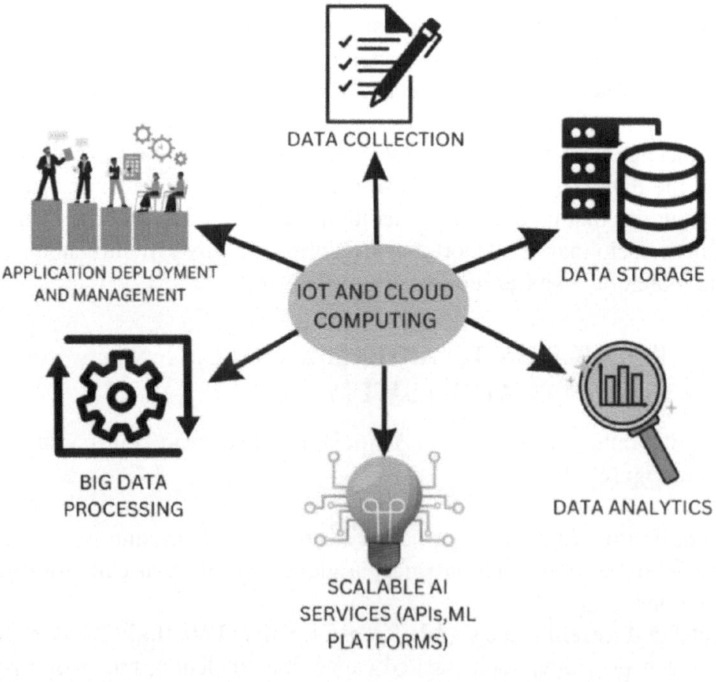

FIGURE 8.1 Introduction to Artificial Intelligence in transportation safety.

The application of Artificial Intelligence (AI) is revolutionising the way that transportation safety is perceived. The creation of algorithms and computational models that allow computers to learn from data, see patterns, and make decisions without explicit human programming is the fundamental activity of Artificial Intelligence (AI). This feature is especially important for the transportation industry, as sensors, cameras, GPS units, and other IoT-enabled equipment produce enormous volumes of data. The research (Ouallane et al., 2021) provides an overview of IoT and AI-powered road traffic control solutions, providing insights into creative methods for improving road safety and streamlining traffic, as reported in Procedia Computer Science, Volume 198. Artificial intelligence (AI)-powered systems in the transportation safety domain use machine learning (Ghandour et al., 2020) methods including deep learning, reinforcement learning, and neural networks to evaluate large, complicated datasets and derive useful insights (Cai et al., 2019). AI algorithms can detect possible dangers and forecast future safety threats with a high degree of accuracy by training (Uma and Eswari, 2021) on historical accident data, traffic patterns, weather conditions, and other pertinent elements. The study (Abduljabbar et al., 2019), which was published in the journal *Sustainability*, gives an overview of the uses of Artificial Intelligence in transportation and offers insights into how these technologies might support sustainable transportation solutions.

Transportation operators can also take advantage of scalable computer resources and storage capacity for real-time data processing and analysis thanks to the integration of AI with Cloud Computing technologies. This makes it possible to quickly

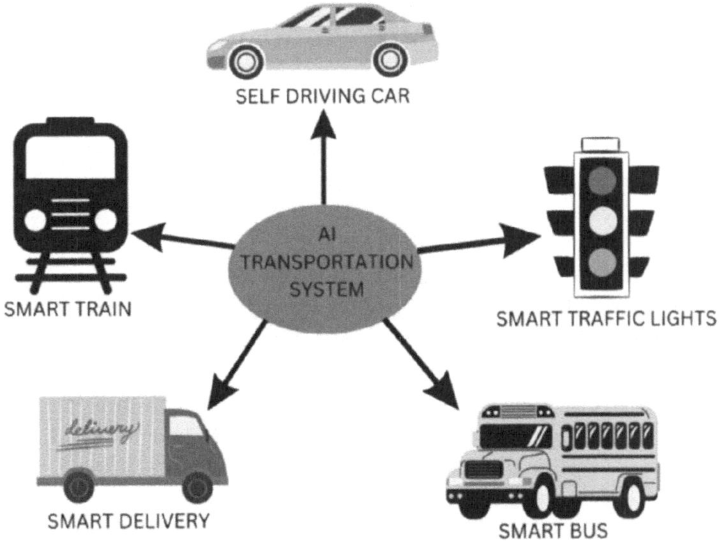

FIGURE 8.2 Artificial Intelligence (AI) and its relevance in transportation safety, IoT, and Cloud.

implement AI-driven solutions throughout dispersed transportation networks, promoting smooth interaction and cooperation between linked systems and devices. According to research published, Bhattacharya et al. (2022) look into how IoT and Artificial Intelligence can be used to improve road safety. They provide insights into creative ways to reduce accidents and enhance overall safety measures.

The capacity of Artificial Intelligence to change and grow with time is one of its main benefits for transportation safety. The study (Kampova et al., 2021) addresses how security management concepts are applied in the transportation industry. It presents conclusions and ideas on how to ensure security measures in the transportation sector, as discussed at the SHS Web Conference in Zilina, Slovakia. The resilience of transportation networks as a whole can be increased by AI algorithms' improved performance and efficacy in spotting safety-critical incidents through ongoing learning and optimisation.

The development of autonomous transportation technologies, such as drones, self-driving automobiles, and unmanned aerial vehicles (UAVs), is made possible by Artificial Intelligence (AI) and has the potential to drastically minimise accidents brought on by human error. As discussed in the OGAI Journal (Oesterreichische Gesellschaft fuer Artif Intell), the research (Kyamakya, 2006) investigates the application of Artificial Intelligence in transportation telematics, offering insights into the utilisation of AI technologies to improve various aspects of transportation systems. Autonomous vehicles can safely and effectively navigate complicated surroundings by combining sensor fusion, computer vision, and decision-making algorithms. This reduces the likelihood of crashes and other safety concerns.

8.4. POTENTIAL BENEFITS OF INTEGRATING ARTIFICIAL INTELLIGENCE (AI), IOT, AND CLOUD TECHNOLOGIES IN TRANSPORTATION SAFETY

1 **Enhanced Predictive Analytics:** By leveraging AI algorithms and advanced data analytics, transportation systems can anticipate safety hazards and proactively mitigate risks before they escalate. Real-time analysis of IoT-generated data, combined with cloud-based processing power, enables predictive modelling of accident-prone areas, contributing to safer routes and reduced collision rates.

2 **Optimised Traffic Management**: AI-driven traffic management systems, supported by IoT sensors and Cloud infrastructure, can dynamically adjust traffic signals, lane configurations, and public transit schedules to optimise traffic flow and minimise congestion. Through real-time data processing and predictive modelling, transportation authorities can implement adaptive traffic control strategies, reducing the likelihood of accidents and improving overall road safety.

3 **Efficient Resource Allocation:** AI-powered predictive maintenance solutions, integrated with IoT-enabled (Rabby et al., 2019) sensors and Cloud platforms, facilitate proactive monitoring of transportation infrastructure, including vehicles, roads, and bridges. By detecting potential equipment

failures before they occur, transportation operators can schedule maintenance activities more efficiently, ensuring the reliability and safety of transportation systems while minimising disruptions to service.

4 **Automated Emergency Response:** AI-driven emergency response systems, supported by IoT sensors and Cloud Computing, enable rapid detection and assessment of safety incidents, such as accidents, natural disasters, or infrastructure failures. By analysing real-time data streams and geospatial information, these systems can accurately identify the location and severity of emergencies, enabling faster response times and more effective allocation of resources to mitigate safety risks.
5 **Better Human-Machine Interaction:** When AI-powered interfaces and decision support systems are combined with Internet of Things gadgets and cloud services, human operators and autonomous transportation technology may communicate and work together more effectively. These technologies enable operators to make well-informed decisions in dynamic contexts, resulting in safer and more efficient transportation operations, by offering real-time insights and practical recommendations.
6 **Developments in Self-Driving Cars:** Autonomous car technologies are becoming more advanced and dependable, thanks to Artificial Intelligence (AI), IoT connection, and Cloud-based services. Autonomous cars can sense their environment, foresee possible safety risks, and make decisions about autonomous driving in real time thanks to machine learning algorithms and sensor fusion techniques. This lowers the likelihood of accidents brought on by human mistake.

8.5. CHALLENGES IN IMPLEMENTING ARTIFICIAL INTELLIGENCE IN TRANSPORTATION SAFETY

1 **Data Quality and Availability:** Real-time, high-quality transportation data is not widely available. The precision of AI models could be impacted by gaps and inconsistencies in data sources.
2 **Interoperability and Standardisation:** Different transportation systems are unable to communicate and share data due to a lack of established standards. Issues with interoperability that arise when combining AI technologies with various transportation modalities.
3 **Cybersecurity Dangers:** Strong cybersecurity measures are necessary, since increased connection increases the potential for cyberthreat vulnerabilities. Safeguarding private information from malevolent intrusions and illegal access is necessary.
4 **Ethical Issues and Bias:** Ethical issues pertaining to the proper application of AI, such as accountability and transparency. Potential biases in AI systems could have a disproportionately negative impact on particular populations.
5 **Infrastructure and Cost Challenges:** Upgrading infrastructure and integrating AI-driven technologies come with high upfront expenditures.

Refitting the integration of AI technology into current transportation systems may provide both financial and logistical obstacles.

6 **Legal and legal Frameworks:** The legal environment is changing, and using AI to improve transportation safety requires specific requirements. There are concerns about liability and legal ramifications in the event of mishaps or system malfunctions.
7 **Public Perception and Acceptance:** The public's perception and acceptance of AI-driven transportation technology are characterised by resistance and mistrust. Worries about monitoring, privacy, and the illusion of losing control must be addressed.

8.6. OBJECTIVES FOR APPLYING ARTIFICIAL INTELLIGENCE (AI) TO THE SAFETY OF TRANSPORTATION

Several important objectives are served by using Artificial Intelligence (AI) to transportation safety:

1 **Accident Prevention:** AI is able to forecast hazardous circumstances and identify possible risks before accidents happen by analysing massive volumes of data from multiple sources, including cameras, sensors, and historical records. AI technologies can assist operators, pilots, and drivers in making safer decisions on the ground, in the air, and while operating rails by giving them access to real-time data.
2 **Improved Decision-Making:** In dynamic contexts, AI systems are able to process intricate data patterns and make snap decisions. This capacity is especially useful in emergency scenarios where human reaction times might not be adequate. Transportation systems can function more safely and effectively if AI-powered recommendations are added to human decision-making.
3 **Predictive Maintenance:** By evaluating sensor data and identifying early indicators of wear and tear, AI-enabled predictive maintenance systems are able to foresee equipment problems before they occur. Transportation companies may lower the chance of unplanned repairs and minimise service interruptions by planning maintenance ahead of time, assuring safer operations for both passengers and cargo.
4 **Traffic Management:** By dynamically modifying lights, route guidance systems, and public transit schedules based on current traffic circumstances, AI algorithms may optimise traffic flow and reduce congestion. AI-powered traffic management systems improve overall transportation safety by minimising traffic congestion and lowering the risk of accidents brought on by crowded roads or unpredictable driving.
5 **Automated Vehicle Safety:** AI is essential to the safe operation of self-driving cars, trucks, drones, and other autonomous vehicles, thanks to improvements in autonomous vehicle technology. These cars can sense their environment, foresee any threats, and make safe and responsible

autonomous driving decisions thanks to AI systems, which lowers the chance of accidents brought on by human mistake.

6 **Emergency Response:** AI-driven emergency response systems have the ability to evaluate incoming distress signals, determine the seriousness of crises, and more quickly send the necessary emergency services. Artificial Intelligence (AI) improves emergency response efficacy by prioritising essential occurrences and giving responders access to real-time information. This eventually saves lives and lessens the impact of accidents on transportation safety.

8.7. APPLICATIONS OF ARTIFICIAL INTELLIGENCE TO TRANSPORTATION SAFETY

Figure 8.3 illustrates the application of artificial intelligence approaches in transportation safety. In a number of fields, Artificial Intelligence (AI) approaches are essential for improving transportation safety. According to the IFC-World Bank Group publication, Conde and Twinn's 2019 study examines how artificial intelligence can improve transportation in emerging markets in terms of safety, cleanliness, dependability, and efficiency. It also offers insights into the revolutionary potential of AI technologies. The following are some important AI methods used in transportation safety:

1 **Machine Learning Algorithms:** Transportation safety makes considerable use of machine learning algorithms, such as supervised learning, unsupervised learning, and reinforcement learning. These algorithms look

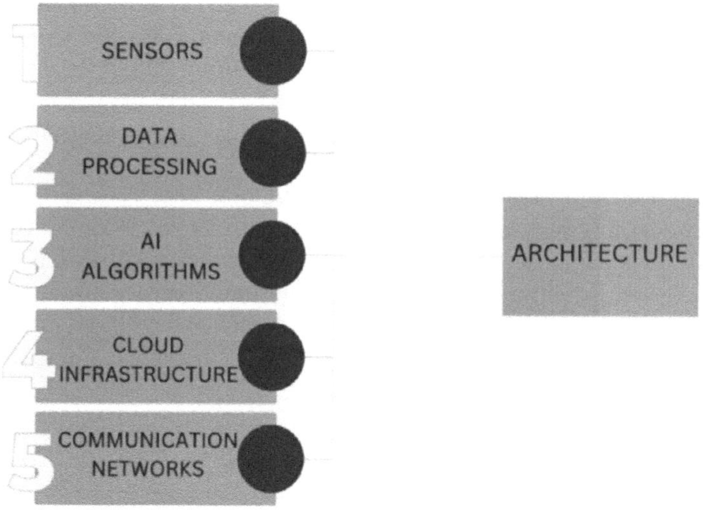

FIGURE 8.3 Artificial Intelligence techniques use for transportation safety.

at a lot of data, including past accident reports, weather reports, traffic patterns, and driving habits, in order to find possible safety hazards and forecast future accidents. For example, unsafe driving behaviours can be classified by supervised learning algorithms, and safer junctions can be achieved by optimising traffic signal timings through reinforcement learning algorithms.

2 **Computer Vision:** Using computer vision techniques, visual data from cameras, LiDAR sensors, and other imaging devices may be analysed to identify objects, identify traffic signs, and evaluate the surrounding environment. Real-time object detection algorithms enable the identification of cyclists, pedestrians, and other vehicles, hence promoting autonomous vehicles and drivers' situational awareness and aiding in collision avoidance systems.
3 **Natural Language Processing (NLP):** Textual data, including accident reports, traffic updates, and driver input, is analysed using NLP approaches in the field of transportation safety. Through the use of NLP algorithms, transportation authorities may better understand unstructured text data, identify reoccurring safety hazards, communicate safety advice, and enhance emergency response protocols.
4 **Predictive Analytics:** Predictive analytics techniques leverage historical and real-time data to forecast safety-related events, such as accidents, breakdowns, or traffic congestion. Time-series forecasting models, Bayesian networks, and deep learning algorithms can predict the likelihood and severity of safety incidents, enabling proactive risk management strategies and resource allocation.
5 **Simulation and Modelling:** Simulation and modelling techniques are used to replicate real-world transportation scenarios and evaluate the safety performance of various interventions and infrastructure designs. Agent-based modelling, traffic simulation software, and virtual reality environments allow transportation planners and engineers to assess the impact of new road layouts, traffic control strategies, and vehicle technologies on safety outcomes.
6 **Deep Reinforcement Learning:** Deep reinforcement learning combines deep learning with reinforcement learning principles to train agents to make sequential decisions in complex environments. In transportation safety, deep reinforcement learning algorithms can optimise driving behaviours, such as lane-keeping, speed control, and collision avoidance, for autonomous vehicles, leading to safer and more reliable transportation systems.

8.8. USE OF IoT AND CLOUD TECHNOLOGY IN TRANSPORT SAFETY

The use of Internet of Things (IoT) and Cloud technology in transportation safety has revolutionised how we approach road safety and manage transportation systems. Here are some key applications:

1. **Real-time Monitoring with IoT Sensors:** Real-time data on traffic flow, road conditions, and vehicle performance is collected by IoT sensors that are put in cars, traffic lights, road signs, and infrastructure. This information is sent to Cloud-based platforms, where it is examined to find possible safety risks like busy junctions, dangerous driving conditions, or strangely behaving cars (Jabbar et al., 2019).
2. **Predictive Maintenance:** Tyre pressure, brake wear, engine temperature, and other equipment performance parameters are continuously monitored by Internet of Things (IoT)-enabled sensors deployed in cars and transportation infrastructure. Transportation operators can reduce the risk of accidents brought on by mechanical problems by anticipating and averting any equipment breakdowns before they happen by analysing this data in the Cloud.
3. **Smart Traffic Management:** Systems that optimise traffic flow and lessen congestion are made possible by IoT devices embedded in traffic lights, road sensors, and automobiles. In order to improve overall road safety and efficiency, Cloud-based algorithms analyse real-time traffic data and dynamically alter traffic signals, reroute vehicles, and prioritise emergency vehicles.
4. **Driver Behaviour Monitoring:** Real-time data on speeding, hard braking, lane departure, and other dangerous driving behaviours is collected by Internet of Things devices like telematics sensors and in-car cameras. By identifying high-risk drivers and offering feedback or interventions to improve driving behaviours, cloud-based analytics solutions analyse this data and ultimately lower the probability of accidents.
5. **Emergency Response and Incident Management:** IoT-enabled emergency call systems automatically detect and report accidents or incidents to emergency responders, providing real-time location data and other critical information. Cloud-based emergency response platforms coordinate the dispatch of emergency services, optimise response routes, and facilitate communication between responders and transportation operators, leading to faster and more effective incident management.
6. **Fleet Management and Optimisation:** Fuel consumption, route planning, and vehicle location can all be tracked in real time by fleet managers, thanks to IoT sensors installed in commercial vehicles. By analysing this data, Cloud-based fleet management platforms can save fuel expenses, maximise vehicle utilisation, and enhance driver safety by offering driver instruction and route optimisation.

8.9. CLOUD, IOT, AND AI FOR EMERGENCY RESPONSE AND INCIDENT MANAGEMENT

1. **Incident Detection in Real-Time:** Talk about the ways in which Internet of Things (IoT) sensors installed in public transportation, automobiles, and infrastructure can instantly identify events like traffic accidents, hazardous

road conditions, or bad weather. These sensors are able to record information on the speed, location, and impact forces of the vehicle. The data is subsequently sent to cloud-based platforms for analysis.

2 **AI-Driven Incident Analysis**: Describe how data from Internet of Things sensors can be analysed by AI algorithms to determine the impact and severity of incidents. Rapid and precise event assessment is made possible by machine learning algorithms, which can classify incidents based on variables including location, time of day, weather, and previous data.

3 **Automatic Emergency Warnings:** Explain how, when events are recognised, AI systems connected with IoT devices may automatically create emergency warnings and messages. These notifications can be distributed to pertinent parties, such as emergency responders, transportation authorities, and surrounding drivers, using Cloud-based communication platforms, enabling a prompt and well-coordinated reaction.

4 **Optimised Resource Allocation:** Examine how event data might be analysed by AI-driven decision support systems to maximise the distribution of emergency resources including police, fire, and medical personnel. Through the consideration of variables, including the intensity of the incident, traffic patterns, and resource availability, these systems can guarantee that the appropriate resources are promptly sent to the correct place.

5 **Predictive Incident Modelling**: Talk about how machine learning and Artificial Intelligence (AI) algorithms can forecast the probability of upcoming incidents by using real-time conditions and previous data. These algorithms can detect high-risk regions and proactively apply safety measures to prevent accidents and minimise their impact by analysing patterns and trends in incident data.

6 **Integrated Incident Response Systems:** To streamline emergency response operations, emphasise the significance of cloud-based incident response systems that incorporate communication, AI, and IoT technologies. These platforms offer a centralised location for gathering, evaluating, and sharing incident data, facilitating easy communication between stakeholders and emergency responders.

7 **Improved Situational Awareness:** Describe how emergency responders can have improved situational awareness during crises with the help of AI-powered dashboards and visualisation tools. Cloud-based collection and analysis of real-time data inputs from traffic cameras, social media platforms, and IoT devices can facilitate decision-making in dynamic contexts by offering actionable insights.

8 **Post-Incident Analysis and Learning:** Stress the value of this process in order to enhance emergency response protocols and avert similar occurrences in the future. In order to discover patterns, underlying causes, and opportunities for development, AI algorithms can evaluate event data. This information can then be used to inform the creation of safer practices and procedures.

8.10. CASE STUDIES AND BEST PRACTICES OF ARTIFICIAL INTELLIGENCE, IoT, AND CLOUD IN TRANSPORTATION SAFETY

8.10.1. City of Los Angeles: Traffic Management With AI and IoT

- Case Study: To improve traffic flow and lessen congestion, the City of Los Angeles installed an AI-driven traffic management system that makes use of IoT sensors built into roads, traffic lights, and automobiles.
- Best Practice: To detect traffic patterns, anticipate hotspots for congestion, and dynamically modify traffic signal timings, real-time data from IoT sensors is gathered and processed in the Cloud. Travel times and accident rates have significantly decreased as a result of this proactive approach to traffic management.

8.10.2. Singapore: Autonomous Vehicle Trials

- Case Study: To increase the efficiency and safety of transportation, Singapore tested driverless cars outfitted with AI and IoT technologies.
- Best Practice: In order to safely navigate urban environments, autonomous vehicles use Artificial Intelligence (AI) algorithms to analyse real-time data from IoT sensors, cameras, and LiDAR systems. Coordinated traffic flow and incident response are made possible by the connection that cloud-based infrastructure allows between vehicles and traffic control systems.

8.10.3. London Underground: Predictive Maintenance

- Case Study: In order to track the state of rolling stock and track infrastructure, London Underground developed a predictive maintenance programme utilising AI and IoT.
- Best Practice: IoT sensors that are mounted on railroads and track elements gather vibration, temperature, and wear data. This information is sent to the Cloud, where Artificial Intelligence (AI) algorithms examine it and forecast equipment faults before they happen. London Underground has reduced service interruptions and increased safety and dependability by proactively resolving maintenance issues.

8.10.4. New York City: Emergency Response Coordination

- Case Study: In order to track the state of rolling stock and track infrastructure, London Underground developed a predictive maintenance programme utilizing AI and IoT.
- Best Practice: IoT sensors that are mounted on railroads and track elements gather vibration, temperature, and wear data. This information is sent to the Cloud, where Artificial Intelligence (AI) algorithms examine it and forecast equipment faults before they happen. London Underground has reduced

service interruptions and increased safety and dependability by proactively resolving maintenance issues.

8.10.5. Tesla: Driver Assistance Systems

- Case Study: Advanced driver assistance features like adaptive cruise control and lane-keeping assistance are provided by Tesla's Autopilot system, which makes use of AI and IoT technology.
- Best Practice: AI systems use information from radar, ultrasonic, and camera sensors to identify obstructions, forecast crash risks, and help drivers avoid collisions. Over-the-air upgrades that regularly add new safety features and enhance system performance are made possible via cloud connectivity.

8.10.6. European Union: Cross-Border Traffic Management

- Case Study: To enable smooth travel between member states, the European Union developed a cross-border traffic control system that makes use of AI, IoT, and Cloud technologies.
- Best Practice: Data on traffic volumes, vehicle movements, and customs procedures are gathered via Internet of Things (IoT) sensors positioned at border crossings and other transportation hubs. These data are analysed by AI systems to optimise border crossing times, lessen traffic, and increase traveller safety.

These case studies demonstrate how proactive traffic management, predictive maintenance, emergency response coordination, driver assistance systems, and cross-border cooperation are utilising AI, IoT, and Cloud technology to improve transportation safety.

8.11. FUTURE DIRECTIONS

1 **Edge Computing:** Using edge computing capabilities to process data closer to the source, minimise latency, and enhance real-time decision-making in transportation safety systems is known as edge computing.

2 **Autonomous Vehicles**: With the development of AI technology, fully autonomous vehicles will be able to safely navigate intricate metropolitan landscapes.

3 **Predictive Maintenance**: By implementing predictive maintenance procedures for infrastructure and vehicles using AI and IoT sensors, downtime is decreased and safety is increased.

4 **Multi-Modal Transportation:** By combining AI and IoT technology, multimodal transportation systems may be optimised to improve efficiency and safety across various modes of transportation.

5 **Ethical AI:** To guarantee equitable and responsible decision-making, ethical issues including bias and transparency in AI algorithms utilised in transportation safety systems are addressed.

8.12. CONCLUSION

The intersection of Cloud, Internet of Things, and Artificial Intelligence (AI) technology with transportation safety offers both formidable obstacles and bright futures. Ongoing technical developments, however, may provide solutions to get above these obstacles. In the future, the trajectory calls for implementing predictive maintenance plans, developing AI for autonomous car navigation, and utilising edge computing for quick decision-making. Furthermore, it is impossible to overestimate how important it is to handle ethical issues, particularly prejudice prevention.

REFERENCES

Abduljabbar, R., H. Dia, S. Liyanage and S. A. Bagloee, 2019. Applications of artificial intelligence in transport: An overview. *Sustainability*, vol. 11.

Azgomi, H. F. and M. Jamshidi, 2018. A brief survey on smart community and smart transportation in IEEE. *30th International Conference on Tools with Artificial Intelligence (ICTAI)*, pp. 932–939. https://ieeexplore.ieee.org/document/8576112

Bhattacharya, Srimantini, Harsh Jha and Radhikesh P. Nanda, 2022. Application of IoT and artificial intelligence in road safety. *Interdisciplinary Research in Technology and Management (IRTM)*, pp. 1–6.

Cai, Q., M. Abdel-Aty, Y. Sun, J. Lee and J. Yuan, 2019. Applying a deep Learning approach for transportation safety planning by using high-resolution transportation and land use data. *Transportation Research Part A: Policy and Practice*, vol. 127, pp. 71–85.

Chavhan, S., D. Gupta, S. Garg, A. Khanna, B. J. Choi, et al., 2020. Privacy and security management in intelligent transportation system. *IEEE Access*, vol. 8, no. 3, pp. 148677–148688.

Conde, M. L. and I. Twinn, 2019. How artificial intelligence is making transport safer, cleaner, more reliable and efficient in emerging markets. *IFC-World Bank Gr.*, vol. 2023, pp 1–8.

Ghandour, A. J., H. Hammoud and S. Al-Hajj, 2020. Analyzing factors associated with fatal road crashes: A machine learning approach. *International Journal of Environmental Research and Public Health*, vol. 17, no. 11, p. 4111.

Iqbal, K., M. A. Khan, S. Abbas, Z. Hasan and A. Fatima, 2018. Intelligent transportation system (ITS) for smart-cities using Mamdani fuzzy inference system. *International Journal of Advanced Computer Science and Applications*, vol. 9, no. 2, pp. 94–105.

Jabbar, R., M. Shinoy, M. Kharbeche, K. Al-Khalifa, M. Krichen and K. Barkaoui, 2019, December. Urban traffic monitoring and modeling system: An IoT solution for enhancing road safety. In *2019 International Conference on Internet of Things Embedded Systems and Communications (IINTEC)*, pp. 13–18. https://ieeexplore.ieee.org/document/9038557

Javaid, S., A. Sufian, S. Pervaiz and M. Tanveer, 2018. Smart traffic management system using Internet of Things. In *20th International Conference on Advanced Communication Technology (ICACT)*, IEEE, 393–398.

Kampova, K., K. Makka and K. Zvarikova, 2021. Implementation of security management principles in transport. In *SHS Web Conference*, Zilina, Slovakia, vol. 92, p. 06016.

Kyamakya, K., 2006 Artificial intelligence in transportation telematics. *OGAI Journal (Oesterreichische Gesellschaft für Artificial Intelligence)*, vol. 25, pp. 2–4

Mahor, V., R. Rawat, A. Kumar, B. Garg and K. Pachlasiya, 2023. IoT and artificial intelligence techniques for public safety and security. In *Smart Urban Computing Applications*. River Publishers, pp. 111–126.

Nanda, S., H. Joshi and S. Khairnar, 2018, August. An IOT based smart system for accident prevention and detection. In *2018 Fourth International Conference on Computing Communication Control and Automation (ICCUBEA)*. IEEE, pp. 1–6.

Ouallane, A. A., A. Bahnasse, A. Bakali and M. Talea, 2021. Overview of road traffic management solutions based on IoT and AI. *Procedia Computer Science*, vol. 198, no. 2021, pp. 518–523.

Qi, C. X., Y. J. Sun and J. M. Cheng, 2010. Transportation management system for ubiquitous computing. In *Proc. 2010 IEEE ICSOLI*, Delhi, India, pp. 311–314.

Rabby, M. K. M., M. M. Islam and S. M. Imon, 2019. A review of IoT application in a smart traffic management system. In *5th International Conference on Advances in Electrical Engineering (ICAEE)*, pp. 280–285. https://ieeexplore.ieee.org/document/9062274

Saarika, P. S., K. Sandhya and T. Sudha, 2017. Smart transportation system using IoT. In *International Conference on Smart Technologies For Smart Nation (SmartTechCon)*, pp. 1104–1107. https://ieeexplore.ieee.org/document/8358507

Torbaghan, M. E., M. Sasidharan, L. Reardon and L. C. MuchangaHvelplund, 2022. Understanding the potential of emerging digital technologies for improving road safety. *Accident Analysis & Prevention*, vol. 166, p. 106543.

Uma, S. and R. Eswari, 2021. Accident prevention and safety assistance using IOT and machine learning. *Journal of Reliable Intelligent Environments*, pp. 1–25.

9 Cyber Security for Personal Data

Rakesh Nayak, Amit Jain, Monika Saxena, and Roopesh Kumar

9.1. INTRODUCTION

The potion of individual information has actually ended up being a pushing problem in an increasingly interconnected as well as technology-driven globe. The fast digitisation of info as well as the expansion of on the internet systems have actually developed brand-new chances for people as well as companies; however, they have, actually, likewise subjected individual information to a wide variety of cyber hazards. Cyber protection, as a result, plays an essential duty in protecting individual information from unapproved gain access, abuse, as well as possible exploitation (Tariq et al., 2023) This chapter checks out the numerous cyber risks that people as well as companies deal with concerning individual information. It discovers the techniques utilised by cybercriminals such as hacking, phishing, as well as social design, to get unapproved accessibility to individual info. In addition, it resolves the possible repercussions of jeopardised individual information, consisting of economic loss, identification burglary, reputational damages, and also violation of personal privacy. The relevance of executing durable cyber safety and security actions is stressed throughout the chapter. It discovers the function of file encryption, solid passwords, multi-factor verification, as well as protected network setups in reducing the threats related to cyber hazards. It likewise highlights the value of routine software application updates, worker education and learning, as well as recognition programs and also event feedback strategies to improve cyber protection durability. Additionally, the short article checks out the lawful coupled with regulative structures that regulate the defence of individual information. It reviews the General Data Protection Regulation (GDPR) plus various other appropriate regulations plus laws, highlighting the obligations companies have in taking care of individual information, together with the legal rights people have in managing their info. Honest factors to consider bordering the collection, storage space, and also use of individual information are additionally dealt with in the chapter. It checks out ideas such as notified authorisation, openness, as well as responsibility in information dealing with techniques. In addition, it highlights the significance of striking an equilibrium in between using individual information for development as well as protecting people' personal privacy via information minimisation and also anonymisation strategies.

DOI: 10.1201/9781003538172-9

The highlights of the chapter are:

- To shield individual information from cyberpunks, people as well as companies should take on durable cybersecurity procedures. This consists of utilising solid, one-of-a-kind passwords, making it possible for multi-factor verification plus maintaining software application together with systems upgraded with the most up to date protection spots. Normal information back-ups are important to alleviate the effect of ransomware strikes, while security can assist safeguard information in transportation together with at rest. Informing people concerning cybersecurity ideal techniques like taking care of dubious e-mails or messages plus preventing unconfident Wi-Fi networks can likewise figure in in stopping individual information exploitation.
- To elaborate connection in between cyber protection as well as individual information, discovering the obstacles as well as effects related to shielding this important property. It intends to supply a thorough understanding of the threats entailed coupled with lost light on the procedures people as well as companies can require to improve their cyber safety pose.
- To highlight the importance of individual information in our modern-day culture: From economic information as well as clinical documents to social networks accounts plus on-line buying routines, individual information includes a wide variety of delicate details that holds tremendous worth. The enhancing dependence on electronic systems, together with the collection of individual information, have actually developed an electronic landscape where personal privacy plus protection go together.
- Extensive expedition of the vital connection in between cyber safety and security and also individual information. By recognising the dangers executing durable safety steps adhering to lawful as well as honest structures, along with advertising individual education and learning and also recognition, people as well as companies can secure individual information in a progressively digitised globe. With each other, we can make every effort to develop a safe electronic setting where individual information continues to be secured from cyber dangers.

This phase is arranged right into six sections. The first section concentrates on information personal privacy in cyber protection. The second section stands for the relevant job plus the third section area stands for the present safety strategy of cyber protection. The fourth section stands for the moral factor to consider coupled with the fifth section stands for the balancing factor with respect to privacy and education. The sixth section describes the collective technique to cyber protection. Lastly, the seventh section stands for the conclusion as well as future obstacles in cyber protection.

9.2. RELATED WORK

In today's electronic age, individual information has actually come to be an important property. From monetary info to clinical documents as well as individual choices to social communications, our lives are progressively linked with the electronic globe. The importance of individual information depends on its capability to form our experiences, allow personalised solutions, and also drive technology (Cremer et al., 2022). Nevertheless, this wide range of info additionally elevates issues concerning personal privacy plus safety as well as the liable handling of individual information. Among the vital factors individual information holds is its capacity to improve customer experiences. Online systems plus solutions gather huge quantities of information to recognise customer behaviour, choices, along with demands. This information allows customised suggestions, individualised material, coupled with a lot more reliable solution distribution. As an example, shopping systems can recommend items based upon previous acquisitions, while streaming solutions can curate playlists based upon private paying attention behaviours. Individual information serves as the gas that powers these customised experiences, making our communications with electronic systems much more pertinent as well as appealing.

In addition, individual information plays an essential function in driving advancement and also financial development. Data-driven understandings as well as analytics supply companies with useful details that can be utilised to establish brand-new items and also enhance existing ones coupled with determine market fads (Shabbir and Gardezi, 2020). The capability to evaluate huge datasets can find patterns coupled with communications that can result in discoveries in numerous areas from health care to transport. Individual information when made use of properly as well as with appropriate approval can sustain development plus add to the growth of brand-new modern technologies and also solutions that profit culture overall. The relevance of individual information, likewise, includes the world of public health as well as clinical study (von Grafenstein et al., 2022). Data accumulated from people can be anonymised as well as accumulated to recognise patterns as well as patterns in condition episodes, track the efficiency of treatments, as well as educate public health plans. This information can be important in discovering, coupled with reacting to arising health and wellness hazards, such as pandemics. In addition, individual information can add to clinical study by offering scientists with accessibility to huge, varied datasets for evaluation and also expedition. While individual information holds tremendous worth, its importance additionally increases problems regarding personal privacy coupled with safety and security. The electronic landscape is widespread with cyber dangers, plus the wrong handling of individual information can cause severe repercussions. Information breaches, identification burglary, together with unapproved accessibility to individual details, can cause economic loss, reputational damages, as well as individual damage. The liable handling of individual information, consisting of durable safety and security steps, security, as well as information security techniques, is necessary to make certain the personal privacy as well as protection of people. The importance of individual information in the electronic age cannot be overemphasised. It has the power to boost individual experiences, drive development, as well as add to public health as well as clinical study. Nonetheless, the liable handling of individual information as well as the defence of personal privacy should be focused on. As people, companies, plus cultures, we have to strike an equilibrium in between using individual information for favourable end results while valuing people's civil liberties to personal privacy coupled with safety and security.

By doing so, we can completely harness the capacity of individual information in the electronic age together with guarantee its value is promoted properly as well as morally.

9.3. CURRENT CYBER SECURITY APPROACHES

The Internet currently is secured primarily through private regulatory activity, defensive strategies and products, national laws and enforcement, and some limited forms of international cooperation and regulation. Some important points are discussed as follows:

9.3.1. Cybersecurity Risks to Personal Data

In today's electronic globe, individual information has actually ended up being a prime target for cybercriminals. The rapid development of innovation, along with interconnectedness, has actually opened brand-new opportunities for harmful stars to make use of susceptibilities, as well as acquire unapproved accessibility to delicate info. Comprehending the danger landscape is important in order to safeguard individual information from cyber-attacks, plus alleviate prospective threats.

Among one of the most common cybersecurity threats to individual information is information violations (Pool et al., 2024). These accompany when authorised people get to data sources or systems consisting of individual info. Cyberpunks can make use of weak safety procedures bypass firewall software and also make use of susceptibilities in software program to accessibility individual information. As soon as gone against, individual information can be cost the dark internet, made use of for identification burglary or leveraged for economic gain. The repercussions of an information violation can be far-reaching, leading to monetary loss, reputation damages, as well as a loss of count on the impacted companies.

9.3.1.1. Phishing

Phishing strikes are one more typical danger to individual information. Phishing includes tricking people right into exposing delicate details such as passwords, bank card information, or login qualifications. Cyberpunks typically mimic relied on entities, such as financial institutions or preferred on the internet solutions, and also send out e-mails or messages having destructive web links or add-ons (Bhavsar et al., 2018). Unwary people might unwittingly supply their individual information, making it possible for cyberpunks to acquire unauthorised accessibility to their accounts or swipe their identifications. Phishing assaults can be extremely advanced, making it essential for people to continue to be alert as well as workout care when connecting with on the internet interactions.

9.3.1.2. Identification Theft

It is a considerable danger connected with cybersecurity. By acquiring individual information such as social safety and security numbers, addresses, or days of birth, cyberpunks can assume a person's identity plus dedicate different deceitful tasks (Virmanil et al., 2020). This can consist of opening up credit scores accounts, requesting loans, or declaring a deceitful income tax return. The effect of identification burglary can be devastating bring about economic spoil, harmed credit history, plus years invested attempting to recover one's identification.

9.3.1.3. Ransomware

Its strikes pose yet one more risk to individual information. Ransomware is a sort of malware that secures information on a sufferer's gadget, making it hard to reach till a ransom money is paid (Robles-Carrillo and García-Teodoro, 2022). Hackers commonly target people or companies with beneficial information, such as doctor or financial institutions, to optimise their possibilities of getting a ransom money repayment. The loss of individual information as a result of ransomware strikes can be tragic, particularly if back-ups are not easily offered.

Comprehending the developing risk landscape is necessary to secure individual information from cyber-attacks. It needs a positive method to cybersecurity that consists of executing solid safety steps, consistently upgrading software application as well as systems, plus educating people concerning finest methods for on-line protection. Using protected passwords allowing multi-factor verification, together with being careful of questionable e-mail accessories or web links, can dramatically decrease the threat of succumbing to cyber hazards. In addition, companies, coupled with people, have to focus on the fostering of durable cybersecurity methods. This consists of carrying out routine safety and security audits executing invasion discovery systems as well as giving recurring training to workers. It is, likewise, important to remain notified concerning the most recent cybersecurity fads, together with arising hazards, as cyberpunks constantly adjust their techniques to make use of brand-new susceptibilities.

The hazard landscape bordering individual information is ever-evolving, and cyberpunks are regularly looking for brand-new methods to manipulate susceptibilities. Recognising the threats related to cybersecurity is critical in securing individual information from information violations, phishing assaults, identification burglary, plus ransomware. By taking on durable safety and security steps, remaining alert, coupled with growing a society of cybersecurity-understanding people as well as companies, can secure individual information and alleviate the prospective threats posed by cyber hazards.

9.3.2. Cybercriminals Exploit Personal Data

In the electronic age, individual information has actually come to be a valuable product demanded by cybercriminals for different wicked objectives. These harmful stars utilise a variety of strategies, together with methods, to make use of individual information placing people, together with companies, in danger. Comprehending exactly how cyberpunks run is important to safeguard individual information and minimise the prospective damages triggered by their activities.

9.3.2.1. Social Engineering

One of the main strategies utilised by cyberpunks is social design. This method counts on manipulating people into revealing delicate details or executing activities that profit

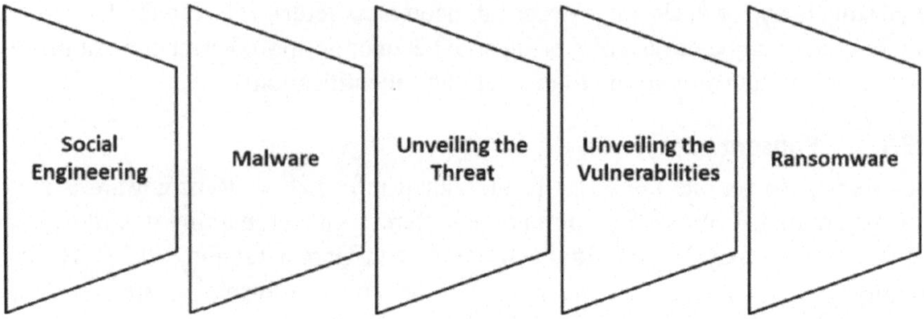

FIGURE 9.1 Tactics and techniques.

the assaulter. Social design can take different types, such as phishing, where cyberpunks send out misleading e-mails or messages claiming relied on entities (Siddiqi et al., 2022). These messages usually have web links or add-ons that, when clicked, can result in malware setup or the collection of individual information. By deceiving people into offering their individual info, cyberpunks can obtain unapproved accessibility to accounts, swipe identifications, or dedicate monetary fraudulence.

9.3.2.2. Malware

It is one more typical device utilised by cyberpunks to make use of individual information. Malware is harmful software applications made to penetrate systems or tools, permitting cyberpunks to obtain control, swipe details, or interfere with procedures (Jang-Jaccard and Nepal, 2014). One sort of malware often used is keyloggers, which videotape keystrokes to catch passwords, bank card information, or login qualifications. Another kind is spyware, which inconspicuously keeps an eye on and accumulates individual information without their understanding. Malware can be dispersed with different methods, consisting of e-mail add-ons, contaminated sites, or endangered software applications.

9.3.2.3. Unveiling the Threat

Data violations are a major technique cyberpunks use to acquire individual information. An information violation takes place when cyberpunks get unauthorised accessibility to data sources or systems, including individual info (Li and Liu, 2021). They make use of weak safety and security actions take advantage of software program susceptibilities or target expert risks to get to delicate information. As soon as acquired, individual information can be put on the dark internet or utilised for identification burglary, monetary scams, or blackmail. Information violations can have extreme effects, consisting of economic loss, reputational damages, and also lawful implications for the influenced people or companies.

9.3.2.4. Unveiling the Vulnerabilities

Cybercriminals, likewise, make use of weak passwords, together with the absence of safety gauges, to get unapproved accessibility to individual information. They make use of methods like brute-force strikes, where they methodically attempt different mixes of passwords until they locate the right one (Dastane, 2020). They additionally manipulate password reuse throughout numerous systems, taking advantage of qualifications acquired from one violation to access to various other accounts. In addition, cyberpunks manipulate unsecured Wi-Fi networks, obstructing information transferred over these networks or releasing man-in-the-middle strikes to record individual info.

9.3.2.5. Ransomware

Another strategy cyberpunks utilise is ransomware strikes. Ransomware is a kind of malware that secures information on a target's tool, making it hard to reach until the ransom money is paid. Cyberpunks usually target people or companies with useful information, such as doctors or banks, to optimise their opportunities of getting ransom money (Maurya et al., 2018). The loss of individual information because of ransomware strikes can be ruinous, as it can bring about economic loss, reputational damages, as well as prospective legal effects.

Cyberpunks utilise numerous strategies to make use of individual information for their advantage. Social design, malware information violations, weak passwords, plus ransomware strikes are simply a couple of instances of their methods. Recognising these methods is necessary to safeguard individual information from falling into the wrong hands. By applying durable cybersecurity steps, remaining watchful and also advertising recognition of cybersecurity ideal techniques, people, together with companies, can protect individual information as well as alleviate the dangers presented by cybercriminals.

9.4. IMPLEMENTING ROBUST CYBERSECURITY MEASURES

In today's electronic landscape, where delicate information is continuously in jeopardy of cyber hazards, executing durable cybersecurity actions is vital. Organisations and people alike have to be aggressive in developing solid protection to protect them from the ever-evolving strategies utilised by cybercriminals. By embracing a thorough method of cybersecurity, we can protect our information plus alleviate possible dangers.

9.4.1. Strong Password

One of the basic columns of a solid cybersecurity support is making use of solid, special passwords. Weak passwords make it much easier for cyberpunks to obtain unapproved accessibility to accounts, together with systems. Executing stringent password plans such as needing a mix of uppercase together with lowercase letters, numbers plus unique personalities, can dramatically boost password toughness (Chanda, 2016). Additionally, urging people to make use of password supervisors can aid in making certain to use special passwords for each and every account without the worry of memorisation.

FIGURE 9.2 Building a strong defence.

9.4.2. Multi-Factor Verification

Enabling multi-factor verification (MFA) is an additional vital way of strengthening cybersecurity defences. MFA includes an additional layer of defence by needing customers to give added evidence of identification, such as a fingerprint check or a distinct confirmation code sent out to a cell phone, along with their password (Williamson and Curran, 2021). This added action makes it much more difficult for cyberpunks to get unapproved access to a customer's password.

9.4.3. Regular Software Program Together With System Updates

Software and also system updates are necessary in keeping a solid cybersecurity stance. Software application updates usually consist of safety and security spots that attend to well-known susceptibilities. Falling short to mount these updates quickly can leave systems vulnerable to exploitation by cyberpunks. Making it possible for automated updates, whenever feasible, makes sure that the most up-to-date safety spots are used immediately, decreasing the danger of succumbing to recognised susceptibilities.

9.4.4. Antivirus as Well as Anti-Malware

Implementing durable anti-virus and also anti-malware remedies is important in spotting and also avoiding the infiltration of harmful software program. These options utilise advanced formulas and also heuristics to recognise as well as reduce malware risks. Frequently upgrading anti-virus software applications makes sure that it keeps up to day with the most recent malware trademarks, boosting its capacity to discover, coupled with mitigating hazards that arise.

9.4.5. Regular Information Back-Ups

Regular information back-ups are crucial in minimising the influence of prospective information violations or ransomware strikes. By consistently supporting information to safeguard, offline or cloud-based storage space people and also companies can recover their information in case of a concession. It is important to confirm the honesty of back-ups on a regular basis and also guarantee they are quickly easily accessible when required.

9.4.6. Use of Cryptography

Implementing file encryption is one more essential element of a durable cybersecurity method. Security transforms information right into an unreadable style that can just be decrypted by licensed celebrations with the proper decryption secrets (Nayak et al., 2008). Encrypting delicate information at rest and also moving supplies an extra layer of defence also if it comes under the incorrect hands.

9.4.7. Educating People

Regarding the best cybersecurity techniques, it is similarly critical to construct solid protection. Several cyber-attacks (Li and Liu, 2021), such as phishing coupled with social design, count on human mistakes or absence of recognition. By supplying thorough training programmes, companies can encourage people to acknowledge and report questionable tasks, stay clear of clicking harmful web links or opening up questionable add-ons, as well as be mindful of divulging delicate details. Lastly, promoting a society of cybersecurity understanding is crucial for constructing a solid protection. Motivating people to report prospective safety occurrences, carrying out safety and security understanding training, as well as producing a risk-free setting for open interaction concerning cybersecurity issues can aid determine together with resolve susceptibilities proactively.

Constructing solid protection versus cyber risks needs a thorough method of cybersecurity. Applying solid, one-of-a-kind passwords, making it possible for multi-factor verification, frequently upgrading software applications as well as systems, utilising durable anti-viruses and also anti-malware services, enlightening people regarding the best cybersecurity methods, executing normal information back-ups, executing security, and also promoting a society of cybersecurity recognition are necessary actions in preventing cyber-attacks. By taking a positive position and also carrying out these steps, companies plus people can construct a solid protection and also secure their useful information in a significantly electronic globe.

9.5. THE ROLE OF LEGAL AND REGULATORY FRAMEWORKS IN DATA PROTECTION

In a period where individual information is gathered, refined, and shared, lawful and also governing structures play an essential function in protecting people' personal privacy plus making certain the accountable handling of information. These structures give standards, guidelines, as well as enforcement systems that regulate exactly how companies, coupled with people, ought to gather, usage, shop, and secure individual information. By developing clear criteria and also liability, they add to the facility of trust, openness, and responsibility in the electronic age.

General Data Protection Regulation as well as various other authorities: One of the considerable lawful structures that have actually had an international influence on information defence is the General Data Protection Regulation (GDPR), executed by the European Union (EU). The GDPR offers a thorough structure for the security of individual information by providing people higher control over their information, together with enforcing stringent commitments on companies that manage individual info. It needs companies to acquire educated permission for information collection, usage, as well as handling and also requires openness relating to information methods. The GDPR additionally gives people the right to gain access to, fix, and eliminate their individual information, along with the right to information mobility as well as the right to be failed to remember.

Beyond the GDPR, lots of nations have actually established their own information security regulations to resolve regional requirements and also problems. As an example, the California Consumer Privacy Act (CCPA) in the United States uses comparable defences to citizens of California, giving them particular legal rights over their information. Various other nations, such as Canada, Japan, and Australia, have actually additionally executed their very own information security legislations to line up with global ideal techniques and also safeguard the personal privacy of their people.

These lawful and also governing structures offer numerous essential functions in information security.

- First of all, they develop clear standards as well as criteria for companies to comply with when gathering and also taking care of individual information. By specifying what comprises authorised and liable information

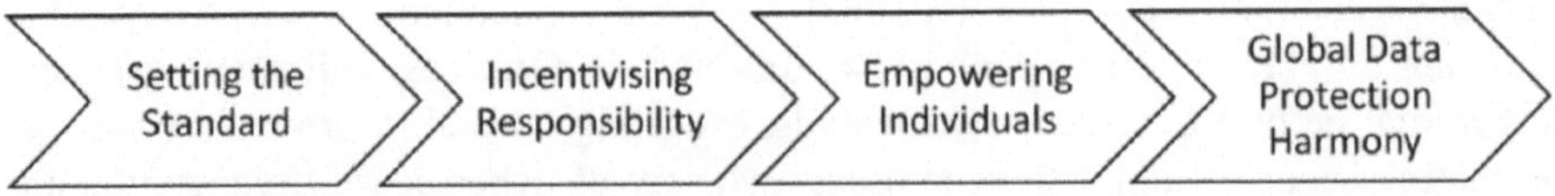

FIGURE 9.3 Legal and regulatory frameworks.

methods, they give a structure for companies to guarantee they are certified as well as responsible. This assists in promoting a society of personal privacy plus information defence within companies, motivating them to take on best methods and focus on the protection of individual information.

- Second of all, lawful structures function as a deterrent for companies that might be attracted to participate in dishonest or manipulative information methods. The hazard of lawful effects such as penalties or lawsuits incentivises companies to take information defence seriously as well as buy the needed sources and also facilities safeguarding individual information. This acts as a secure versus prospective misuses or violations that might cause damage for people and also damages to a company's credibility.
- Finally, lawful structures offer people the option and also legal rights to shield their individual information. By approving people's right to accessibility, fixing, and also removing their information, they encourage people to have control over their individual info. This aids in developing a much better, balanced partnership between people and also companies, where people have a say exactly how their information is made use of as well as can hold companies responsible for any kind of abuse or violations.
- Ultimately, lawful together with governing structures, likewise, add to harmonisation and also interoperability in the worldwide information defence landscape. With the enhancing electronic interconnectedness of our globe, information streams throughout boundaries and also various territories need to have suitable information security requirements. Lawful structures help with this by giving an integrated collection of concepts as well as policies that companies can comply with when handling information throughout various areas.

Legal as well as governing structures play an essential role in information defence by offering standards, criteria, and also enforcement devices to guard individual information. They develop clear regulations for companies to adhere to, incentivise liable information methods, empower people with legal rights and also options, combined with adding to harmonisation in the worldwide information defence landscape. By sticking to these structures, companies can construct and foster openness plus make sure of the accountable handling of individual information in the electronic age.

9.6. ETHICAL CONSIDERATIONS IN CYBER SECURITY

In the electronic age, where individual information is continuously gathered, refined, and shared, moral factors to consider concerning educated authorisation and also liable information handling have actually come to be significantly essential. As well as companies browse the complicated landscape of information personal privacy, it is crucial to promote moral concepts that focus on openness, regard for freedom, and the liable use individual information.

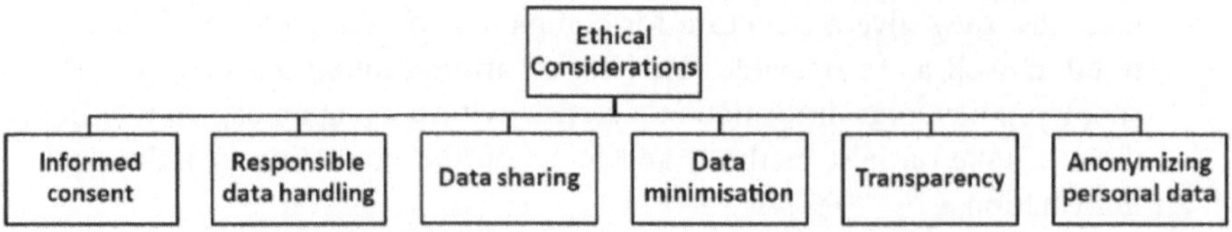

FIGURE 9.4 Ethical considerations.

- **Informed Consent**: At the heart of honest information handling is the principle of educated authorisation. Educated authorisation is the concept that people need to have the right to comprehend together with regulate exactly how their individual information is accumulated, utilised, and shared. It entails giving people clear along with reasonable details concerning the function of information collection, the sorts of information being accumulated, as well as just how it will certainly be utilised. Educated authorisation encourages people to make educated choices regarding sharing their individual details and makes certain that they have the chance to exercise their freedom and personal privacy legal rights.
- **Responsible Data Handling**: It goes hand in hand with notified approval. It needs companies to embrace techniques that value the personal privacy, together with safety of individual information throughout its lifecycle. This consists of carrying out durable safety steps to shield information from unauthorised access, making certain information is exact, as well as making use of information just for the functions for which authorisation was gotten. Accountable information handling additionally entails consistently examining along with upgrading information, taking care of methods to develop personal privacy requirements, as well as keeping clear documents of information-handling tasks.
- **Data Sharing**: Responsible information handling reaches information-sharing techniques also. When companies share individual information with third parties, they have a moral responsibility to make certain that the recipients of the information follow the very same concepts of educated authorisation and also liable information handling. This can be attained via information handling arrangements, which detail the assumptions as well as obligations of all celebrations associated with the information sharing procedure. Companies must additionally make certain that people are educated regarding information sharing methods and also have the choice to pull out if they are not comfy with their information being shared.
- **Data Minimisation**: Another moral factor to consider in information handling is the principle of information reduction. Information decrease includes accumulating as well as keeping just the minimum quantity of individual information essential to accomplish the designated objective. By decreasing the collection as well as retention of individual information, companies minimise the danger of information violations, together with

unapproved accessibility. This concept coheres with the moral responsibility of companies to regard people' personal privacy plus secure their individual info from unneeded direct exposure.

- **Transparency**: It is an essential facet of moral information handling. Organisations must be clear concerning their information care techniques consisting of exactly how individual information is accumulated, utilized, and shared. This can be attained with clear, together with conveniently obtainable, personal privacy plans and also solution papers. Openness builds trust between businesses and individuals, allowing people to make informed decisions about sharing their information while also holding businesses accountable for their information management procedures.
- **Anonymising individual information**: Ethical factors to consider additionally encompass using individual information for research study or analytics objectives. Organisations must make sure that individual information is anonymised or de-identified whenever feasible to secure peoples' personal privacy. In addition, companies ought to get different grant-making use of individual information for research study functions, making certain that people are totally notified concerning just how their information will certainly be made use of, the prospective dangers plus advantages, as well as their legal rights relating to engagement or withdrawal.

Moral factors to consider, bordering notified authorisation and also accountable information handling, are vital in the electronic age. Maintaining moral concepts makes certain that people have company as well as control over their individual information as well as that companies manage information in a way that appreciates personal privacy as well as safety. We may build trust, foster positive relationships with people, and contribute to a far more moral and privacy-conscious electronic society by concentrating on informed approval, responsible information handling transparency, information minimisation, and moral study approaches.

9.7. STRIKING THE BALANCE: USER EDUCATION, AWARENESS, AND PRIVACY IN CYBERSECURITY INNOVATION

In today' s data-driven world, where big quantities of private details are accumulated as well as saved, the suggestions of info decrease, plus anonymisation, play a crucial function in striking an equilibrium between development and personal privacy. These techniques are important in securing peoples' personal privacy legal rights while still allowing organisations to acquire important understandings from information. By using detail decrease along with anonymization strategies, organisations can browse the intricate landscape of information personal privacy plus cultivate moral concepts. Detail decrease is the concept of accumulating as well as keeping just the minimum quantity of individual information needed to accomplish a particular function. It includes a calculated coupled with thoughtful techniques of information collection, making certain that companies do not accumulate too much or unneeded individual info (Mukta et al., 2022). By decreasing the collection of individual information, companies lower the danger of information violations, unapproved accessibility, along with prospective misuse of info. Information decrease, likewise, coheres with personal privacy policies, such as the General Data Protection Regulation (GDPR), which highlights the requirement for companies to restrict the handling of individual information to what is purely essential.

Carrying out detail decrease requires companies to meticulously take a look at the objective for which information is being gathered, combined with recognise the particular information components that are vital to accomplish that objective. Unnecessary or non-relevant information need not be gathered or preserved, as it presents an unneeded danger to peoples' personal privacy. By taking on information decrease strategies, companies can show their dedication to personal privacy and assure people that their individual info is being dealt with correctly. Anonymisation is one more essential method in stabilising development along with personal privacy. Anonymisation entails the elimination or change of individual identifiers from data collection, making the details no more associated with specifics. By anonymising information, companies can get important understandings as well as carry out evaluation without endangering peoples' personal privacy. Anonymisation strategies consist of getting rid of straight identifiers, such as names or social safety and security numbers, together with using analytical techniques to additional safeguard peoples' identifications.

Nonetheless, it is necessary to keep in mind that anonymisation is not sure-fire. Sometimes, re-identification or the mix of anonymised information with various other details might still make it feasible to recognise people. Hence, companies have to very carefully analyse the threats related to re-identification, together with added safeguards such as information gathering or using differential personal privacy methods to additionally improve personal privacy protection. While information decrease, paired with anonymisation, is essential, techniques in personal privacy defence should be stabilised with the demand for development as well as data-driven understandings. Striking this equilibrium needs companies to locate methods to obtain worth from information while valuing peoples' personal privacy. Techniques, such as differential personal privacy, that include regulated sound to answer actions to shield personal privacy can make it possible for companies to draw out helpful understandings while keeping information private.

Organisations need to, likewise, think about applying personal privacy using layout concepts. Personal privacy must be incorporated into the whole lifecycle of information, from the preliminary style of systems to refinement throughout the recurring tracking, together with disposal of information. This positive method guarantees that personal privacy factors to consider are installed into the material of a company's procedures, making it possible for personal privacy in addition to development to exist side by side.

Detail decrease as well as anonymisation are effective devices in stabilising development, along with personal privacy. By reducing the collection, along with retention, of individual information plus anonymising datasets, companies can shield peoples' personal privacy and legal rights while still making use of the capacity of data-driven understandings (Tomás et al., 2022). Organisations need to embrace personal privacy by layout concepts, very carefully examine the dangers connected with re-identification, and regularly take another look at their information-handling techniques to guarantee they are lined up with advancing personal privacy criteria. By inviting these methods, companies can browse the complicated landscape of information personal privacy in addition to promoting a society of liable information usage as well as personal privacy defence.

Cyber dangers are extensive, and also, specific education and learning, as well as understanding, play an essential function in keeping a durable cybersecurity pose. As advancement grows and cyberpunks come to be a lot more sophisticated, it is important for people to comprehend the dangers they encounter and take positive activities to secure themselves as well as their electronic possessions. By purchasing private education and learning plus cultivating a society of cybersecurity recognition, people can come to be the frontline of protection against cyber dangers. Among key factors, private education and learning and also recognition are important in cybersecurity, since numerous cyber-attacks depend on human mistakes or absence of understanding. Phishing, social design, and malware circulation typically make use of people's inquisitiveness or absence of knowledge to acquire unapproved accessibility or concession systems. By informing individuals regarding these techniques, coupled with increasing understanding regarding the prospective threats, people can come to be extra watchful and much better outfitted to identify and prevent these hazards.

Specific education and learning assists people in recognising best techniques for protecting their on-line existence as well as safeguarding their individual details. This consists of subjects such as producing solid special passwords for each and every account, making it possible for multi-factor verification, coupled with being conscious of dubious e-mails or messages. By enlightening people on these basic protection techniques, companies can encourage people to take possession of their cybersecurity plus lower the chance of falling under cyber-attacks. In enhancement to securing peoples' individual info, customer education and learning likewise aids in shielding business possessions. Several cyber-attacks target people within companies as a way to acquire unapproved gain access to or concede delicate information. By notifying staff members concerning the threats, coupled with supplying training on just how to recognise plus reply to cyber threats, companies can significantly minimise the possibilities of effective strikes. This not just shields delicate information but additionally aids in keeping the track record plus economic security of the company.

Private education and learning, likewise, plays a vital role in advertising liable on-line actions. By enlightening people concerning moral factors to consider in the electronic globe, such as valuing others' personal privacy, preventing cyberbullying, and adhering to copyright legislations, companies can foster a society of regard and also duty. This aids in producing a more secure and extra comprehensive atmosphere for every person.

Furthermore, individual education and learning is not a single initiative but a recurring procedure. Cyber risks plus assault techniques are continually advancing, and people need to remain educated concerning the current fads as well as ideal methods. Companies must frequently supply training sessions, workshops, and sources to maintain individuals current with the most up-to-date cybersecurity growth. This additionally consists of informing people concerning brand-new hazards, arising modern technologies, and the relevance of software programme updates to resolve vulnerabilities. Individual education and learning, coupled with recognition, are vital parts of a durable cybersecurity method. By informing people regarding cyber risks, ideal methods for safeguarding individual together with company details as well as advertising liable on-line habits companies can equip people to end up being energetic individuals in securing themselves and their electronic possessions. Private education and learning are recurring procedures that ought to be focused on by companies and people alike, as they play a vital role in preserving a solid cybersecurity position and developing a much safer electronic atmosphere for everybody.

9.8. COLLABORATIVE APPROACHES TO CYBERSECURITY

In the ever-evolving landscape of cybersecurity, the requirement for collective techniques, including federal governments, companies, as well as people, has actually come to be progressively vital. Cyber risks go beyond boundaries and also impact people, organisations and federal governments. By interacting, these stakeholders can take advantage of their special toughness, together with sources, to develop a safer electronic atmosphere for every person. Federal governments play an important function in cybersecurity by producing, along with enforcing, regulations, laws, and plans that shield people and also companies from cyber dangers. They develop lawful structures such as the General Data Protection Regulation (GDPR) in the European Union or the California Consumer Privacy Act (CCPA) in the United States, to guarantee the liable handling of individual information plus the enforcement of cybersecurity criteria. Federal governments additionally purchase cybersecurity r & d, accept global companions, and develop nationwide cybersecurity methods to attend to rising hazards.

Organisations, both public and exclusive, get on the cutting edge of cybersecurity. They are accountable for protecting their networks, systems, as well as information along with shielding the delicate info of their consumers as well as customers. Organisations buy durable cybersecurity procedures, such as firewall programmes, security, and breach discovery systems to safeguard against cyber hazards. They, likewise, execute safety and security recognition training programmes for workers to advertise accountable online habits as well as enlighten them on the most up-to-date hazards as well as best methods. Additionally, companies usually team up as well as share details within their sector markets to jointly enhance their supports versus cyber-attacks. People are an important part of the cybersecurity community. Their activities both online and offline can affect the safety and security of their tools, individual info, and the wider electronic landscape. People need to take individual responsibility for their cybersecurity by exercising excellent electronic health, such as utilising solid as well as special passwords, allowing multi-factor verification, and being careful of dubious e-mails or web links. By remaining educated concerning the most recent dangers as well as best techniques, coupled with applying safety steps, people can shield themselves as well as add to a more secure on the internet setting.

Partnership between federal governments, organisations, and people is vital for efficient cybersecurity. Federal governments can offer support, policies, and sources to sustain companies and also people in their cybersecurity initiatives. They can assist in detail sharing and also work with reactions to cyber risks. Organisations, on the other hand, can share risk knowledge best techniques as well as lessons found out with each various other and also with federal government firms. They can, likewise, work together with federal governments to establish cybersecurity criteria and also standards that mirror the advancing danger landscape. Last but not least, people can remain notified concerning best cybersecurity techniques, record dubious tasks, and also actively join initiatives to develop a society of cybersecurity recognition. These stakeholders additionally reach worldwide teamwork. Cyber risks frequently come from various components of the globe as well as need an international reaction. Federal governments as well as companies work together with global companions to share hazard intelligence, collaborate on case actions, and also create worldwide cybersecurity standards. International partnership assists in the recognition and also acknowledgment of cyber opponents and brings about raised deterrence as well as responsibility.

Collective techniques, including federal governments, companies, and also people, are important in dealing with the obstacles positioned by cyber dangers. By interacting, these stakeholders can take advantage of their distinct stamina along with sources to produce a more secure electronic setting. Federal governments can develop lawful structures as well as supply sources, companies can execute durable cybersecurity actions as well as share info, and people can exercise great electronic health as well as remain educated. With partnership, we can construct a more powerful cybersecurity ecological community that shields people, companies, and federal governments from cyber dangers in an interconnected globe.

9.9. CONCLUSION AND FUTURE CHALLENGES IN CYBERSECURITY

Cybersecurity as well as individual information defence come across brand-new patterns plus problems as innovation developments swiftly. These advancements show the requirement for consistent advancement, along with adjustment to shield individuals and also organisations in an electronic age. The development of IoT gadgets is a cybersecurity pattern. IoT devices consisting of clever family home appliances, wearables, and also commercial sensing units are coming to be progressively usual. Nevertheless, wide use of these devices develops extra dangers and also problems. IoT tools are susceptible to cyberattacks because of their weak safety. Establishing risk-free plus durable IoT communities with security, verification, and routine safety and security upgrades to shield individual information and also stop unapproved accessibility is challenging. Cybersecurity is additionally seeing the development of AI as well as ML. Risk recognition, violation discovery, and automated reaction are encouraging with AI and also ML. These modern technologies might possibly be made use of by cyberpunks to embark on much more complicated attacks. AI as well as ML are coming to be significantly usual in cybersecurity for that reason cybersecurity needs to stabilise their benefits along with dangers. This necessitates making AI formulas clear and also reasonable as well as structuring solid defences against enemies. Remote jobs as well as cloud computers, likewise, elevate cybersecurity plus information security problems. As even more information is saved and also refined in the cloud, organisations have to protect delicate information throughout remote systems. As employees attach to service networks from various tools as well as areas, remote jobs have actually boosted the strike surface area. Safe and secure accessibility limitations, file encryption, as well as personnel training are required to guard information as well as stop unapproved access.

The increase of information analytics, together with huge information, offers individual information security opportunities as well as problems. Organisations utilise information analytics to obtain understandings and also boost procedures. Nonetheless, comprehensive individual information gathering plus evaluation produce personal privacy concerns. Data-driven advancement as well as personal privacy should be well balanced. Carrying out personal privacy deliberately, anonymizing information, and also getting notified authorisation for information collection along with handling are instances.

The future difficulties in cybersecurity, along with individual information security, are more enhanced by the expanding refinement of cyber risks. Cyberpunks are constantly advancing their techniques, leveraging social design, ransomware, and also innovative consistent dangers to go against networks plus swipe delicate info. Furthermore, state-sponsored cyber-attacks as well as geopolitical stress enhance the intricacy of the cybersecurity landscape. Resolving these difficulties calls for recurring financial investment in research study as well as growth, cooperation between federal governments and companies, and also the application of innovative safety and security gauges to spot, stop, and also react to cyber risks successfully. Arising patterns, together with future difficulties in cybersecurity and also individual information defence, need continuous watchfulness plus adjustment. By remaining aware of the progressing danger landscape, companies as well as federal governments can apply durable safety steps, accept arising innovations properly, and foster a society of cybersecurity understanding. Partnership, technology, and also a dedication to personal privacy as well as safety are essential to browsing the intricate cybersecurity landscape as well as securing individual information in the electronic age.

REFERENCES

Bhavsar, Vaishnavi, Aditya Kadlak, Shabnam Sharma, "Study on Phishing Attacks", *International Journal of Computer Applications*, Vol. 182, Issue 33, 2018.

Chanda, Katha, "Password Security: An Analysis of Password Strengths and Vulnerabilities", *International Journal of Computer Network and Information Security*, Vol. 8, Issue 7, PP. 23–30, July 2016.

Cremer, Frank, Barry Sheehan, Michael Fortmann, Arash N. Kia, Martin Mullins, Finbarr Murphy, Stefan Materne, "Cyber Risk and Cybersecurity: A Systematic Review of Data Availability", *Springer Nature*, Vol. 47, Issue 3, PP. 698–736, 2022.

Dastane, Omkar, "The Effect of Bad Password Habits on Personal Data Breach", *International Journal of Emerging Trends in Engineering Research*, Vol. 8, Issue 10, Oct. 2020.

Jang-Jaccard, Julian, Surya Nepal, "A Survey of Emerging Threats in Cybersecurity", *Journal of Computer and System Sciences*, Vol. 80, Issue 5, PP. 973–993, 2014.

Li, Yuchong, Qinghui Liu, "A Comprehensive Review Study of Cyber-Attacks and Cyber Security; Emerging Trends and Recent Developments", *Energy Reports*, Vol. 7, Nov. 2021.

Maurya, Awadhesh, Neeraj Kumar, Alka Agrawal, Raees Ahmad Khan, "Ransomware Evolution, Target and Safety Measures", *International Journal of Computer Sciences and Engineering*, Vol. 6, Issue 1, PP. 80–85, 2018.

Mukta, Rahma, Hye-young Paik, Qinghua Lu, Salil S. Kanhere, "A Survey of Data Minimisation Techniques in Blockchain-Based Healthcare", *Computer Networks*, Vol. 205, March 2022.

Nayak, Rakesh, C. V. Sastry, Jayaram Pradhan, "A Matrix Formulation for NTRU Cryptosystem", *Proceedings 16th IEEE, International Conference on Networks* (ICON-2008), New Delhi. http://doi.org/10.1109/ICON.2008.4772602

Pool, Javad, Saeed Akhlaghpour, Farhad Fatehi, Andrew Burton-Jones, "A Systematic Analysis of Failures in Protecting Personal Health Data: A Scoping Review", *International Journal of Information Management*, Vol. 24, 2024.

Robles-Carrillo, M., P. García-Teodoro, "Ransomware: An Interdisciplinary Technical and Legal Approach", *Security and Communication Networks*, Vol. 2022, 2022.

Shabbir, Muhammad Qasim, Syed Babar Waheed Gardezi, "Application of Big Data Analytics and Organizational Performance: The Mediating Role of Knowledge Management Practices", *Springer Journal of Big Data*, Vol. 7, 2020.

Siddiqi, Murtaza Ahmed, Wooguil Pak, Moquddam A. Siddiqi, "A Study on the Psychology of Social Engineering-Based Cyberattacks and Existing Countermeasures", *Applied Sciences*, Vol. 12, Issue, 12, 2022.

Tariq, Usman, Irfan Ahmed, Ali Kashif Bashir, Kamran Shaukat, "A Critical Cybersecurity Analysis and Future Research Directions for the Internet of Things: A Comprehensive Review", *Journal of Sensors*, Vol. 23, Issue 9, 2023.

Tomás, Joana, Deolinda Rasteiro, Jorge Bernardino, "Data Anonymization: An Experimental Evaluation Using Open-Source Tools", *Future Internet*, Vol. 14, Issue 6, 2022.

Virmani, Charu, Neha Kaushik, Mohak, Vishnu Mathur, Sanskar Saxena, "Analysis of Cyber Attacks and Securityintelligence: Identity Theft", *Indian Journal of Science and Technology*, Vol. 13, Issue 25, PP. 2529–2536, 2020.

von Grafenstein, Max, Timo Jakobi, Gunnar Stevens, "Effective Data Protection by Design Through Interdisciplinary Research Methods: The Example of Effective Purpose Specification by Applying User-Centred UX-Design Methods", *Computer Law & Security Review*, Vol. 46, 2022.

Williamson, Joseph, Kevin Curran, "Best Practice in Multi-factor Authentication", *Semiconductor Science and Information Devices*, Vol. 3. Issue 1, May 2021.

10 A Lightweight Fast-Four Q-Key Generation for Embedded Devices on Women's Safety

Suryya Farhat, Manoj Kumar, Anshul Srivastava, and Arti Vaish

10.1. INTRODUCTION

The need to know the identity and legitimacy of the individual in which we interact and maintain users' privacy has become important in the age of ubiquitous computing. For low-resource devices such as sensor networks, RFID tags, smart phones, and smart cards, this new age has introduced new cryptography. This is called "cryptography lightweight". It is a challenge to develop an efficient protocol that meets all the security demands of small devices with limited resources. According to Hoopad (2010), a balance between performance and protection, performance and cost, or cost and security is possible but difficult to find. In recent years, therefore, a significant number of researchers have been engaged in the search for protection and privacy solutions in these smart devices Markku et al. (2012). Much of the research on the safety of these devices focuses more on protocols of identification Istvan et al. (2003), Hung-Yu (2009).

Elliptic curve cryptography (ECC) is a common public-key method that has become an attractive candidate for restricted devices to allow strong cryptography (Ciet, 2003; Ciet et al., 2002). Its reduced key sizes and excellent performance are well balanced by its strong safety foundation, focused on the discrete logarithm problem of the elliptic curve (ECDLP). Therefore, ECC-based mechanisms that could boost efficiency and power limitations in order to make ECC acceptable for restricted applications are mainly applicable to research Chung et al. (2015).

The FourQ curve of Costello and Longa [10.5], a special example of the endomorphism-based constructions studied by Smith (2016) and Guillevic and Ionica (2013), is a high-performance elliptical curve that provides around 128 bits of protection and allows scalar multiplications to be efficient and safe. Implementations based on this curve have shown that the fastest variable-base, fixed-base, and double scalar multiplication computations to date have been performed on a wide range of x64 and ARMv7 A processors (Longa, 2016). Furthermore, Jarvinen et al. have recently published.

DOI: 10.1201/9781003538172-10

For example, since many of these heterogeneous objects interact with each other or with other computer systems, they do not have a clear view of their interlocutors, the first FourQ-based hardware implementation, and set a speed record for curves over large prime characteristic fields on FPGAs (Prou and Rivain, 2007). It is therefore necessary to recognise the various actors in a conversation in order to identify them. Nevertheless, the identity of the consumer becomes a key element in a scheme. In order to prevent circumstances such as identity fraud or theft of identity and non-repudiation, it is important to maintain the authenticity of the asserted identity. We not only have to recognise the individual but also authenticate and protect its identity.

Indeed, the authors propose a set of extremely lightweight authentication schemes in Lejla et al. (2012), such as challenge-response using logic and simple arithmetic operations, that can be used to authenticate tags in RFID systems. It was noticed that certain protocols of the latter were weak and crypt analysed Stinson and Mashatan (2008).

Most protocols used for identification using standard cryptographic primitives that are most frequently based on the random oracle model are used in RFID systems, sensor networks, smart cards, Idots (Avanzi, 2005). The solid support of cryptographic primitives is not optimal due to the limitations of these devices (Istvan et al., 2003). Beyond the capabilities of these devices is the use of traditional cryptographic hash functions. There is, therefore, a strong need for new FourQ cryptographic primitives to support restricted resources such as deterministic randomness extractors on elliptical curves (Bernstein et al., 2008) with these methods.

In environments with limited resources, Schnorr's identification protocol is used because it provides a reasonable level of protection while respecting the constraints of these technologies. The security of this protocol is based on the difficulty of extracting in suitable finite fields the discrete logarithm.

In this chapter, for limited-resources devices, we propose a new FourQ identification protocol. In fact, our protocol is designed to be a prime or a binary field for any elliptic curve identified over the finite field K. However, to achieve complexity and contract side channel attacks, we used the Edwards elliptic curve. Deterministic encodings are also used to map random elements of the base field to a curve point Biehl et al. (2000), as well as deterministic randomness extractors, to derive an appropriate random bit-string from a random elliptical curve point (Brier et al., 2004). Under the standard model, our protocol is stable, assuming that the discrete logarithm problem is difficult.

In this chapter, we are going present a secure cloud storage and resource algorithm based on a hybrid cryptosystem; our proposed algorithm is a combination of Elliptic Curve Cryptography (ECC) and one-way hash function based on FourQ an optimisation-based, secure model. This algorithm and model help us secure resources effectively. Cloud storage must provide a high level of security and efficiency. The ECC cryptosystem, a form of public key or asymmetric encryption, uses different keys for encryption and decryption. There are various data sources for military databases' confidential video conferencing, medical imaging systems, and online personal photograph albums. To store information on a cloud server, we need robust security and advanced cryptography. This algorithm will help secure cloud resources as well. Protecting sensitive image data from unauthorized access is essential.

10.1.1. Identification Protocols

It is well recognised that patterns of recognition are very important for cryptography and computer protection.

An authentication protocol is a portion of an identification pattern (Chari, et al., 1999). An identification method is associated with two protocols designated for registration and acceptance between two parties. In a fundamental identification process, evidence concludes with the exchange, by all parties, of a secret key, all of which need to be stored securely. Usually, one or more of the following variables depend on protocols for authentication.

1 Are you what? By biometrics.
2 What do you have? It works on appliances like mobile phones, SIM cards, etc.
3 Hey, you know, what? Passwords, keys that are hidden, PIN codes.

We focus on purely cryptographic authentication protocols in this chapter, where a good prover must know where a secret key should be accessible. The general objective of authentication protocols in cryptographic constructions is to decrease the computation time of the prover and/or verifier.

Usually, three or four rounds of these protocols happen.

The goal of the adversary in an identification scheme is to identity theft or assault the computer so that it behaves like a cheater prover and tries to locate the true verifier. In general, passive, violent, and simultaneous attacks are considered with the involvement of the adversary seeking to imitate three traditional assaults. Therefore, protection against these attacks has become a major concern in cryptography, where the research and development of identification systems is widely studied.

The conception of zero-knowledge is used as an authentication device (Guillevic and Ionica, 2013). It is implemented, in particular, in the form of digital signatures, often on smart cards. Many protocols remain, despite the findings of some security defects, and many variants evolve.

First, Fiat and Shamir introduced an interactive method of acknowledgement of zero intelligence that also includes two components: a prover P and a prover V, where the prover convinces the spinels of a secret without revealing any information other than that they are aware of the secret.

A great deal of identification was then proposed on the basis of knowledge of the zero-knowledge protocol: Feige-Fiat-Shamir (FFS), Schnorr and Guillou-Quisquater (GQ) or Ohta-Okamoto are included in particular. We detail the Schnorridenti-cation on elliptic curves in the protocol below.

The scheme of Guillou-Quisquater (QM) is based on the problem of RSA inversion. They show that, given the difficulty of factorisation, their approach is safe from passive attacks, quite close to the Schnorr protocol. Ohta and Okamoto (OO) suggest a modification of the Fiat-Shamir technique based on the difficulty of extracting the ith root and showing that their method is safe as the Fiat-Shamir system.

In it, you find three variations of the Okamoto name scheme. The first is based on the discrete logarithm problem; the second is based on the RSA problem; and the third, on the factorisation problem.

It has been shown that both of these systems are shielded from passive aggression.

In recent years, there has been a growing concern globally regarding women's safety, particularly in urban environments, where incidents of harassment, assault, and violence against women are alarmingly prevalent. To address this pressing issue, there is an urgent need for innovative technological solutions that can empower women to protect themselves and access help efficiently in times of distress. One promising approach involves the development of lightweight and fast cryptographic algorithms tailored for embedded devices, enabling the implementation of secure communication and location tracking systems that can be seamlessly integrated into everyday accessories such as smart jewellery, wearable gadgets, or mobile applications.

This chapter focuses on proposing a lightweight and fast key generation scheme based on the FourQ elliptic curve cryptography for deployment on embedded devices, with a specific emphasis on enhancing women's safety. The FourQ curve offers several advantages, including its efficiency in terms of computation, compact representation, and suitability for resource-constrained environments typical of embedded systems. By leveraging this cryptographic framework, we aim to facilitate the rapid generation of secure cryptographic keys, which are fundamental for establishing secure communication channels, encrypting sensitive data, and verifying the authenticity of users in women safety applications.

The key objectives of this research include:

1 **Efficiency**: Designing a key generation scheme that minimises computational overhead and memory requirements, ensuring compatibility with low-power embedded devices commonly used in wearable technology and smart accessories.
2 **Security**: Ensuring robust cryptographic security to protect the confidentiality, integrity, and authenticity of communication and location data transmitted by women safety devices, thereby safeguarding user privacy and thwarting potential adversaries.
3 **Accessibility:** Creating a user-friendly solution that can be easily deployed and utilised by individuals without specialised technical knowledge, fostering widespread adoption and empowerment among women from diverse socioeconomic backgrounds.
4 **Scalability**: Developing a scalable architecture capable of supporting a large number of users and devices within a decentralised network, enabling effective collaboration and coordination in emergency situations while preserving system performance and reliability.

By addressing these objectives, we envision the proposed lightweight and fast FourQ key generation scheme to serve as a foundational building block for the development of next-generation women safety applications, empowering women to navigate urban environments with confidence and peace of mind. Through the integration of advanced cryptographic techniques into wearable devices and mobile applications, we aspire to contribute to the creation of safer and more inclusive communities where everyone, regardless of gender, can thrive without fear of violence or harassment.

10.2. LITERATURE STUDY

In this literature survey, we evaluation the diverse research papers, which can guide us for greater secure safety version for cloud computing environments and ECC encryption systems; in the current scenario, it plays a vital role, and well defined, suitable public-key encryption/decryption is best for cloud computing environments. One of the other current public key cryptosystems is ECC (Elliptic Curves Cryptography), used for security.

In the current landscape of cloud computing, many cloud storage solutions employ advanced cryptography to ensure user authentication. Chari, et al. (2002) developed side-channel attacks on implementations of curve-based cryptographic systems, demonstrating strong overall performance in exploiting vulnerabilities. However, the rapidly growing demand for cloud computing is driving a shift towards more advanced cloud environments. A review of the literature indicates that ECC cryptography generally outperforms other cryptographic systems. We compared various standard public-key cryptosystems, such as Diffie-Hellman and RSA.

ECC provides the security with smaller key sizes; this algorithm has performed faster calculation, and this reduces time for encryption techniques. ECC is useful for cloud computing, which can be commonly specific in terms in their CPU, electricity, and community connectivity. Elliptic curve-based totally zero-know-how proof techniques are effective tools in such packages for providing secure and private cloud computing storage applications (Fan and Verbauwhede, 2012). The improvement of security is due to the better complexity of fixing the discrete logarithm hassle over elliptic curves than over the multiplicative institution Zn. A new security for secure cloud computing storage, Elliptic Curve-based key era for rotation cipher is proposed through S. Maria Celestin Vigila et al. and Costello and Longa (2015) and Faz-Hernández et al. (2015). We did lots of research on cryptosystem, and we find the best cryptosystem, the most secure and efficient, is the Elliptic curve cryptosystem (Clavier, 2010; Cooper, 2013).

Literature Review: A Lightweight Fast FourQ Key Generation for Embedded Devices on Women Safety.

The intersection of cryptographic techniques, embedded systems, and women's safety has emerged as a crucial area of research, driven by the imperative to develop innovative solutions that empower women to protect themselves in diverse urban environments. In this literature review, we explore existing studies related to lightweight cryptography, fast key generation methods, embedded systems, and women's safety applications to provide a comprehensive understanding of the state-of-the-art in this field.

10.2.1. Lightweight Cryptography for Embedded Systems

Lightweight cryptography has gained significant attention due to the proliferation of resource-constrained devices such as wearable gadgets and Internet-of-Things (IoT) devices. Researchers have proposed various lightweight cryptographic algorithms and protocols optimised for low-power, low-memory embedded systems. Notable works include the development of lightweight block ciphers, hash functions, and elliptic curve cryptography (ECC) variants tailored for constrained environments. These efforts aim to strike a balance between security, efficiency, and resource consumption, making them particularly relevant for applications targeting women safety on embedded devices.

10.2.2. Fast Key Generation Techniques

Efficient key generation is essential for establishing secure communication channels and ensuring the confidentiality and integrity of data exchanged by women safety devices. Several studies have explored fast key generation techniques, especially in the context of elliptic curve cryptography. Techniques such as key precipitation, scalar multiplication algorithms, and curve parameter selection strategies have been investigated to accelerate key generation processes while maintaining cryptographic security. These advancements are crucial for enabling real-time encryption and authentication mechanisms on resource-constrained embedded devices.

10.2.3. Elliptic Curve Cryptography (ECC) for Women's Safety

ECC has emerged as a preferred cryptographic framework for women's safety applications due to its strong security properties and efficient computational performance. ECC offers compact key sizes and faster cryptographic operations, compared to traditional public-key cryptosystems, making it well-suited for deployment on wearable devices and mobile applications. Researchers have explored the application of ECC in women's safety solutions, including secure messaging systems, location tracking mechanisms, and emergency response platforms. These studies underscore the importance of lightweight ECC implementations for ensuring seamless integration into embedded devices aimed at enhancing women's safety.

10.2.4. Challenges and Opportunities

Despite significant progress in lightweight cryptography and embedded systems, several challenges remain in the development of effective women safety solutions. These challenges include balancing security and efficiency trade-offs, addressing privacy concerns, ensuring interoperability across diverse device ecosystems, and promoting user acceptance and adoption. Furthermore, the dynamic nature of urban environments and evolving threat landscapes necessitate continuous innovation and collaboration among researchers, policymakers, and stakeholders to design robust and user-centric women safety technologies.

10.2.5. Future Directions

Future research directions in this domain may include the exploration of post-quantum cryptographic algorithms suitable for embedded systems, the integration of machine learning and artificial intelligence techniques for threat detection and risk assessment, and the development of decentralised and privacy-preserving communication protocols. Additionally, efforts to engage with end-users through participatory design approaches and community-driven initiatives can help tailor women's safety solutions to meet the unique needs and preferences of diverse user demographics.

In summary, the literature highlights the importance of lightweight, fast key generation techniques based on elliptic curve cryptography for enhancing women's safety on embedded devices. By leveraging advancements in cryptographic research, embedded systems engineering, and user-centred design principles, researchers can contribute to the development of innovative and impactful solutions that empower women to navigate urban environments safely and confidently.

10.2.6. Key Generation

As per Elliptic Equation:

$$y^2 = x^3 + ax + b \tag{10.1}$$

Elliptic Curve is denoted by E Point on the curve is denoted by p Upper limit for selecting the random number and should be a prime number is denoted by N.

The equation (1) for an elliptic curve shows that the curve is symmetrical about the x axis. If we take square root of both sides x and y then:

$$y = \pm\sqrt{x^2}\ ax + b \tag{10.2}$$

This equation shows or proves that x is same but y is varying from –y to +y value.

For the purpose of data security key generation playing a vital role, for the purpose of more secure data public and private key generation is more secure as encryption is done by using public key of receiver and decryption is done by using receiver private key. This Elliptic curve we are using here for key generation for encryption

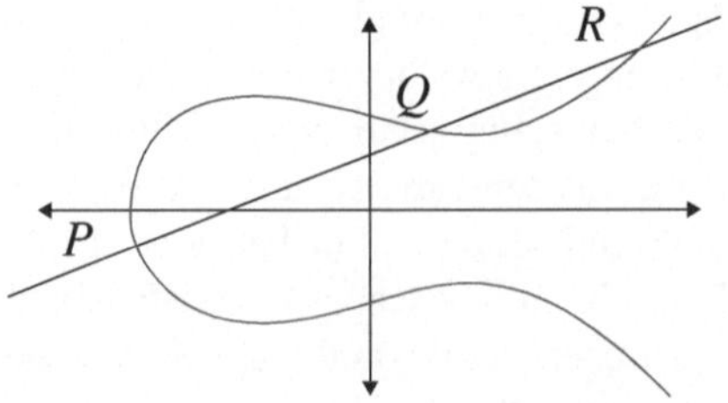

FIGURE 10.1 Elliptic curve.

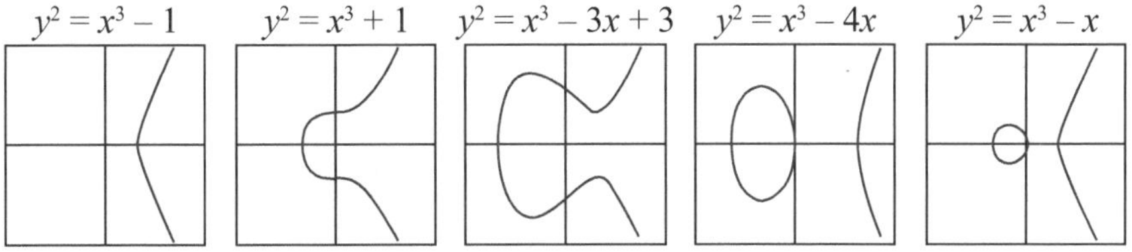

FIGURE 10.2 Different elliptic curves.

and decryption function, key generation is an important process and to generate both public key and private key.

Firstly is to select a random number "D". Our selected number is not greater than "N".

$$Q_k = D{*}P \tag{10.3}$$

Equation 10.3 helps to generate the public key, and where D is random number selected from range 1 to N-1 and P is the point of the curve. This equation is used to derive both the private and public keys. In this context, 'D' represents the private key, and 'Q_k' can be computed using the above equation.

ENCRYPT THE MESSAGE

For the purpose of encrypt the message, we generate the public and private key. Suppose, on the curve "E", MX has the point. *Next step is to select* select "k_i" from [1—(N-1)], where k_i is randomly selected.

Now, we will complete the process by generating cipher texts CM_1 and CM_2.

$$CM_1 = k_i{*}P \tag{10.4}$$

$$CM_2 = MX{*}k_i{*}QK \tag{10.5}$$

This generated message CM_1 and CM_2 is now ready to send.

DECRYPTION

Now, our process is for decryption message "MX" that was sent to us,

$$MX = CM_2 - D{*}CM_1 \tag{10.6}$$

This MX is the original message that is sent using Elliptic curve techniques.

Proof: Now we are discussing the proof

$$MX = CM_2 - D{*}CM_1$$

"MX" can be represented as $CM_2 - D * CM_1$

$$CM_2 - D^*CM_1 = (MX + k_i{}^*QK) - D^*(k_i{}^*P) \tag{10.7}$$

This message is original message that we send by encryption process. The Elliptic curve for the encryption/decryption process is for message that we described previously, But, in cloud computing, we need more security. As cloud computing is popular due to providing the data storage space, we need a model that will provide more security.

10.2.7. FourQ Curve

The researcher Costello and Longa did research on various Elliptic Curves and invented a best Curve FourQ in 2015, defined by a twisted Edwards equation Costello and Longa (2015). The FourQ is defined by the equation

$$-x^2 + y^2 = 1 + dx^2y^2 \tag{10.8}$$

FourQ is functionality based on two efficiently computable endomorphism, ψ and φ, that will generate the four-dimensional decompositions. FourQ is defined over the quadratic extension field $p = 2^{127} - 1$.

FourQ is an Elliptic curve that is more popular due to providing more security and faster compared to Curve25519 and the quadratic extension field.

$$F_p^2 = F_{P(i)} F_p^2 = F_{P(i)} \; for \; i^2 = -1$$

where p is the Mersenne prime

$$p = 2^{127} - 1.$$

$$R(F_p^2) = [N] \text{ related to } R(F_p^2) = 392$$

The FourQ curve equation 2 is a prime order subgroup, where N represents the 246 bit prime $R(F_p^2) = [N]$ related to $R(F_p^2) = 392 \cdot N$, is used to carry out encryption/decryption key generation computations. In this subgroup, the O_E= (0, 1) is for neutral element, and the inverse of a point (x, y) is given by ($-x$, y).

10.3. OUR PROTOCOL

We propose a new FourQ weak-strong identification protocol that is safe, using elliptic curves and biometric data, under the standard model.

The principle is to combine two forms of identity systems: authentication based on biometrics and recognition of challenge-response.

Over the finite field Fq, where q is a prime power, let E be an elliptical curve defined. E(Fq) over E is denoted as the set of Fq-rational points. Let

$$h : D \rightarrow E\left(F_q\right)z \rightarrow Q = \left(x, y\right)$$

D denotes the set of biometric data in the elliptic curve that can be interpreted as bit-strings as a function of hash. H may be the Icart function for elliptic curves in Weierstrass form or the Elligator when dealing with Edwards elliptic curves.

Alice, the claimant (the prover) uses function h to map her biometric data b to point B of the elliptic curve E (a bit-string consisting of a fingerprint and retinal scan combination or voice scan). We also choose a random integer, calculate s = Extk (?? D), where the Lk or Dk function may be Extk, and apply the pair (D; s) to the verifier via asymmetric cryptography methods (Bob). B may be encrypted using, for example, the public key of the verifier. Consequently, the claimant and the verifier share the same secret (D; s) that is used for poor authentication. Here, D plays the role of a password.

The process accepted two important points:

1 The verification process is correct.
2 Presume the randomness of the hardness and biometric information by the DLP, and then the proposed recognition protocol is protected by impersonation from direct attacks.

Designing a lightweight and fast key generation scheme for embedded devices focused on women's safety is a crucial endeavour, given the need for efficient and secure communication channels in potentially dangerous situations. Here's a proposal for such a scheme:

10.3.1. Algorithm Selection

Choose a lightweight cryptographic algorithm suitable for embedded devices. FourQ is a good candidate due to its efficiency and security properties.

10.3.2. Key Generation

Implement a key generation process tailored for embedded devices as above:

Utilise the FourQ elliptic curve to generate public-private key pairs as shown earlier.

1 Employ a secure random number generator suitable for embedded systems to generate private keys.
2 Derive public keys from the corresponding private keys using the elliptic curve scalar multiplication.
3 Store the generated keys securely in the device's memory.

10.3.3. Integration With Women's Safety Applications

Integrate the key generation scheme into women safety applications on embedded devices:

1. Ensure seamless integration with existing safety applications such as panic buttons, safety alarms, or communication apps.
2. Provide an intuitive interface for users to initiate key generation and manage their keys securely.
3. Implement features for key backup and recovery to prevent data loss in case of device damage or loss.

10.3.4. Performance Optimisation

Optimise the key generation process for speed and efficiency:

1. Minimise computational overhead by leveraging hardware-accelerated cryptographic primitives if available.
2. Implement parallelisation techniques to distribute key generation tasks across multiple processing units if applicable.
3. Conduct thorough performance testing and optimization to ensure the scheme meets the stringent resource constraints of embedded devices.

10.3.5. Security Considerations

Prioritise security throughout the key generation process:

1. Utilise robust cryptographic primitives and algorithms to withstand potential attacks.
2. Implement countermeasures against common cryptographic threats such as side-channel attacks and fault injections.
3. Regularly update the embedded device's firmware to patch any security vulnerabilities and ensure ongoing protection.

10.3.6. User Education and Awareness

Educate users on the importance of key management and safe communication practices:

1. Provide guidance on securely storing and managing generated keys.
2. Raise awareness about potential risks and threats associated with unsafe communication channels.
3. Offer training sessions or educational materials to empower users in utilizing the safety features effectively.

10.4. CONCLUSION

We discussed FourQ and its role as a standard model of security functions. By combining, for example, biometrics that provide better efficiency, based on the complexity of the discrete logarithm and the rarity of an authentication protocol based on the standard FourQ cryptography model, we suggested defining zero-knowledge protocols. A hash function or Elligator, Icart, and randomness extractor, as indicated, are used in this protocol. This makes it possible to enhance identification efficiency, protection, and cost. We have also shown that our protocol is secure from impersonation by active attacks. Thus, the proposed recognition scheme is more suitable for these light technologies than the existing systems. A lightweight and fast key generation scheme can be developed and integrated into embedded devices, contributing to enhanced women's safety in various scenarios. Regular updates and community feedback should be solicited to ensure continuous improvement and adaptation to evolving security needs.

REFERENCES

Avanzi, R. M (2005). Side channel attacks on implementations of curve-based cryptographic primitives. *IACR Cryptology ePrint Archive, Report 2005/017.*

Bernstein, D. J., P. Birkner, et al. (2008). Twisted Edwards curves. In S. Vaudenay, editor, *Progress in Cryptology—AFRICACRYPT 2008*, Volume 5023 of Lecture Notes in Computer Science, pages 389–405. Springer.

Biehl, B. Meyer, and V. Müller (2000). Differential fault attacks on elliptic curve cryptosystems. In M. Bellare, editor, *Advances in Cryptology—CRYPTO 2000*, Volume 1880 of Lecture Notes in Computer Science, pages 131–146. Springer.

Brier, E., C. Clavier, and F. Olivier (2004). Correlation power analysis with a leakage model. In M. Joye and J. Quisquater, editors, *Cryptographic Hardware and Embedded Systems—CHES 2004*, Volume 3156 of Lecture Notes in Computer Science, pages 16–29. Springer.

Chari, S., C. S. Jutla, J. R. Rao, and P. Rohatgi (1999). Towards sound approaches to counteract power-analysis attacks. In M. J. Wiener, editor, *Advances in Cryptology—CRYPTO '99*, Volume 1666 of Lecture Notes in Computer Science, pages 398–412. Springer.

Chari, S., J. R. Rao, and P. Rohatgi (2002). Template attacks. In B. S. Kaliski, çetin K. Koç and C. Paar, editors, *Cryptographic Hardware and Embedded Systems—CHES 2002*, Volume 2523 of Lecture Notes in Computer Science, pages 13–28. Springer.

Chung, P. N., C. Costello, and B. Smith (2015). Fast, uniform, and compact scalar multiplication for elliptic curves and genus 2 Jacobians with applications to signature schemes. *IACR Cryptology ePrint Archive, Report 2015/983.* https://ia.cr/2015/983

Ciet, M. (2003). *Aspects of Fast and Secure Arithmetics for Elliptic Curve Cryptography.* PhD thesis, Universit´eCatholique de Louvain, Louvain-la-Neuve.

Ciet, M., J. Quisquater, and F. Sica (2002). Preventing differential analysis in GLV elliptic curve scalar multiplication. In B. S. Kaliski, çetin K. Koç and C. Paar, editors, *Cryptographic Hardware and Embedded Systems CHES 2002*, Volume 2523 of Lecture Notes in Computer Science, pages 540–550. Springer.

Clavier, C., B. Feix, G. Gagnerot, M. Roussellet, and V. Verneuil (2010). Horizontal correlation analysis on exponentiation. In M. Soriano, S. Qing, and J. López, editors, *Information and Communications Security ICICS 2010*, Volume 6476 of Lecture Notes in Computer Science, pages 46–61. Springer.

Cooper, J., E. DeMulder, G. Goodwill, J. Jaffe, G. Kenworthy, and P. Rohatgi (2013). Test Vector Leakage Assessment (TVLA) methodology in practice. *International Cryptographic Module Conference*.

Costello, C., and P. Longa (2015). FourQ: Four-dimensional decompositions on a Q-curve over the Mersenne prime. In T. Iwata and J. H. Cheon, editors, *Advances in Cryptology—ASIACRYPT 2015*, Volume 9452 of Lecture Notes in Computer Science, pages 214–235. Springer.

Dang, D., M. Plant, and M. Poole (2014). Wireless connectivity for the Internet of Things (IoT) with MSP430 microcontrollers (MCUs). *Texas Instruments White Paper*, available at: www.ti.com/lit/wp/slay028/slay028.pdf.

Fan, J., and I. Verbauwhede (2012). An updated survey on secure ECC implementations: Attacks, countermeasures and cost. In D. Naccache, editor, *Cryptography and Security: From Theory to Applications—Essays Dedicated to Jean-Jacques Quisquater on the Occasion of His 65th Birthday*, Volume 6805 of Lecture Notes in Computer Science, pages 265–282. Springer.

Faz-Hernández, P. Longa, and A. H. Sánchez (2015). Efficient and secure algorithms for GLV-based scalar multiplication and their implementation on GLV-GLS curves (extended version). *Journal of Cryptographic Engineering*, 5(1):31–52.

Guillevic, A., and S. Ionica (2013). Four-dimensional GLV via the Weil restriction. In K. Sako and P. Sarkar, editors, *Advances in Cryptology—ASIACRYPT 2013*, Volume 8269 of Lecture Notes in Computer Science, pages 79–96. Springer.

Hoopad, M. (2010). Authentication and lightweight cryptography in low cost r_d. In *Software Technology and Engineering (ICSTE), 2010 2nd International Conference on*, Volume 2, pages V2123. IEEE.

Hung-Yu, C. (2009). The study of RFID authentication protocols and security of some popular RFID tags. *Development and Implementation of RFID Technology*, Department of Information Management, National Chi Nan University, pages 261–290.

Istvan, V., B. Levente, et al. (2003). Lightweight authentication protocols for low-cost RFID tags. In *Second Workshop on Security in Ubiquitous Computing-Ubicomp*.

Lejla, B., S. Stefaan, et al. (2012). Hierarchical ecc-based RFID au-thentication protocol. In *RFID. Security and Privacy*, pages 183–201. Springer.

Longa, P. (2016). FourQ: Faster elliptic curve scalar multiplications on ARM processors. In R. Avanzi and H. Heys, editors, *Selected Areas in Cryptography—SAC 2016 (to appear), Lecture Notes in Computer Science*. Springer.

Markku, J., et al. (2012). A do-it-all-cipher for rifd: Design requirements. *IACR Cryptology ePrint Archive*, 2012:317.

Paris, K., and Z. Yan (2008). *RFID Security: Techniques, Protocols and System-on-Chip Design*. Springer.

Prou, E., and M. Rivain (2007). A generic method for secure sbox implementation. In S. Kim, M. Yung, and H. Lee, editors, *Information Security Applications, WISA 2007*, Volume 4867 of Lecture Notes in Computer Science, pages 227–244. Springer.

Smith, B. (2016). The Q-curve construction for endomorphism-accelerated elliptic curves. *Journal of Cryptology*, 29(4):806–832.

Stinson, D., and R. Mashatan (2008). Interactive two-channel message authentication based on interactive-collision resistant hash functions. *International Journal of Information Security*, 8:49–60.

11 Navigating Legal and Ethical Dimensions in AI, IoT, and Cloud Solutions for Women's Safety

Priyanka Prabhakar, Peeta Basa Pati, and Shantipriya Parida

11.1. INTRODUCTION

The safety and well-being of women in various facets of life, whether in public spaces, workplaces, or within their own homes, have long been a concern shaped by societal norms, cultural attitudes, and systemic inequalities (Roy and Bailey, 2021). In recent years, the advancement of technology has offered new avenues for addressing these concerns (Cardoso et al., 2019), with AI (Artificial Intelligence), IoT (Internet of Things), and cloud computing emerging as pivotal tools in enhancing women's safety. However, while these technologies hold promise in providing innovative solutions, their implementation raise many legal and ethical considerations that necessitate careful examination.

In this chapter, we embark on a journey to explore the intersection of women's safety and technology, focusing on the safety implications of deploying AI, IoT, and cloud computing tools. The goal is to shift the narrative from solely addressing primary safety concerns to critically examining the secondary safety issues that arise from utilising these technologies. By delving into the complexities of legal and ethical dimensions, we aim to provide insights into navigating the deployment of these technologies with trust and confidence, ultimately ensuring comprehensive protection for women.

At the heart of this discussion lies the recognition that, while technology has the potential to empower women and create safer environments (Hariharan et al., 2021), it also introduces new challenges and risks (Kabir and Tasneem, 2020). Take, for example, the context of workplace sexual harassment—a pervasive issue that affects women across industries and sectors. Traditional reporting mechanisms often fail to provide a safe and confidential avenue for victims to come forward, leading to underreporting and perpetuating a culture of silence. Organisations have turned to technological solutions such as AI-powered reporting tools to facilitate reporting and addressing incidents in real-time.

DOI: 10.1201/9781003538172-11

However, introducing such technologies brings forth a host of secondary safety concerns (Mason and Magnet, 2012). For instance, the data collected through these reporting tools may be vulnerable to misuse or unauthorized access, raising questions about privacy and confidentiality (Michota, 2013; Bani Issa et al., 2020). Moreover, the reliance on AI algorithms introduces the risk of bias or discrimination in handling reported incidents, potentially exacerbating existing inequalities within the workplace. Beyond workplace safety, similar challenges emerge in other contexts where technology is deployed to enhance women's safety. In public spaces, IoT-enabled surveillance systems may offer real-time monitoring and response mechanisms to prevent incidents (Prabhakar, 2018) of harassment or violence. However, the widespread deployment of such systems raises concerns about privacy invasion and the potential for misuse or abuse of surveillance data. In the domestic sphere, smart home devices equipped with AI capabilities promise to enhance safety and security for women (Schaefer et al., 2006) living alone or in vulnerable situations (Gayathri et al., 2022). From smart locks that offer remote monitoring and access control to AI-powered virtual assistants that can alert authorities in emergencies, these technologies offer a sense of reassurance (Schomakers et al., 2021) and peace of mind. However, the collection and storage of sensitive personal data by these devices raise significant privacy concerns (Chhetri and Motti, 2019), especially in cases where data may be accessed or exploited by unauthorised parties (Guhr et al., 2020; Zimmermann et al., 2019).

As we navigate these complexities, it becomes evident that deploying AI, IoT, and cloud computing for women's safety requires a nuanced understanding of legal and ethical considerations (Naik et al., 2022). It is not enough to simply focus on the primary safety concerns; rather, we must also critically examine the implications of these technologies (Singh et al., 2015) on secondary safety issues such as privacy, data security, and algorithmic bias. Through a comprehensive analysis of relevant laws, regulations, and ethical frameworks, we aim to provide a roadmap for stakeholders involved in deploying these technologies for women's safety. By highlighting the potential risks and challenges and strategies for mitigating them, we seek to ensure that these technologies can be harnessed responsibly and ethically to create safer environments for women (Crabtree and Geara, 2018; Sharma et al., 2022).

Involving end-users and communities in the design process ensures that the technology (Prabhakar et al., 2022) is contextually relevant, respectful of cultural nuances, and aligns with the actual needs and expectations of the users (Bach and Twidale, 2010). The collaborative development model, incorporating community feedback and insights, fosters a sense of ownership and trust among the end-users (Lindberg, 2018). Transparency and accountability frameworks constitute the bedrock upon which ethical technology governance stands (Doridot, 2013). Establishing clear mechanisms for transparency ensures that users understand the technology's functionalities, limitations, and implications (Carroll and Rosson, 2007). Simultaneously, robust accountability mechanisms, including ethics review boards and regular audits, serve as checks and balances (Kurt and Duquenoy, 2013) against potential misuse or unintended consequences. This governance structure becomes a guiding framework, aligning the development and deployment of technology (Sivan et al., 2022a) with ethical imperatives and societal expectations (Nathan, 2015; Zimmerman, 1995).

The following sections and subsections will delve deeper into specific legal and ethical considerations surrounding deploying AI, IoT, and cloud computing for women's safety. Through case studies and real-world examples, we will explore the nuances of navigating these complexities and provide practical insights for practitioners, policymakers, and stakeholders. Ultimately, our goal is to foster a dialogue that promotes the responsible and ethical use of technology to enhance women's safety while ensuring that the rights and dignity of individuals are upheld.

11.2. GUARDIAN GRACE: WOMEN'S SAFETY SPACE

This section delves into the multifaceted realm of women's safety, examining various dimensions that encompass physical, emotional, socioeconomic, and health-related aspects. Safety holds profound significance in women's lives (Moser, 2012), influencing their ability to pursue opportunities and live fulfilling lives free from fear and harm. However, achieving comprehensive safety for women necessitates a holistic approach addressing immediate threats alongside broader social, economic, and psychological factors.

11.2.1. Physical Safety

Ensuring the physical safety of women is crucial for their overall well-being and empowerment. It protects them from immediate harm and allows them to participate fully in society, pursue opportunities, and thrive in various aspects of life. Physical safety is essential for women to feel secure and confident in navigating public spaces, workplaces (Forssberg et al., 2022), and interpersonal relationships (Velonis et al., 2017). Additionally, safeguarding women's physical safety is a fundamental human right that promotes dignity, autonomy, and equality. By prioritising women's physical safety, we create environments that foster trust, respect, and inclusivity, benefiting individuals, communities, and society.

- Assault and Violence: Instances of assault and violence against women persist in both public and private spheres, posing serious threats to their physical safety (Yu et al., 2020). Community-based support programmes for survivors of domestic violence and sexual assault highlight the importance of tailored interventions. Research insights shed light on the prevalence and impact of different forms of violence, informing initiatives aimed at prevention and support (Ellsberg et al., 2015).
- Safe Public Spaces: Public spaces are essential for social interaction and community engagement, yet women often experience harassment and fear when navigating these environments (Rosenbaum et al., 2020). Initiatives, such as implementing gender-sensitive urban planning strategies and community-led safety walks, demonstrate efforts to create safer public spaces. Research insights uncover the spatial dynamics of harassment and the

efficacy of interventions like improved lighting and surveillance systems (Conrey and Zurbriggen, 2023).

- Workplace Safety: Women's safety in the workplace is paramount (Sadler et al., 2003; Kauppinen and Tuomola, 2008) for their professional advancement and well-being (Sorrentino et al., 2016). Corporate policies on sexual harassment prevention and response showcase organisational efforts to create safer work environments. Research into the prevalence and impact of workplace harassment inform the development of comprehensive training programs and reporting mechanisms.

11.2.2. Emotional and Psychological Safety

Emotional and psychological safety forms the bedrock of women's well-being, particularly for those from underrepresented backgrounds. For example, invalidating women's capabilities based on gender can engender discomfort and self-doubt (Altun et al., 2017), highlighting the critical need for psychological safety in diverse settings (Schmitt et al., 2003). This section delves into the complex terrain of emotional and psychological safety, examining women's unique challenges and the imperative to create inclusive and affirming environments.

- Mental Health: Mental health is a cornerstone of women's overall well-being (Dixon et al., 2021), profoundly shaping their ability to navigate life's challenges, pursue personal aspirations, and cultivate fulfilling relationships. For instance, consider the prevalence of mental health issues such as depression, anxiety, and trauma among women worldwide. These conditions impact individuals on a personal level and reverberate through their interactions within families, workplaces, and communities (Oram et al., 2017). Moreover, the pervasive stigma surrounding mental health often prevents women from seeking the support they need, compounding their struggles. This stigma manifests in various forms, from societal expectations that undermine women's emotional vulnerability to cultural norms that discourage open discussions about mental well-being (Nair and Menon, 2023). As a result, women from diverse backgrounds may face significant barriers in accessing appropriate mental health resources and services tailored to their unique needs (Kuehner, 2017).
- Cyberbullying and Online Safety: Women often find themselves subjected to a barrage of online abuse, ranging from persistent harassment to explicit threats and invasive cyberstalking (Bossler and Holt, 2012). Such experiences not only inflict immediate emotional distress but also leave lasting scars on their emotional balance (Prabhakar et al., 2023) and overall well-being (Carvalho et al., 2021). Safeguarding personal information and privacy online is particularly challenging, as cyber attackers continually devise new tactics to exploit vulnerabilities and breach security measures. Addressing cyberbullying and ensuring online safety for women is imperative, as it directly impacts their emotional resilience and sense of security in both virtual and real-world environments.

- Safe Relationships: Safe relationships are essential for women's emotional well-being and sense of security. However, women may face challenges in fostering safe relationships (Ludermir et al., 2010) due to various factors, including power dynamics, gender-based violence, and unhealthy relationship patterns (Ludermir et al., 2008). Building trust and setting boundaries within relationships, both intimate and platonic, can be complex, particularly in environments where gender norms and societal expectations impact interpersonal dynamics (Almış et al., 2020).

11.2.3. Socioeconomic Safety

Socioeconomic safety is a pivotal component encompassing the structural determinants (Jayachandran, 2021) significantly influencing individuals' quality of life. By addressing the foundational elements, socioeconomic safety aims to create environments conducive to promoting social justice, reducing inequalities, and enhancing the overall resilience of individuals and communities.

- Financial Independence: Financial independence is intricately linked to women's safety, as it enables them to make autonomous decisions and reduces their vulnerability to economic exploitation (Baxter and Kane, 1995) and dependence on others for financial support. Societal expectations and gender norms often restrict women's access to opportunities for economic advancement (Kanyagui et al., 2023), perpetuating their reliance on others for financial stability (Lerner, 1983). This dependence can make women more susceptible to financial abuse (Into, 2003) and manipulation within relationships, compromising their safety and autonomy.
- Access to Resources: Access to resources such as education (García-Moreno et al., 2015), housing, and social support services is crucial for women's socio-economic safety and overall well-being. Limited access to education and employment opportunities can trap women in cycles of poverty and dependency, increasing their vulnerability to various forms of exploitation and abuse (Fitzpatrick and Gomez, 1997; Vickery, 2012; Kasearu et al., 2017). Additionally, disparities in housing availability and quality can expose women to unsafe living conditions and exacerbate their socio-economic insecurities, further compromising their safety and well-being.
- Legal and Policy Frameworks: Legal and policy frameworks play a significant role in shaping women's socioeconomic safety by providing protections, rights, and avenues for recourse against discrimination and exploitation (Hyland et al., 2021). For example, in countries with strong labour laws (Arun et al., 2020) and anti-discrimination policies, women are better protected against workplace harassment and unequal pay practices. However, challenges persist in enforcing these laws, especially in regions with weak governance structures and patriarchal legal systems (Martin and Hashi, 1992). Additionally, cultural norms and societal attitudes may undermine the implementation of gender-sensitive policies, posing obstacles to women's socio-economic empowerment (Joshi, 2019).

11.2.4. Health and Well-Being

The health and well-being of women are vital components of a thriving society. By prioritising their health, women not only empower themselves but also foster the well-being of their families, ultimately contributing to the health and prosperity of our nation.

- Reproductive Health Rights: Ensuring reproductive health rights is essential for women's autonomy and well-being (Uberoi and De Bruyn, 2013). Access to comprehensive reproductive healthcare services, including family planning, maternal care, and reproductive education, empowers women to make informed decisions about their bodies and reproductive futures (Espey et al., 2019). However, challenges persist, particularly in regions where restrictive laws, cultural norms, and limited access to healthcare services impede women's ability to exercise their reproductive rights (Silvers et al., 2016). For example, in some countries, women face legal barriers to accessing contraception or safe abortion services, leading to adverse health outcomes and violations of their reproductive rights.
- Access to Healthcare Services: Access to healthcare services is fundamental for promoting women's health and well-being. Adequate healthcare infrastructure, trained healthcare professionals, and affordable healthcare services are essential components of a comprehensive healthcare system (Carter et al., 2020). However, disparities in access to healthcare services persist, particularly in rural and marginalised communities (Hooda et al., 2021), where women often face barriers such as transportation costs, lack of healthcare facilities, and cultural stigmatisation (Sundari, 2020). For instance, in remote areas of developing countries (Dahab and Sakellariou, 2020), women may have limited access to maternal care services, leading to higher maternal mortality rates and adverse health outcomes.
- Intersection of Health and Safety: The intersection of health and safety is a critical consideration in addressing women's well-being (Trench et al., 1992). Women's health is intricately linked to their safety and security, with factors such as gender-based violence, environmental hazards, and socioeconomic inequalities impacting their health outcomes. For example, women experiencing intimate partner violence may suffer from physical injuries, mental health issues (Lavanya et al., 2023), and reproductive health problems as a result of abuse. Additionally, women from low-income communities are disproportionately affected by environmental pollution and lack of access to clean water and sanitation, leading to adverse health consequences (van der Ham et al., 2021). Addressing the intersection of health and safety requires comprehensive approaches that address underlying social determinants, promote gender equality, and prioritise women's health needs in policy and programming (Tyer-Viola and Cesario, 2010).

Recognising the paramount importance of women's safety for the overall well-being of communities worldwide, there is a pressing need to prioritise addressing the myriad challenges that impede the implementation of safety measures. From cultural barriers to systemic inequalities, these obstacles hinder progress in ensuring women's safety and empowerment. However, amidst these challenges, technology is a promising ally in advancing women's safety initiatives. Through innovative solutions such as AI-powered reporting tools and IoT-enabled safety devices, technology offers practical avenues to overcome barriers (Sivan et al., 2022b) and enhance the effectiveness of safety measures. By leveraging technological advancements, we can bridge gaps in access, improve response mechanisms, and ultimately create safer environments where women can thrive without fear of harm or discrimination.

11.3. THE INTERSECTION OF TECHNOLOGY AND WOMEN'S SAFETY

This section explores the dynamic intersection of technology and women's safety, focusing on innovative solutions to enhance safety measures. Through advanced technology, stakeholders are empowered to address safety concerns effectively and prioritise the well-being of women. Figure 11.1 illustrates a hierarchical structure for

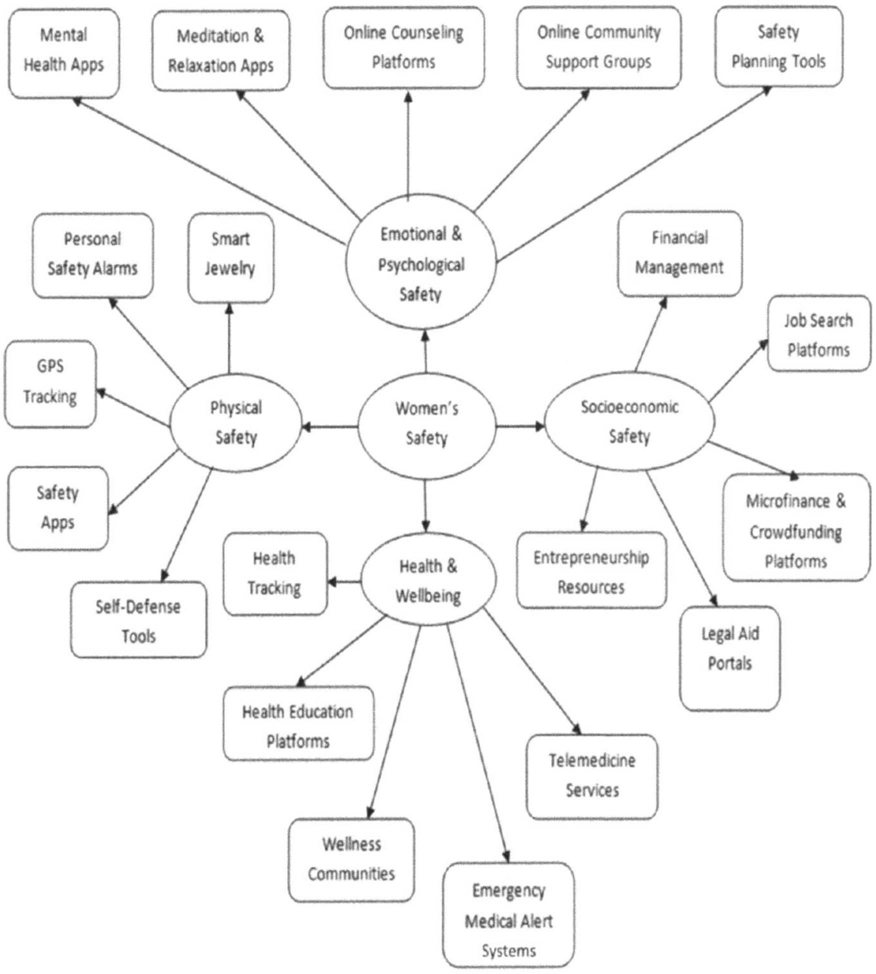

FIGURE 11.1 Hierarchical structure for addressing women's safety concerns through technology.

addressing women's safety concerns, with Women's Safety branching into sub-categories. Table 11.1 showcases a diverse range of technologies specifically designed to enhance women's safety across various domains. From personal safety alarms and self-defence tools to mental health apps and financial management platforms (Jacob and Vivek, 2019), these technologies cater to different aspects of women's safety needs, providing support, resources, and empowerment in navigating their daily lives.

TABLE 11.1
Diverse Technologies and Their Uses Designed to Address Women's Safety Concerns Across Multiple Safety Categories

Safety Name	Technology Use
Physical Safety:	
SheAlarm Personal Safety Alarm	Personal safety alarm with loud sound alert
Safelet Smart Jewellery	Smart jewellery with SOS alert feature
bSafe Safety App	Safety app with SOS alerts and real-time location sharing
Taser Self	Self-defence tool with electroshock capabilities
Nimb Ring	Smart ring with emergency alert feature
Revolar Instinct	Wearable safety device with alert functionality
ROAR for Good Athena	Smart wearable with safety features
Pepper Spray with Smart Technology	Pepper spray with additional safety features
Emotional and Psychological Safety:	
Shine	Mental health app offering support and resources
BetterHelp for Women	Online counselling platform for women
Women's Safety App by Safetipin	Safety app with reporting and alert features
MyPlan App	Safety planning tool for individuals at risk
Socioeconomic Safety:	
Ellevest	Financial management app tailored for women
Fairygodboss	Job search platform focusing on women's career needs
iFundWomen	Crowdfunding platform specifically for women entrepreneurs
WEConnect International	Resources for women entrepreneurs
Ellevest	Financial management app for women
Fairygodboss	Job search platform for women
WEConnect International	Resources for women entrepreneurs
Health and Well-Being:	
Flo Health	Health tracking app designed for women
Nurx	Telemedicine services tailored for women
Glow	Wellness community focusing on women's health
Healthline	Health education platform providing resources for women
Flo App	Women's health tracking app
Tia	Women's health and wellness platform
Maya	Women's health and wellness platform

11.3.1. Utilising Technology for Enhanced Safety of Women

Innovations in technology are revolutionising the landscape of women's safety, offering novel solutions to address longstanding concerns. From smart surveillance systems in public spaces to AI-powered risk assessment tools, these advancements provide a multifaceted approach to enhancing security for women. Through integrating mobile apps, wearable devices (Kannan et al., 2020), and digital hotlines, technology enables swift responses to emergencies and fosters a culture of prevention and awareness. By leveraging the capabilities of technology in innovative ways, we are reshaping the narrative of women's safety, ushering in an era where empowerment and security intersect seamlessly (Prabhakar, 2018).

11.3.1.1. Current Technological Solutions

Technological solutions for women's safety have seen significant advancements globally, including in India, addressing various categories such as personal safety, emergency response, and community support. Here are some current technological solutions:

a Personal Safety Apps
  - India: Apps like *Safetipin* and *Himmat* (Delhi Police's women safety app) provide features such as GPS tracking, emergency helplines, and crowd-sourced safety ratings for areas.
  - International: Apps like *bSafe* and *Circle of 6* offer similar features with added functionalities like real-time location sharing and quick SOS alerts to trusted contacts.

b Smart Wearables
  - India and International: Devices like *Safer Pro* and *ROAR for Good's Athena* are wearable safety devices that can be discreetly activated to send distress signals and location information to pre-set contacts or authorities.

c Emergency Response Systems
  - India: *Nirbhaya* and *iFollow* are emergency response systems that utilise GPS and mobile networks to send distress signals to emergency contacts and local authorities.
  - International: Systems like *911 Shield* in the US and *112* in the EU provide centralised emergency response services with location tracking and two-way communication features.

d Crowdsourcing Platforms
  - India and International: Platforms like *Safecity* and *Hollaback!* allow users to report incidents of harassment or violence anonymously, contributing to data collection for identifying high-risk areas and patterns.

e Digital Safety Education
  - India: Initiatives like *SheSafe* and *Chetna* focus on educating women about digital safety, including securing online profiles, recognising cyber threats, and utilising safety features on digital platforms.
  - International: Organisations like *Take Back the Tech!* and *TechSafety.org* offer resources and campaigns to raise awareness about online harassment and provide tools for digital self-defence.

f Transportation Safety Solutions
- India: Services like *Uber's Safety Toolkit* and *Ola's Guardian* offer in-app safety features such as real-time ride tracking, emergency assistance buttons, and driver screening.
- International: Similar safety features are integrated into ride-hailing apps globally, including Uber's *Safety Center* and Lyft's *Smart Trip Check-In*.

g Community Support Platforms
- India: Platforms like *Sakhi* and *Shakti on Wheels* provide online and offline support networks for women, offering counselling, legal aid, and community engagement initiatives.
- International: Initiatives like *UN Women's Safe Cities and Safe Public Spaces* program and *Rape Crisis England & Wales* provide community-based support services and advocacy efforts.

11.3.1.2. Upcoming Technological Developments

Upcoming Technological Solutions for Women's Safety in India and Internationally (within 2 or 3 years) are anticipated to leverage emerging technologies to enhance safety measures for women. Some potential advancement includes the following.

- Artificial Intelligence (AI) for Predictive Policing: AI-powered predictive policing algorithms are expected to be deployed in India and internationally to anticipate and prevent crimes against women. These algorithms analyse historical crime data to identify high-risk areas and predict potential incidents, allowing law enforcement agencies to allocate resources more effectively and respond proactively to threats.
- Smart Wearable with Enhanced Features: Within the next few years, smart wearables designed specifically for women's safety will hit the market. These wearables may incorporate advanced features such as real-time GPS tracking, biometric authentication for access to emergency services, and integrated self-defence mechanisms. Such devices provide women with discreet yet effective tools to ensure their safety in various situations (Hemasagar et al., 2022).
- Blockchain-Based Safety Platforms: Blockchain technology is anticipated to be utilised in developing secure and decentralised safety platforms for women. These platforms may enable secure data sharing and communication between individuals, law enforcement agencies, and support services, enhancing privacy and confidentiality in reporting incidents of violence or seeking assistance.
- Augmented Reality (AR) Safety Apps: AR-powered safety applications are expected to emerge, offering immersive experiences to educate women about safety measures and self-defence techniques. These apps may simulate real-life scenarios, providing interactive training sessions and empowering women with the skills and knowledge to protect themselves in different situations.

- Internet of Things (IoT) Devices for Smart Homes: IoT devices integrated into smart home systems are anticipated to enhance women's safety within their residences significantly. These devices may include smart door locks with facial recognition technology, motion sensors linked to alarm systems, and voice-activated emergency alerts, creating a comprehensive security ecosystem tailored to women's safety needs.

As technology continues to evolve, these upcoming solutions hold the potential to revolutionise the landscape of women's safety (Kommineni et al., 2023), offering innovative approaches to address existing challenges and empower women to navigate the world with greater confidence and security.

11.3.1.3. Future Technological Innovations

Futuristic Technological Solutions for Women's Safety in India and Internationally (after 3 years) are envisioned to harness cutting-edge technologies to revolutionise safety measures for women. Some speculative advancements include:

- Advanced Artificial Intelligence (AI) Surveillance Systems: In the future, AI-driven surveillance systems are expected to become more sophisticated (Scatiggio, 2022), leveraging facial recognition (Baytamouny et al., 2022), behavioural analysis, and predictive algorithms to identify and prevent potential threats to women's safety. These systems may be integrated into public spaces, transportation networks, and smart cities to enhance security and enable rapid response to emergencies.
- Biometric Authentication for Personal Safety Devices: Within the next few years, personal safety devices are anticipated to incorporate biometric authentication features such as fingerprint or iris scanning to ensure authorized access and prevent misuse. This technology could enhance the security of wearable devices and enable seamless activation of emergency features in critical situations (Khan et al., 2020).
- Quantum Cryptography for Secure Communication: Futuristic advancements in quantum cryptography are expected to offer unparalleled levels of security for communication networks, ensuring confidential and tamper-proof data transmission related to women's safety. Quantum-encrypted communication channels may be utilised in emergency response systems, online platforms, and wearable devices (Gautam et al., 2022) to safeguard sensitive information and protect women's privacy.
- Neuro-Technology for Personal Defence: Emerging neuro-technologies, such as brain-computer interfaces (BCIs) (Gao et al., 2021), may be leveraged to develop innovative personal defence systems for women. BCIs could enable individuals to control wearable safety devices using their brain signals (Mudgal et al., 2020), allowing for swift and precise responses to potential threats without the need for physical interaction.
- Space-Based Surveillance and Communication Networks: Future advancements in satellite technology may lead to the deployment of space-based surveillance and communication networks dedicated to women's safety.

These satellites could provide global coverage for monitoring and responding to emergencies (Pecorella et al., 2015), offering real-time support and coordination in remote or inaccessible areas.

While these futuristic technological solutions hold immense potential to revolutionise women's safety measures, their implementation may require careful considerations (Kodheli et al., 2020) of ethical, legal, and privacy implications. Additionally, collaboration between governments, technology companies, and civil society organisations will be crucial to ensure these technologies' responsible and inclusive development to benefit women worldwide.

11.3.2. Implications of Technological Advancements

In 2024, as we navigate a world driven by technological progress, examining its implications is imperative, particularly in light of the ongoing issue of women's safety. Though the road to comprehensive solutions may be long, we must act now to prevent future tragedies and create a world where women can thrive without fear. It's imperative to prioritise women's safety and work towards building a society where every woman feels secure in pursuing her aspirations in 2024.

11.3.2.1. Privacy and Data Security Risks

Advances in technology raise concerns about the privacy and security of personal information (Williams et al., 2017), with risks of data breaches, surveillance, and tracking that could expose women to stalking, doxing, or identity theft. Developing protections for digital privacy (Mukhopadhyay and Vinayaka, 2021) and cybersecurity is crucial to prevent technology from further facilitating gender-based violence and abuse.

i Impacts of Current Technological Solutions
- Existing technological solutions often require collecting and storing sensitive personal data, raising concerns about privacy breaches and unauthorized access.
- Data security vulnerabilities in current apps and platforms may expose users to risks such as identity theft, stalking, and harassment, compromising their safety (Alabdan, 2020).

ii Anticipated Implications of Upcoming Developments
- Upcoming technologies, such as AI-powered predictive policing algorithms and blockchain-based safety platforms, may raise concerns about the privacy and security of sensitive data collected and shared (Gupta et al., 2023).
- Inadequate safeguards against unauthorised access or data breaches could compromise the confidentiality of information related to women's safety, exposing them to risks such as identity theft or surveillance.

iii Potential Impacts of Future Technological Innovations
- The deployment of advanced AI-driven surveillance systems (Bhavyasri et al., 2023) raises significant privacy concerns, as facial recognition and

behavioural analysis technologies may lead to extensive monitoring and tracking of individuals, compromising their privacy rights.

- Integrating biometric authentication features in personal safety devices may raise concerns about unauthorised access and potential misuse of sensitive biometric data, leading to privacy breaches and identity theft.

11.3.2.2. Technological Dependence and Reliability Issues

While technology can provide new tools for women's empowerment and safety, over-reliance on flawed systems also presents dangers like critical safety apps failing when needed most. Achieving equitable access and avoiding exclusion requires technology that is reliable, accountable and focused on inclusiveness.

i Impacts of Current Technological Solutions
- Over-reliance on current technological solutions for safety may lead to complacency and a false sense of security among users, potentially putting them at risk in situations where technology fails or malfunctions.
- Reliability issues with current mobile apps, wearable devices, or online platforms may hinder their effectiveness in providing timely assistance or support during emergencies.

ii Anticipated Implications of Upcoming Developments
- The reliance on upcoming smart wearables and IoT devices for safety may lead to overdependence (Marrington et al., 2016) on technology, potentially resulting in a false sense of security and reduced vigilance in real-world safety practices.
- Concerns regarding the reliability and accuracy of upcoming augmented reality (AR) safety apps in simulating real-life scenarios (D'Mello et al., 2018) and providing effective training sessions may impact their usefulness in empowering women with practical self-defence techniques.

iii Potential Impacts of Future Technological Innovations
- Futuristic advancements in quantum cryptography for secure communication networks may introduce new security vulnerabilities (Huang et al., 2018), as hackers and malicious actors may target quantum-encrypted channels to intercept or tamper with sensitive data related to women's safety (Waks et al., 2002).
- Emerging neuro-technologies like brain-computer interfaces (BCIs) (Blain-Moraes et al., 2012) for personal defence systems could pose risks of exploitation, as unauthorised access or manipulation of BCI-controlled safety devices may lead to unintended consequences or physical harm.

11.3.2.3. Digital Gender Divide and Accessibility Challenges

Persistent digital divides are reinforced by biases in technology design and implementation risk, excluding marginalised genders from safety resources and innovations. Prioritising inclusive technology access and literacy is critical to ensuring that all can benefit from technology for empowerment.

i Impacts of Current Technological Solutions
- Limited access to current technology, especially among marginalised communities and rural populations (Kalyan et al., 2020), exacerbates existing inequalities and restricts women's ability to benefit from safety solutions (Egard and Hansson, 2023).
- Current technological solutions may not be accessible to women with disabilities or those lacking digital literacy skills, further widening the digital gender gap (Davaki, 2018), and excluding vulnerable groups from safety measures.

ii Anticipated Implications of Upcoming Developments
- The introduction of advanced technologies like upcoming smart wearables and IoT devices may exacerbate existing technological access inequalities, particularly among marginalised communities and rural populations.
- Limited affordability and accessibility of upcoming solutions could widen the digital gender gap, excluding vulnerable groups of women from benefiting from innovative safety measures.

iii Potential Impacts of Future Technological Innovations
- Adoption of neuro-technologies like brain-computer interfaces (BCIs) for personal defence systems may raise concerns about accessibility and inclusivity, as individuals with disabilities or limited cognitive abilities may face barriers in using or accessing BCI-controlled safety devices (Burwell et al., 2017).
- Deployment of space-based surveillance and communication networks may exacerbate inequalities in access to safety resources, as remote or marginalised communities may have limited access to satellite technology and emergency response services.

11.3.2.4. Misuse and Abuse of Technology

Digital spaces present new avenues for misogyny, harassment and abuse, with real-world consequences for women's safety and well-being. Monitoring and mitigating harmful behaviour enabled by technology is essential to creating an ethical digital environment.

i Impacts of Current Technological Solutions
- Perpetrators may exploit current technological tools, such as GPS tracking features or online communication platforms, to monitor, harass, or intimidate women, undermining their safety and autonomy (Can and Alatas, 2019).
- The anonymity afforded by current digital platforms may embolden individuals to engage in cyberbullying (Burke et al., 2015), online harassment (Freeman et al., 2022), or revenge porn, posing significant threats to women's mental and emotional well-being.

ii Anticipated Implications of Upcoming Developments
- Safety apps and wearable devices designed to empower women may face the risk of manipulation. Hackers or malicious actors could compromise these technologies, diverting emergency signals or exploiting

vulnerabilities (Kabir and Tasneem, 2020), thereby rendering the safety features ineffective or turning them into tools for potential harm.
- The use of facial recognition technology in upcoming smart home devices and safety platforms may raise privacy concerns and spark debates about the ethical implications (Selinger and Leong, 2021) of widespread surveillance in residential environments.

iii Potential Impacts of Future Technological Innovations
- Future technological innovations may introduce new forms of social engineering tactics, where perpetrators use deceptive methods to exploit women's trust (Salahdine and Kaabouch, 2019). This could include the creation of fake support networks or the use of AI-driven chatbots to manipulate victims into compromising situations, eroding the trust in online spaces meant to be safe.
- Integrating AI-driven predictive algorithms into public spaces and smart cities may raise questions about algorithmic bias (Kim et al., 2023) and discriminatory outcomes (Pandey and Caliskan, 2021), as predictive technologies may disproportionately target certain communities or individuals based (Žliobaitė, 2017) on biased data inputs.

11.3.2.5. Ethical and Legal Concerns

Emerging technology generates ethical dilemmas around gender-based discrimination, consent, surveillance and autonomous systems affecting women's safety. Developing governance and oversight to align technology with ethical values (Coeckelbergh, 2019) the following impacts should be considered.

i Impacts of Current Technological Solutions
- Ethical dilemmas surrounding using AI algorithms for predictive policing or surveillance raise questions about bias, discrimination, and the potential for wrongful accusations or targeting of certain communities (Gstrein et al., 2019; Babuta et al., 2018).
- Legal ambiguities regarding jurisdiction, data ownership, and accountability in cases of technology-enabled crimes against women pose challenges for law enforcement agencies and regulatory bodies (Bailey and Mathen, 2017).

ii Anticipated Implications of Upcoming Developments
- The deployment of AI-powered predictive policing algorithms raises ethical concerns related to algorithmic bias and discriminatory outcomes, potentially exacerbating existing biases in law enforcement practices (Asaro, 2019).
- The use of facial recognition technology in upcoming smart home devices and safety platforms may raise privacy concerns and spark debates about the ethical implications (Almeida et al., 2022) of widespread surveillance in residential environments.

iii Potential Impacts of Future Technological Innovations
- The integration of AI-driven predictive algorithms into public spaces and smart cities may raise questions about algorithmic bias and

discriminatory outcomes (Pandey and Caliskan, 2021), as predictive technologies may disproportionately target certain communities or individuals based on biased data inputs.
- The widespread deployment of space-based surveillance and communication networks dedicated to women's safety raises ethical concerns about mass surveillance and potential violations of privacy rights.

11.3.2.6. Cultural and Societal Implications

Technology does not exist in a vacuum, often reflecting and amplifying broader gender biases and inequities (Harris and Vitis, 2020). Examining and addressing how technology interacts with culture is key to catalysing positive change for gender justice.

i Impacts of Current Technological Solutions
- Technological solutions designed and implemented without considering cultural sensitivities and societal norms may inadvertently reinforce existing gender stereotypes or perpetuate cultural barriers (Bhat and Himaan, 2022) to seeking help or reporting violence.
- The normalisation of surveillance and monitoring in the name of safety may erode trust in interpersonal relationships and contribute to a culture of fear and suspicion among women.

ii Anticipated Implications of Upcoming Developments
- The introduction of augmented reality (AR) safety apps and immersive training experiences may inadvertently reinforce gender stereotypes or cultural norms surrounding women's roles in self-defence and safety practices (Sharma et al., 2022).
- Integrating biometric authentication features in upcoming smart wearables and safety devices could raise cultural sensitivities regarding the collection and use of biometric data, especially in regions with strict privacy regulations or cultural norms.

iii Potential Impacts of Future Technological Innovations
- The introduction of advanced AI-driven surveillance systems and biometric authentication features may raise cultural sensitivities and concerns about government overreach, as invasive surveillance technologies may infringe upon cultural norms and values related to privacy and autonomy.
- Integrating space-based surveillance and communication networks into women's safety initiatives may raise societal concerns about militarisation and securitisation of public spaces, as satellite technology enables real-time monitoring and response to emergencies globally.

By examining these negative impacts and implications across different dimensions, stakeholders can better understand the complexities surrounding the use of technology for women's safety and work towards mitigating potential risks while maximizing the benefits.

11.4. ENSURING ETHICAL AND LEGAL COMPLIANCE IN THE DEVELOPMENT OF AI, IOT, AND CLOUD COMPUTING TOOLS AND APPLICATIONS FOR WOMEN'S SAFETY

Developing AI, IoT, and cloud computing tools and applications for women's safety demands a meticulous focus on ethical considerations and legal compliance. Striking a balance between innovation and responsible development is crucial to avoid potential misuse and abuse of these technologies. Ensuring adherence to ethical guidelines and legal frameworks will foster trust, protect privacy, and empower women through the effective and secure utilization of these advancements.

11.4.1. Legal Frameworks

As the development of technologies for women's safety unfolds, a critical lens is cast on the legal frameworks that govern these innovations. The intricate tapestry of legal considerations spans across international, national, and regional levels, each layer contributing to the overarching governance of technology development.

11.4.1.1. Data Privacy and Protection Laws

Data privacy and protection laws are essential regulatory frameworks designed to safeguard individuals' personal data from unaüthorised access, use, or disclosure. These laws dictate how organisations collect, store, process, and share personal information, ensuring individuals retain control over their data and promoting transparency and accountability in data handling practices.

a Existing Legislation

  Existing data privacy and protection legislation encompasses laws that establish rights for individuals regarding their personal data and impose obligations on organisations to protect this data.

  i International Regulations

  - General Data Protection Regulation (GDPR): Enforced by the European Union, GDPR provides comprehensive data protection and privacy regulations for individuals within the EU and the European Economic Area (EEA). It includes provisions regarding the processing of personal data, consent requirements, and the rights of data subjects, including the right to access and rectify personal data.
  - Convention on Cybercrime (Budapest Convention): Addresses cybercrime, including offenses against the confidentiality, integrity, and availability of computer systems, which can impact women's safety. It provides a framework for international cooperation on investigating and prosecuting cybercrimes, contributing to global efforts to enhance digital safety for women (Van der Wilk, 2021)

  ii National Legal Considerations

  - The Digital Personal Data Protection Act, 2023 (DPDP Act or DPDPA-2023) is legislation passed by the Indian Parliament to regulate the processing of digital personal data. It aims to balance the rights of individuals to safeguard their personal data with the legitimate need to process such data for lawful purposes. The act addresses various matters related to the handling of personal data and includes provisions for its lawful processing. Notably, this act marks a departure from the traditional use of "he/him" pronouns in legislative language, opting instead for inclusive "she/her" pronouns, reflecting a progressive approach to gender representation in legal texts.

iii Regional Legal Considerations

- Kerala Police Act (Amendment) Ordinance, 2020: Introduced amendments, including Section 118A, to curb offensive content and fake news on social media. Addresses online harassment and the spread of false information, contributing to women's digital safety in the state of Kerala.
- Maharashtra Cyber Digital Crime Unit (MCDCU): Established to investigate and combat cybercrimes, including offenses against women. Provides a regional focus on tackling cybercrimes affecting women's safety in Maharashtra.
- Telangana Women Safety Wing: Dedicated police unit focusing on the safety and security of women. Addresses women's safety concerns at the regional level in Telangana, incorporating technological solutions and law enforcement efforts.

b Developing Legislation

Developing legislation refers to ongoing efforts to enact or amend data privacy and protection laws to address evolving technological landscapes and emerging privacy concerns. Governments and regulatory bodies worldwide continually review and update legislation to enhance data protection measures and adapt to new challenges posed by technological advancements.

i International Regulations

- E-Privacy Regulation (EU): The European Union is in the process of finalising the E-Privacy Regulation, which aims to enhance privacy protections for electronic communications. This regulation complements the GDPR and addresses specific privacy concerns related to electronic communications, including messaging apps, email, and internet voice calls.

ii National Legal Considerations

- Amendments to Information Technology Act, 2000: The Indian government is also considering amendments to the Information Technology Act, 2000, under the Jan Vishwas Act, 2023, to strengthen data privacy and protection measures. These amendments may introduce new provisions or modify existing ones to address emerging privacy concerns in the digital era.

c Compliance with Data Protection Regulations

Compliance with data protection regulations involves ensuring that organisations adhere to the requirements outlined in existing data privacy laws (Pereira et al., 2020). This includes implementing measures to secure personal data, obtaining consent for data processing activities, and providing individuals with rights to access, rectify, or delete their data as mandated by law (Lonzetta and Hayajneh, 2020).

- Secure Personal Data: Organisations must implement robust measures to secure personal data from unauthorised access, disclosure, or misuse. This involves implementing encryption, access controls, and other security measures to protect data from cyber threats.
- Obtaining Consent: Organisations must obtain explicit consent from individuals before processing their personal data. This consent must be freely given, specific, informed, and unambiguous, and individuals can withdraw consent at any time.
- Purpose Limitation: Personal data should be collected and processed only for specified, explicit, and legitimate purposes. Organisations must ensure they do not use data for purposes beyond what individuals have consented to or what is necessary for the performance of a contract or legal obligation.
- Data Minimisation: Organisations should limit the collection and processing of personal data to what is necessary for the intended purpose. They should avoid collecting excessive or irrelevant data and regularly review and delete data that is no longer necessary.
- Data Accuracy: Organisations are responsible for ensuring the accuracy and currency of the personal data they process. They should take reasonable steps to update or rectify inaccurate or incomplete data and inform relevant parties of any corrections made.
- Data Subject Rights: Individuals have rights concerning their personal data, including the right to access, rectify, erase, or restrict the processing of their data. Organisations must have procedures in place to facilitate the exercise of these rights and respond to requests from data subjects promptly.
- Data Transfer: When transferring personal data outside the jurisdiction, organisations must ensure adequate safeguards to protect the data's security and privacy. This may involve implementing standard contractual clauses, binding corporate rules, or relying on data protection adequacy decisions from regulatory authorities.
- Data Breach Notification: Organisations must promptly notify data protection authorities and affected individuals in case of a personal data breach. They should have procedures to assess the risk to individuals' rights and freedoms and take appropriate measures to mitigate any adverse effects.

11.4.1.2. Surveillance Laws and Regulations

Surveillance laws and regulations govern the monitoring, collection, and use of data for surveillance purposes by government agencies, law enforcement, and other authorised entities.

a Existing Legislation

Existing surveillance legislation outlines the legal framework for surveillance activities, including the scope of permissible surveillance, the conditions under which surveillance can be conducted, and the rights of individuals regarding surveillance.

i International Regulations

- International Covenant on Civil and Political Rights (ICCPR): The ICCPR outlines principles related to privacy rights (Margulies, 2013) and restrictions on arbitrary surveillance (Humble, 2021), which indirectly contributes to women's safety by safeguarding individuals' rights against intrusive surveillance practices. India is a signatory to ICCPR.
- European Convention on Human Rights (ECHR): The ECHR includes privacy and data protection provisions, which impact surveillance activities affecting women's safety in European countries.
- United Nations Convention on the Elimination of All Forms of Discrimination Against Women (CEDAW): While not specifically focused on surveillance, CEDAW addresses gender-based discrimination and promotes gender equality, indirectly influencing surveillance practices concerning women's safety.

ii National Legal Considerations

- Information Technology (Reasonable Security Practices and Procedures and Sensitive Personal Data or Information) Rules, 2011: These rules prescribe security standards for handling sensitive personal data, which can include information related to women's safety.
- The Indian Telegraph Act, 1885: This act provides the legal framework for intercepting telegraphic messages, which may be relevant to surveillance activities related to women's safety.
- The Protection of Children from Sexual Offences (POCSO) Act, 2012: While primarily focused on protecting children, this act includes provisions related to surveillance and monitoring of offenders, which may indirectly impact women's safety.

iii Regional Legal Considerations

- Delhi Surveillance Rules: Delhi has its own rules and regulations governing surveillance activities within the territory, which may include provisions aimed at ensuring women's safety through surveillance measures.
- Maharashtra Control of Organised Crime Act (MCOCA), 1999: While not exclusively focused on women's safety, MCOCA includes provisions related to surveillance and monitoring of organised crime, which can indirectly impact women's safety in the region.

b Compliance with Surveillance Laws

Compliance with surveillance laws involves ensuring that surveillance activities conducted by government agencies or private entities are lawful and authorised under relevant legislation. This includes obtaining proper warrants, adhering to specified procedures, and respecting individuals' privacy rights.

- Obtaining Proper Warrants: Law enforcement agencies or other authorised entities must obtain warrants from judicial authorities before conducting surveillance (Gray, 2015). Warrants specify the scope and purpose of surveillance activities, including the type of information to be collected and the duration of surveillance. Warrants are issued based on probable cause, ensuring that surveillance is conducted in a targeted and lawful manner.
- Adhering to Specified Procedures: Surveillance activities must be conducted in accordance with specified procedures outlined in relevant legislation or regulations. These procedures may include requirements for obtaining consent from individuals subject to surveillance, notifying individuals of surveillance activities, and documenting the reasons for conducting surveillance. Adherence to specified procedures helps ensure transparency and accountability in surveillance practices which is crucial (Koskela, 2002).
- Respecting Individuals' Privacy Rights: Surveillance activities must respect individuals' privacy rights as guaranteed by law. This includes minimising the collection of personal data to the extent necessary for lawful purposes, such as investigating criminal activities or ensuring public safety. Individuals subject to surveillance have rights to access, rectify, or delete their personal data collected through surveillance activities, as mandated by data protection laws.
- Implementing Safeguards: Organisations conducting surveillance must implement appropriate safeguards to protect the security and integrity of surveillance data. This may include measures such as encryption, access controls, and data retention policies to prevent unauthorised access or misuse of surveillance data. Safeguards help mitigate the risk of data breaches or unauthorised disclosure of sensitive information collected through surveillance.
- Oversight and Accountability: Surveillance activities are subject to oversight and accountability mechanisms to ensure compliance with relevant laws and regulations. Oversight bodies, such as judicial review committees or independent monitoring agencies, may review surveillance practices to assess their legality and appropriateness. Accountability mechanisms, such as audits or reporting requirements, help hold organisations accountable for their surveillance activities and ensure transparency in their operations.

c. Restrictions on Data Collection and Monitoring

   Surveillance laws may impose restrictions on data collection and monitoring to protect individuals' privacy and civil liberties. These restrictions may include limitations on the types of data that can be collected (Voss, 2013), the duration of surveillance activities, and the purposes for which data can be used.

- Purpose Limitations: Surveillance laws specify the permissible purposes for data collection and monitoring, ensuring that surveillance activities are conducted solely for lawful and legitimate reasons. Organisations must adhere to these purpose limitations to prevent unauthorised surveillance for unrelated objectives, thereby preserving individuals' privacy rights.
- Scope of Data Collection: Regulations define the types of data that can be collected through surveillance activities, restricting the collection of unnecessary or overly intrusive information. By limiting the scope of data collection, surveillance laws help minimise the risk of privacy infringement and ensure that only relevant data is obtained for lawful purposes.
- Consent Requirements: Some jurisdictions require organisations to obtain explicit consent from individuals before collecting or monitoring their data. Consent ensures that individuals are aware of and agree to the surveillance activities, empowering them to make informed decisions about their privacy.
- Duration of Data Retention: Surveillance laws limit the duration for which collected data can be retained, ensuring that data is not stored indefinitely and is only retained for as long as necessary to fulfil the specified purposes. This restriction helps mitigate the risk of data misuse or unauthorized access over time, enhancing individuals' privacy protection.
- Transparency Obligations: Regulations may mandate transparency requirements, compelling organisations to inform individuals about the purposes of data collection, the types of data being collected, and how the data will be used or processed. Transparency promotes accountability and enables individuals to control their personal data more.
- Security Measures: Surveillance laws may require organisations to implement security measures to protect collected data from unauthorized access, disclosure, or misuse. By imposing security requirements, these regulations help safeguard individuals' privacy and prevent data breaches or cyberattacks.
- Access and Rectification Rights: Individuals may have rights to access and rectify their personal data collected through surveillance activities, allowing them to review the accuracy and completeness of their data and request corrections or deletions as necessary. These rights empower individuals to control their personal information, enhancing privacy protection.

Effective surveillance laws and regulations balance the legitimate interests of law enforcement and national security agencies and the protection of individual's privacy rights and civil liberties. By establishing clear legal frameworks, oversight mechanisms, and accountability measures, surveillance laws ensure surveillance activities are conducted legally, proportionately, and transparently.

11.4.1.3. Cybersecurity Regulations

Cybersecurity regulations encompass laws and regulations that protect digital systems, networks, and data from cyber threats and attacks. These regulations aim to establish standards and requirements for ensuring the security and resilience of information systems (Kipker and Pagel, 2020), as well as safeguarding sensitive data from unauthorized access or manipulation.

a Existing Legislation
 i International Regulations
  - The Online Safety Act: It introduces a duty of care for providers of user-to-user services, requiring risk assessments and mitigation measures to address various forms of online harm. The Act addresses a longstanding gap in legislation by enabling action against service providers facilitating online abuse and applies extraterritorially, albeit with exemptions for certain services.

 ii National Legal Considerations
  - The Indian Penal Code, 1860: The 2013 Criminal Amendment Act introduced Sections 354A to 354D to address online harassment and crimes against women in cyberspace. These sections criminalise sexual harassment, voyeurism, stalking, and other forms of online harassment against women.
  - Other Relevant Sections of the Indian Penal Code: Sections such as 499, 503, 507, and 509 provide legal remedies for defamation, criminal intimidation, and insult to modesty, applicable to cybercrimes targeting women.
  - The Information Technology Act, 2000 (amended in 2008): Sections 66C, 66E, 67, 67A, and 67B of the Information Technology Act address identity theft, privacy violations, and the publication of obscene material, including content depicting children.
  - Indecent Representation of Women (Prohibition) Act: This act regulates and prohibits the indecent portrayal of women through various media, including the Internet. The Indecent Representation of Women (Prohibition) Amendment Bill, 2012 extends the scope of the law to cover audio-visual and electronic media, including online distribution.

b Developing Legislation

 The Ministry of Home Affairs established the Cyber Crime Prevention against Women and Children (CCPWC) scheme, involving a dedicated Expert Group to address gaps and challenges in combating cybercrime. The scheme, formulated to prevent crimes against women and children, was examined by the National Commission for Women (NCW). Inputs from the NCW included proposals for an Online Women-specific Crime Reporting Unit to streamline complaints, a Monitoring Unit for Cyber Crimes to provide regular reports, and an emphasis on expediting investigations through the National Forensic Laboratory. Capacity building initiatives, especially for protection officers under the Domestic Violence Act, 2005, were also highlighted to enhance effectiveness in addressing cybercrime against women and children.

11.4.2. Ethical Considerations in Technology Development

In the rapidly evolving landscape of technology development, ethical considerations play a pivotal role in shaping the design, deployment, and impact of innovative solutions. As we navigate the complexities of integrating Artificial Intelligence (AI), Internet of Things (IoT), and cloud computing technologies into women's safety initiatives, we must adhere to ethical principles prioritising human rights, fairness, transparency, and accountability (Clayton and Sibbald, 2020). In this section, we delve into the ethical dimensions of technology development, specifically focusing on AI, and present an Ethical AI Framework that visually represents the principles and components guiding responsible innovation.

11.4.2.1. Principles of Ethical AI

The Ethical AI Framework presented herein encapsulates a holistic approach to embedding ethical principles into developing and deploying AI technologies for women's safety. At its core, the framework is grounded in four foundational principles:

- Human Rights-Centric Design: AI systems must be designed and implemented in a manner that upholds and respects fundamental human rights, including but not limited to privacy, non-discrimination, and freedom from harm.
- Transparency and Explicability: AI systems should be transparent in their operations and decision-making processes, enabling users to understand how decisions are reached and explaining algorithmic outcomes.
- Fairness and Accountability: AI systems must be designed to mitigate biases, ensure decision-making fairness, and establish accountability mechanisms when errors or biases occur.
- Beneficence and Non-Maleficence: AI systems should prioritise the well-being of individuals, aiming to maximise benefits while minimising potential harm or adverse consequences.

The framework comprises several key components, each addressing specific ethical considerations in AI development:

- Data Governance: Establishing robust data governance practices to ensure the responsible collection, storage, and usage of data, focusing on privacy, consent, and data security.
- Algorithmic Bias Mitigation: Implementing techniques and methodologies to detect, mitigate, and prevent biases in AI algorithms, including bias-aware data collection, algorithmic auditing, and fairness-aware machine learning.

- Explainable AI (XAI): Incorporating mechanisms for explicability and interpretability into AI systems, enabling users to understand how algorithms make decisions and providing transparency into decision-making processes.
- Ethical Use Cases and Impact Assessment: Conducting comprehensive ethical impact assessments to evaluate the potential societal impact of AI technologies, identifying and mitigating potential risks and harms to vulnerable populations.
- User-Centric Design: Prioritising user-centric design principles ensures that AI systems are inclusive, accessible, and respectful of diverse user needs and preferences.
- Accountability Mechanisms: Establishing clear mechanisms for accountability (McGregor et al., 2019), including accountability for AI developers, operators, and users, with mechanisms for addressing errors, biases, and adverse outcomes.
- Continuous Monitoring and Evaluation: Implementing ongoing monitoring and evaluation processes to assess AI systems' ethical implications and performance throughout their lifecycle, with iterative improvement and adaptation mechanisms.

11.4.2.2. Bias and Fairness

- Addressing Bias in AI Algorithms: Addressing bias in AI algorithms is crucial to ensure fair and equitable outcomes (Ntoutsi et al., 2020). This involves identifying and mitigating biases that may be present in training data or algorithmic decision-making processes. Techniques such as bias detection, data preprocessing, and algorithmic fairness interventions mitigate biases and promote fairness in AI systems. By addressing bias, AI algorithms can provide more accurate and equitable results across diverse populations.
- Ensuring Fair Treatment Across Gender and Socioeconomic Groups: Ensuring fair treatment across gender and socioeconomic groups is essential to prevent discriminatory outcomes in technology development. This involves designing AI algorithms and systems that do not perpetuate or exacerbate existing inequalities based on gender or socioeconomic status. By prioritising fairness and inclusivity in technology development, developers can contribute to creating more equitable and accessible solutions for all users.

11.4.2.3. Transparency and Explicability

- Transparency in Data Collection and Processing: Transparency in data collection and processing involves providing users with clear and understandable information about how their data is collected, processed, and used. This includes disclosing data collection practices, data processing methods, and the purposes for which data is utilised. Transparent data practices empower users to make informed decisions about their data and build trust in technology systems.

- Providing Explanations for AI Decisions: Explaining AI decisions ensures transparency and accountability in algorithmic decision-making processes (Lee et al., 2019). Explainable AI (XAI) techniques enable users to understand how AI systems make specific decisions or recommendations. By explaining AI decisions, developers can enhance trust and confidence in AI technologies and facilitate better user understanding and acceptance.

11.4.2.4. User Empowerment and Autonomy

- Providing User Control Over Data and Settings: Providing users with control over their data and settings is essential for promoting user empowerment and autonomy. This involves implementing user-friendly interfaces and features that enable users to manage their privacy preferences, control data sharing settings, and customise their user experience according to their preferences. Empowering users with control over their data enhances trust and confidence in technology systems (Blasgen, 1982).
- Ensuring Informed Consent and Respect for Autonomy: Ensuring informed consent and respect for autonomy involves obtaining explicit consent from users before collecting or processing their personal data. This includes providing clear and understandable information about data collection practices, purposes, and potential risks to users. Respecting user autonomy also entails allowing users to opt-in or opt-out of data collection and processing activities and honouring their preferences regarding data usage.

11.4.2.5. Social Impact and Equity

- Assessing Impact on Vulnerable Communities: Assessing the impact of technology on vulnerable communities is essential to mitigate potential harms and promote social equity. This involves conducting thorough impact assessments to identify potential risks and benefits of technology deployment on marginalised or vulnerable populations (Huda, 2019). By understanding the social impact of technology, developers can design interventions that address societal challenges and promote equitable outcomes.
- Promoting Equity in Access and Usage: Promoting equity in access and usage involves designing technology solutions that are accessible and inclusive for all users, regardless of their background or circumstances. This includes considering diverse user needs and preferences in the design and development process and ensuring that technology solutions are accessible to users with disabilities. By prioritising equity in access and usage, developers can create technology solutions that benefit a wide range of users and contribute to social inclusion.

11.4.2.6. Accessibility and Inclusivity

- Designing Tools for Diverse User Needs: Designing tools for diverse user needs involves considering users' diverse abilities, preferences, and circumstances (Obrenovic et al., 2007) in the design and development process. This includes implementing inclusive design principles and accessibility features that accommodate a wide range of user needs, including those with disabilities or unique requirements. By designing for diversity, developers can create technology solutions that are usable and inclusive for all users.

- Ensuring Accessibility for Persons with Disabilities: Ensuring accessibility for persons with disabilities involves implementing accessibility features and standards that enable individuals with disabilities to access and use technology effectively. This includes providing alternative formats, assistive technologies, and accessible interfaces accommodating various disabilities and impairments. By prioritising accessibility, developers can ensure that technology solutions are usable and inclusive for persons with disabilities, promoting equal participation and opportunities for all users.

11.4.3. Intersectionality of Legal and Ethical Frameworks

Legal and ethical frameworks intersect at various levels, reflecting cultural, societal, and global perspectives while shaping policy implications. Understanding this intersectionality is crucial (Vesnic-Alujevic et al., 2020) for developing comprehensive approaches to address complex challenges in technology governance.

11.4.3.1. Cultural and Societal Norms

Cultural and societal norms play a significant role in shaping legal and ethical frameworks related to technology. These norms vary across different regions and communities, influencing perceptions of privacy, data protection, and ethical considerations in technology development and deployment. Cultural and societal norms inform the design of regulatory policies and ethical guidelines, reflecting diverse perspectives on issues such as data privacy, surveillance, and algorithmic bias.

11.4.3.2. Global Perspectives

Global perspectives on legal and ethical frameworks for technology governance reflect the diversity of approaches and priorities across countries and regions. International agreements, conventions, and standards provide a framework for addressing global challenges in technology regulation, including data protection, cybersecurity, and human rights considerations. Global perspectives inform discussions on harmonising legal and ethical standards to ensure interoperability and consistency in technology governance while respecting cultural and regional differences.

11.4.3.3. Policy Implications

The intersectionality of legal and ethical frameworks has significant policy implications for technology governance at national and international levels. A complex interplay of legal, ethical, and societal factors influences data privacy, cybersecurity, and AI regulation policy decisions. Balancing competing interests, such as individual rights, economic interests, and national security concerns, requires policymakers to navigate diverse cultural, societal, and global perspectives while developing regulatory frameworks and ethical guidelines for technology governance (Hine, 2021). Addressing policy implications involves fostering multistakeholder dialogue, promoting transparency, and advancing inclusive decision-making processes to ensure that legal and ethical frameworks align with societal values and promote the common good.

11.5. PRIVACY AND DATA PROTECTION

In the context of developing technologies for women's safety, ensuring privacy and data protection is paramount. This section focuses on privacy considerations and strategies for safeguarding personal data in AI, IoT, and cloud computing-based tools.

11.5.1. Data Flow: A Visual Trace

The Data Flow Diagram Figure 11.2 illustrates the flow of data within women's safety tools, highlighting key points of data collection, storage, and usage. This visual representation provides insights into how personal data is processed throughout the system, facilitating the identification of potential privacy risks and informing

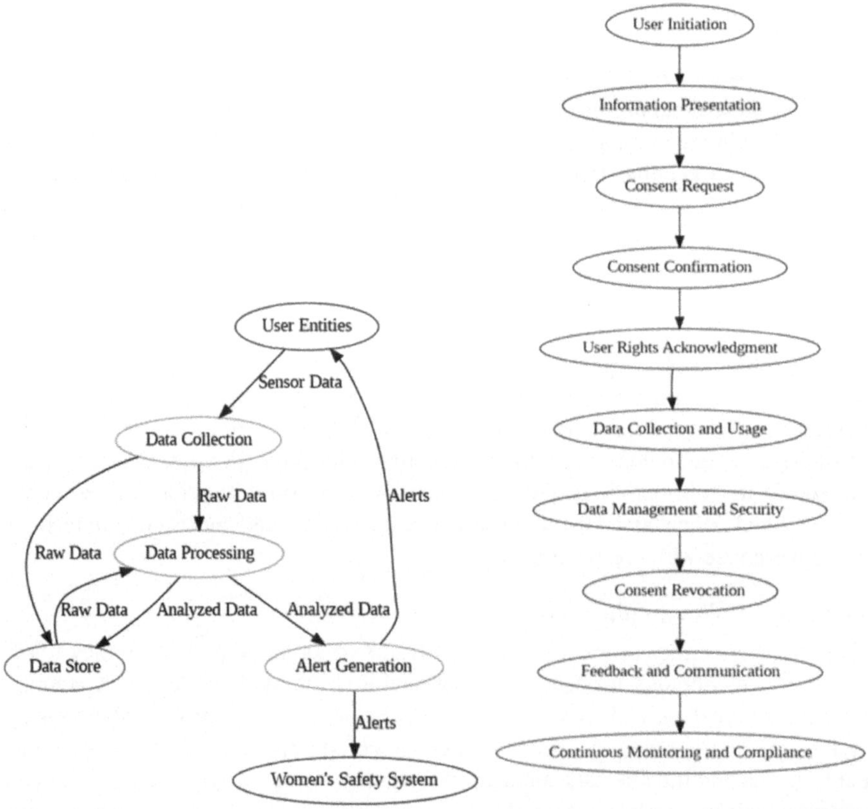

a. Data flow within women's safety tools.

b. Informed consent work flow diagram of women's safety.

FIGURE 11.2 Privacy and data protection in women's safety.

data protection measures. The data flow diagram encompasses external entities, data sources, data collection processes, data stores, and alert systems, all contributing to the functionality and objectives of the system.

External entities supply inputs to the system, including users engaging with mobile applications or wearable devices, emergency services receiving alerts, and organisations with vested interests. Data sources, including sensors, surveillance systems, external databases, and user inputs, provide the necessary data for analysis and processing. Data collection processes encompass acquiring pertinent data from these sources, involving sensor data collection, user input collection, surveillance data collection, external data integration, historical data retrieval, and automated data collection. These processes gather data concerning safety incidents, environmental conditions, user interactions, and contextual information vital for enhancing women's safety.

The collected data is then pre-processed to ensure data quality, consistency, and compatibility with the system's algorithms or models. Data preprocessing steps involve cleaning, transforming, integrating, and scaling the raw data to improve its suitability for analysis or modelling. Missing values are handled, outliers are addressed, features are selected or engineered, and data is normalised or encoded as needed. Pre-processed data is then stored in data stores such as database systems, data warehouses, file systems, cloud storage services, local storage devices, data lakes, or blockchain technology. These data stores serve as repositories for the cleaned, transformed, and integrated data, ensuring its persistence, accessibility, and security within the system.

Alerts are generated from the pre-processed data. Alert generation involves defining criteria or thresholds indicative of safety incidents or emergencies, which are often predefined based on factors like sensor data thresholds, user input, surveillance data analysis, or external data integration. Once established, the system continuously monitors data streams from various sources, applying analysis and processing algorithms to evaluate if predefined criteria are met. The system evaluates incoming data against these criteria in real time, triggering the alert generation process when thresholds are exceeded. This process generates alerts, such as notifications or messages, to notify relevant stakeholders, identified based on predefined rules. Alerts are delivered through specified communication channels like mobile applications or text messages. These alerts provide timely warnings or notifications about safety incidents, enabling proactive responses and interventions to enhance women's safety. Feedback collection post-alert delivery enables evaluation and improvement of the alert generation process for future incidents.

11.6. REAL-TIME RESILIENCE: A WOMEN'S SAFETY CASE STUDY

In implementing the Cyber Crime Prevention against Women and Children (CCPWC) scheme, significant progress has been achieved in bolstering cybercrime prevention measures and enhancing safety for women. Let's consider a case study to illustrate the impact of these initiatives.

- Case Study:

  An individual reported a case of online harassment and stalking to the Online Women-specific Crime Reporting Unit established under the CCPWC scheme. The complaint was promptly forwarded to the Monitoring Unit for Cyber Crimes, which conducted a thorough investigation. Utilising advanced forensic technology and expertise from the National Forensic Laboratory, crucial evidence was gathered, leading to the identification and apprehension of the perpetrator. Additionally, capacity-building initiatives ensured that protection officers were equipped with the necessary skills to support and guide the victim through the legal process, providing a comprehensive support system.

- Challenges and Advancements:
  Despite the progress in cybercrime prevention for women's safety, several challenges persist. These include the evolving nature of cyber threats, the need for continuous capacity building, and ensuring seamless coordination among various stakeholders. Moreover, advancements in technology bring both opportunities and challenges. While AI, IoT, and cloud computing offer innovative solutions for enhancing women's safety, they also pose challenges (Poster, 2018) such as data privacy concerns (Gupta and Mishra, 2022), algorithmic biases, and the potential misuse of technology for malicious purposes.

11.7. CONCLUSION

In conclusion, developing AI, IoT and cloud computing-based tools and applications for women's safety represents a dynamic and evolving field that requires a multidisciplinary approach. While significant challenges exist in navigating legal and ethical complexities, technological advancements and regulatory compliance efforts offer promising opportunities for enhancing women's safety. By addressing bias, promoting transparency, and empowering users, technology can play a transformative role in preventing and responding to gender-based violence. Moving forward, continued collaboration among stakeholders and a commitment to human-centric design principles are essential for realizing the full potential of technology in promoting women's safety and advancing gender equality.

There is a vast scope for further research and development in this field. As technology intersects with women's safety and empowerment, we must pursue human-centred innovation that embeds ethical principles of privacy, accessibility, and justice. This requires ongoing research to enhance data protections, establish governance for emerging technologies, and bridge digital divides through inclusive design and literacy programs. Ultimately, the goal should be developing technology responsibly and equitably so all people, regardless of gender, can benefit from advanced tools that uphold privacy and autonomy while preventing harm.

REFERENCES

Alabdan, R. (2020). Phishing attacks survey: Types, vectors, and technical approaches. *Future Internet*, 12(10), 168.

Almeida, D., Shmarko, K., & Lomas, E. (2022). The ethics of facial recognition technologies, surveillance, and accountability in an age of artificial intelligence: A comparative analysis of US, EU, and UK regulatory frameworks. *AI and Ethics*, 2(3), 377–387.

Almiş, B. H., Gümüştaş, F., & Kütük, E. K. (2020). Effects of domestic violence against women on mental health of women and children. *Psikiyatride Guncel Yaklasimlar*, 12(2), 232–242.

Altun, S., Abas, M., Zimmerman, C., Howard, L. M., & Oram, S. (2017). Mental health and human trafficking: Responding to survivors' needs. *BJPsych International*, 14(1), 21–23.

Arun, K., Krishnakumar, U., & Das, D. (2020). Convergence of CSR and industry 4.0. recent trends in Indian public sector enterprises. In *Proceedings of the 5th NA International Conference on Industrial Engineering and Operations Management* (pp. 3955–3961). Detroit, MI.

Asaro, P. M. (2019). AI ethics in predictive policing: From models of threat to an ethics of care. *IEEE Technology and Society Magazine*, 38(2), 40–53.

Babuta, A., Oswald, M., & Rinik, C. (2018). Machine learning algorithms and police decision making: Legal, ethical and regulatory challenges. *Whitehall Reports RUSI*. https://rusi.org/explore-our-research/publications/whitehall-reports/machine-learning-algorithms-and-police-decision-making-legal-ethical-and-regulatory-challenges

Bach, P. M., & Twidale, M. (2010, April). Involving reflective users in design. In *Proceedings of the SIGCHI Conference on Human Factors in Computing Systems* (pp. 2037–2040). https://doi.org/10.1145/1753326.1753636

Bailey, J., & Mathen, C. (2017). Technologically-facilitated violence against women and girls: If criminal law can respond, should it? *Ottawa Faculty of Law Working Paper (2017–44)*. Available at SSRN: https://ssrn.com/abstract=3043506 or http://dx.doi.org/10.2139/ssrn.3043506

Bani Issa, W., Al Akour, I., Ibrahim, A., Almarzouqi, A., Abbas, S., Hisham, F., & Griffiths, J. (2020). Privacy, confidentiality, security and patient safety concerns about electronic health records. *International Nursing Review*, 67(2), 218–230.

Baxter, J., & Kane, E. W. (1995). Dependence and independence: A cross-national analysis of gender inequality and gender attitudes. *Gender & Society*, 9(2), 193–215.

Baytamouny, M., Kolandaisamy, R., & ALDharhani, G. S. (2022, April). AI-based home security system with face recognition. In *2022 6th International Conference on Trends in Electronics and Informatics (ICOEI)* (pp. 1038–1042). IEEE.

Bhat, V., & Himaan, A. S. (2022). Distortions in the Indian scriptural image of women–an elucidation. *Journal of Veda Samskrita Academy*, I. ISSN 2250–1711, UGC-CARE Listed Journal Centenary Commemoration Volume.

Bhavyasri, J., Ramaiah, G. K., & Rasadurai, K. (2023). AI based smart surveillance system. *International Journal of Scientific Research in Science, Engineering and Technology (IJSRSET)*, 10(1), 10–15. https://doi.org/10.32628/IJSRSET229672

Blain-Moraes, S., Schaff, R., Gruis, K. L., Huggins, J. E., & Wren, P. A. (2012). Barriers to and mediators of brain–computer interface user acceptance: Focus group findings. *Ergonomics*, 55(5), 516–525.

Blasgen, M. (1982). Database systems. *Science*, 215, 869–872.

Bossler, A. M., & Holt, T. J. (2012). Online abuse: Cyberbullying, harassment, and stalking. In *Encyclopedia of Cyber Behavior* (pp. 911–917). IGI Global.

Burke WinkelmAn, S., Oomen-Early, J., Walker, A. D., Chu, L., & Yick-Flanagan, A. (2015). Exploring cyber harassment among women who use social media. *Universal Journal of Public Health*, 3(5), 194.

Burwell, S., Sample, M., & Racine, E. (2017). Ethical aspects of brain computer interfaces: A scoping review. *BMC Medical Ethics*, 18(1), 1–11.

Can, U., & Alatas, B. (2019). A new direction in social network analysis: Online social network analysis problems and applications. *Physica A: Statistical Mechanics and Its Applications*, 535, 122372.

Cardoso, L. F., Sorenson, S. B., Webb, O., & Landers, S. (2019). Recent and emerging technologies: Implications for women's safety. *Technology in Society*, 58, 101108.

Carroll, J. M., & Rosson, M. B. (2007). Participatory design in community informatics. *Design Studies*, 28(3), 243–261.

Carter, S. M., Rogers, W., Win, K. T., Frazer, H., Richards, B., & Houssami, N. (2020). The ethical, legal and social implications of using artificial intelligence systems in breast cancer care. *The Breast*, 49, 25–32.

Carvalho, M., Branquinho, C., & de Matos, M. G. (2021). Cyberbullying and bullying: Impact on psychological symptoms and well-being. *Child Indicators Research*, 14, 435–452.

Chhetri, C., & Motti, V. G. (2019). Eliciting privacy concerns for smart home devices from a user centered perspective. In *Information in Contemporary Society: 14th International Conference, iConference 2019, Washington, DC, USA, March 31–April 3, 2019, Proceedings 14* (pp. 91–101). Springer International Publishing.

Clayton, J., & Sibbald, S. (2020). Privacy and ethics are fundamental to tech development. *International Review of Information Ethics*, 28. https://doi.org/10.29173/irie379

Coeckelbergh, M. (2019). Artificial intelligence: Some ethical issues and regulatory challenges. *Technology and Regulation*, 2019, 31–34.

Conrey, S. C., & Zurbriggen, E. L. (2023). Surveillance and gender-based power dynamics: Psychological considerations. In *The Palgrave Handbook of Power, Gender, and Psychology* (pp. 129–150). Springer International Publishing.

Crabtree, K., & Geara, P. (2018). Safety planning for technology: Displaced women and girls' interactions with information and communication technology in Lebanon and harm reduction considerations for humanitarian settings. *Journal of International Humanitarian Action*, 3(1), 1–12.

Dahab, R., & Sakellariou, D. (2020). Barriers to accessing maternal care in low income countries in Africa: A systematic review. *International Journal of Environmental Research and Public Health*, 17(12), 4292.

Davaki, K. (2018). The underlying causes of the digital gender gap and possible solutions for enhanced digital inclusion of women and girls. *FEMM: Women's Rights and Gender Equality.* www.europarl.europa.eu/RegData/etudes/STUD/2018/604940/IPOL_STU2018)604940_EN.pdf

Dixon, K., Fossey, E., & Petrakis, M. (2021). Safety for women when accessing mental health services: A scoping review of the link between safety and recovery. *Australian Health Review*, 45(5), 554–561.

D'Mello, O., Gelin, M., Khelil, F. B., Surek, R. E., & Chi, H. (2018). Wearable IoT security and privacy: A review from technology and policy perspective. In *Future Network Systems and Security: 4th International Conference, FNSS 2018, Paris, France, July 9–11, 2018, Proceedings 4* (pp. 162–177). Springer International Publishing.

Doridot, F. (Ed.). (2013). *Ethical Governance of Emerging Technologies Development.* IGI Global.

Egard, H., & Hansson, K. (2023). The digital society comes sneaking in. An emerging field and its disabling barriers. *Disability & Society*, 38(5), 761–775.

Ellsberg, M., Arango, D. J., Morton, M., Gennari, F., Kiplesund, S., Contreras, M., & Watts, C. (2015). Prevention of violence against women and girls: What does the evidence say? *The Lancet*, 385(9977), 1555–1566.

Espey, E., Dennis, A., & Landy, U. (2019). The importance of access to comprehensive reproductive health care, including abortion: A statement from women's health professional organizations. *American Journal of Obstetrics and Gynecology*, 220(1), 67–70.

Fitzpatrick, J. A., & Gomez, T. R. (1997). Still caught in a trap: The continued povertization of women. *Affilia*, 12(3), 318–341.

Forssberg, K. S., V¨anje, A., & Parding, K. (2022). Bringing in gender perspectives on systematic occupational safety and health management. *Safety Science*, 152, 105776.

Freeman, G., Zamanifard, S., Maloney, D., & Acena, D. (2022). Disturbing the peace: Experiencing and mitigating emerging harassment in social virtual reality. *Proceedings of the ACM on Human-Computer Interaction*, 6(CSCW1), 1–30.

Gao, X., Wang, Y., Chen, X., & Gao, S. (2021). Interface, interaction, and intelligence in generalized brain–computer interfaces. *Trends in Cognitive Sciences*, 25(8), 671–684.

García-Moreno, C., Zimmerman, C., Morris-Gehring, A., Heise, L., Amin, A., Abrahams, N., & Watts, C. (2015). Addressing violence against women: A call to action. *The Lancet*, 385(9978), 1685–1695.

Gautam, C., Patil, A., Podutwar, A., Agarwal, M., Patil, P., & Naik, A. (2022, October). Wearable women safety device. In *2022 IEEE Industrial Electronics and Applications Conference (IEACon)* (pp. 214–217). IEEE.

Gayathri, P., Stalin, A., & Anand, S. (2022). Intelligent smart home security system: A deep learning approach. In *2022 IEEE 10th Region 10 Humanitarian Technology Conference (R10-HTC)* (pp. 438–444). IEEE. https://ieeexplore.ieee.org/abstract/document/9929516

Gray, D. (2015). Fourth amendment remedies as rights: The warrant requirement. *Boston University Law Review*, 96, 425.

Gstrein, O. J., Bunnik, A., & Zwitter, A. (2019). Ethical, legal and social challenges of Predictive Policing. *Católica Law Review, Direito Penal*, 3(3), 77–98.

Guhr, N., Werth, O., Blacha, P. P. H., & Breitner, M. H. (2020). Privacy concerns in the smart home context. *SN Applied Sciences*, 2, 1–12.

Gupta, A., & Mishra, M. (2022). Ethical concerns while using artificial intelligence in recruitment of employees. *Business Ethics and Leadership*, 6(2), 6–11. https://doi.org/10.21272/bel.6(2).6-11.2022

Gupta, C., Vinchurkar, T., Chavan, S., & Waware, P. G. (2023). Channelizing machine learning towards early threat detection and prevention against women using surveillance cameras. *International Journal for Research in Applied Science & Engineering Technology (IJRASET)*, 11(5).

Hariharan, K., Jain, R. R., Prasad, A., Sharma, M., Yadav, P., Poorna, S. S., & Anuraj, K. (2021). A comprehensive study toward women safety using machine learning along with android app development. In *Sustainable Communication Networks and Application: Proceedings of ICSCN 2020* (pp. 321–330). Springer.

Harris, B., & Vitis, L. (2020). Digital intrusions: Technology, spatiality and violence against women. *Journal of Gender-Based Violence*, 4(3), 325–341. https://doi.org/10.1332/239868020X15986402363663

Hemasagar, K., Manoj Kumar, R., Sai Manojna, V., & Priya, B. K. (2022). Ingenious bracelet for women safety and security using IoT. In *Emerging Research in Computing, Information, Communication and Applications: ERCICA 2020*, Volume 2 (pp. 253–265). Springer.

Hine, C. (2021). Evaluating the prospects for university-based ethical governance in artificial intelligence and data-driven innovation. *Research Ethics*, 17(4), 464–479.

Hooda, M., Ramesh, M., Gupta, A., Nair, J., & Nandanan, K. (2021, September). Need assessment and design of an IoT based healthcare solution through participatory approaches or a rural village in Bihar, India. In *2021 IEEE 9th Region 10 Humanitarian Technology Conference (R10-HTC)* (pp. 1–6). IEEE.

Huang, A., Barz, S., Andersson, E., & Makarov, V. (2018). Implementation vulnerabilities in general quantum cryptography. *New Journal of Physics*, 20(10), 103016.

Huda, M. (2019). Empowering application strategy in the technology adoption: Insights from professional and ethical engagement. *Journal of Science and Technology Policy Management*, 10(1), 172–192.

Humble, K. P. (2021). International law, surveillance and the protection of privacy. *The International Journal of Human Rights*, 25(1), 1–25.

Hyland, M., Djankov, S., & Goldberg, P. (2021). Do gendered laws matter for women's economic empowerment? *Peterson Institute for International Economics Working Paper (21–5)*. Available at SSRN: https://ssrn.com/abstract=3827165 or http://dx.doi.org/10.2139/ssrn.3827165

Into, F. H. (2003). Older women and financial management: Strategies for maintaining independence. *Educational Gerontology*, 29(10), 825–839.

Jacob, J. V., & Vivek, S. (2019, June). A work on women empowerment with special reference to Kerala. *International Journal of Innovative Technology and Exploring Engineering (IJITEE)*, 8(8).

Jayachandran, S. (2021). Social norms as a barrier to women's employment in developing countries. *IMF Economic Review*, 69(3), 576–595.

Joshi, V. (2019). Gender discrimination at work place: A significant barrier for women empowerment. *International Journal of Humanities and Social Science*, 6(1), 12–15 https://doi.org/10.14445/23942703/IJHSS-V6I1P103

Kabir, A. T., & Tasneem, T. (2020, June). Safety solution for women using smart band and CWS app. In *2020 17th International Conference on Electrical Engineering/Electronics, Computer, Telecommunications and Information Technology (ECTI-CON)* (pp. 566–569). IEEE.

Kalyan, K. S., Barnala, K. K., Rajeevan, A., Ajay, R., Nair, A. M., Frey, L. M., & Mohan, R. (2020, December). Women empowerment through productivity, rural development and technology: Assessment of cross linkages within a village of Maharashtra, India. In *2020 IEEE 8th R10 Humanitarian Technology Conference (R10-HTC)* (pp. 1–6). IEEE.

Kannan, M. R., Jyothsna, K., Aparna, T. S., Anjali, T., Meera, M., & Amrutha, S. D. (2020). IoT-based women security system. In *Inventive Communication and Computational Technologies: Proceedings of ICICCT 2019* (pp. 1369–1378). Springer.

Kanyagui, M. K., Sajithkumar, K. J., Velankar, Y., Mohan, R., Viswanathan, P. K., & Magnani, N. (2023). Livelihood challenges faced by women in rural India: Exploration of solutions using participatory action research. *Development in Practice*, 34(4), 1–15.

Kasearu, K., Maestripieri, L., & Ranci, C. (2017). Women at risk: The impact of labour-market participation, education and household structure on the economic vulnerability of women through Europe. *European Societies*, 19(2), 202–221.

Kauppinen, K., & Tuomola, T. (2008). Work-related violence, bullying, and sexual harassment. In *Promoting Health for Working Women* (pp. 161–182). Springer.

Khan, R., Mahfuz, N., & Nowshin, N. (2020, December). A novel approach of women safety assistant device with biometric verification in real scenario. In *2020 IEEE International Women in Engineering (WIE) Conference on Electrical and Computer Engineering (WIECON-ECE)* (pp. 426–431). IEEE.

Kim, S., Lee, J., & Oh, P. (2023). Rethinking artificial intelligence: Algorithmic bias and ethical issues—questioning artificial intelligence: How racial identity shapes the perceptions of algorithmic bias. *International Journal of Communication*, 18, 23.

Kipker, D., & Pagel, P. (2020). Editorial. *International Cybersecurity Law Review*, 1–5.

Kodheli, O., Lagunas, E., Maturo, N., Sharma, S. K., Shankar, B., Montoya, J. F. M., & Goussetis, G. (2020). Satellite communications in the new space era: A survey and future challenges. *IEEE Communications Surveys & Tutorials*, 23(1), 70–109.

Kommineni, K. K., Basha, S. J., Sandeep, M., Vadana, P. S., Sai, T. S. R., & Kumar, D. S. (2023, March). A review on IoT-based defensive devices for women security. In *2023 9th International Conference on Advanced Computing and Communication Systems (ICACCS)* (Vol. 1, pp. 99–104). IEEE.

Koskela, H. (2002). Video surveillance, gender, and the safety of public urban space: "Peeping Tom" goes high tech? *Urban Geography*, 23(3), 257–278.

Kuehner, C. (2017). Why is depression more common among women than among men? *The Lancet Psychiatry*, 4(2), 146–158.

Kurt, A., & Duquenoy, P. (2013). Governance in technology development. In *Ethical Governance of Emerging Technologies Development* (pp. 149–165). IGI Global.

Lavanya, S. D., Aiswarya, I. V., Vishnu, U., Kadambari, P. B., Vishnu, S., & Namboothiri, P. K. (2023). Critical analysis on the role of Panchakarma in the management of psychological manifestations during menopause. *European Chemical Bulletin*, 12(11). https://doi.org/10.48047/ecb/2023.12.10.918

Lee, M., Jain, A., Cha, H., Ojha, S., & Kusbit, D. (2019). Procedural justice in algorithmic fairness. *Proceedings of the ACM on Human-Computer Interaction*, 3, 1–26.

Lerner, H. E. (1983). Female dependency in context: Some theoretical and technical considerations. *American Journal of Orthopsychiatry*, 53(4), 697–705. https://doi.org/10.1111/j.1939-0025.1983.tb03412.x

Lindberg, S. (2018). *Ethics of User Involvement in Sensitive Design Situations* (Doctoral dissertation, Halmstad University Press).

Lonzetta, A. M., & Hayajneh, T. (2020). Challenges of complying with data protection and privacy regulations. *EAI Endorsed Transactions on Scalable Information Systems*, 8(30). https://doi.org/10.4108/eai.26-5-2020.166352

Ludermir, A. B., Lewis, G., Valongueiro, S. A., de Araújo, T. V. B., & Araya, R. (2010). Violence against women by their intimate partner during pregnancy and postnatal depression: A prospective cohort study. *The Lancet*, 376(9744), 903–910.

Ludermir, A. B., Schraiber, L. B., D'Oliveira, A. F., França-Junior, I., & Jansen, H. A. (2008). Violence against women by their intimate partner and common mental disorders. *Social Science & Medicine*, 66(4), 1008–1018.

Margulies, P. (2013). The NSA in global perspective: Surveillance, human rights, and international counterterrorism. *Fordham Law Review*, 82, 2137.

Marrington, A., Kerr, D., & Gammack, J. (Eds.). (2016). *Managing Security Issues and the Hidden Dangers of Wearable Technologies*. IGI Global.

Martin, D. M., & Hashi, F. O. (1992). Law as an institutional barrier to the economic empowerment of women (No. 2). In *Poverty and Social Division, Technical Department, Africa Region*. World Bank.

Mason, C. L., & Magnet, S. (2012). Surveillance studies and violence against women. *Surveillance & Society*, 10(2), 105–118.

McGregor, L., Murray, D., & Ng, V. (2019). International human rights law as a framework for algorithmic accountability. *International and Comparative Law Quarterly*, 68, 309–343.

Michota, A. (2013). Digital security concerns and threats facing women entrepreneurs. *Journal of Innovation and Entrepreneurship*, 2(1), 1–11.

Moser, C. (2012). Mainstreaming women's safety in cities into gender-based policy and programmes. *Gender & Development*, 20(3), 435–452.

Mudgal, S. K., Sharma, S. K., Chaturvedi, J., & Sharma, A. (2020). Brain computer interface advancement in neurosciences: Applications and issues. *Interdisciplinary Neurosurgery*, 20, 100694.

Mukhopadhyay, A., & Vinayaka, R. (2021). A smart-contract-based blockchain for a healthcare IoT network. *International Journal of Electronic Healthcare*, 11(3), 256–270.

Naik, N., Hameed, B. M., Shetty, D. K., Swain, D., Shah, M., Paul, R., & Somani, B. K. (2022). Legal and ethical consideration in artificial intelligence in healthcare: Who takes responsibility? *Frontiers in Surgery*, 9, 266.

Nair, P., & Menon, J. (2023). Role of Amrita Vishwa Vidyapeetham in integrated holistic health policy actions of civil 20 India 2023. *Amrita Journal of Medicine*, 19(4), 204–208.

Nathan, G. (2015). Innovation process and ethics in technology: An approach to ethical (responsible) innovation governance. *Journal on Chain and Network Science*, 15(2), 119–134.

Ntoutsi, E., Fafalios, P., Gadiraju, U., Iosifidis, V., Nejdl, W., Vidal, M., Ruggieri, S., Turini, F., Papadopoulos, S., Krasanakis, E., Kompatsiaris, I., Kinder-Kurlanda, K., Wagner, C., Karimi, F., Fernandez, M., Alani, H., Berendt, B., Kruegel, T., Heinze, C., Broelemann, K., Kasneci, G., Tiropanis, T., & Staab, S. (2020). Bias in data-driven artificial intelligence systems—An introductory survey. *Wiley Interdisciplinary Reviews: Data Mining and Knowledge Discovery*, 10.

Obrenovic, Z., Abascal, J., & Starcevic, D. (2007). Universal accessibility as a multimodal design issue. *Communications of the ACM*, 50(5), 83–88.

Oram, S., Khalifeh, H., & Howard, L. M. (2017). Violence against women and mental health. *The Lancet Psychiatry*, 4(2), 159–170.

Pandey, A., & Caliskan, A. (2021). *Disparate Impact of Artificial Intelligence Bias in Ridehailing Economy's Price Discrimination Algorithms*. Association for Computing Machinery.

Pecorella, T., Ronga, L. S., Chiti, F., Jayousi, S., & Franck, L. (2015). Emergency satellite communications: Research and standardization activities. *IEEE Communications Magazine*, 53(5), 170–177.

Pereira, L., Gewehr, M., & Alves, M. (2020). Enhancing organizational compliance programs: The impact of data protection implementation under the personal data protection law. *ESG Law Review*. https://doi.org/10.37497/esg.v3issue.1612

Poster, W. R. (2018). Cybersecurity needs women. *Nature*, 555(7698), 577–580. https://doi.org/10.1038/d41586-018-03327-w

Prabhakar, P., Gupta, D., & Pati, P. B. (2022, December). Abstractive summarization of Indian legal judgments. In *2022 OITS International Conference on Information Technology (OCIT)* (pp. 256–261). IEEE.

Prabhakar, P., Palaniswamy, S., & Pati, P. B. (2023, April). Stress analysis in online examination using deep learning approach. In *2023 IEEE 8th International Conference for Convergence in Technology (I2CT)* (pp. 1–7). IEEE.

Prabhakar, S. (2018). Techniques for women safety based on Internet of Things (IoT). *Global Journal for Research Analysis*, 7(2), 624–626.

Rosenbaum, M. S., Edwards, K. L., Malla, B., Adhikary, J. R., & Ramírez, G. C. (2020). Street harassment is marketplace discrimination: The impact of street harassment on young female consumers' marketplace experiences. *Journal of Retailing and Consumer Services*, 57, 102220.

Roy, S., & Bailey, A. (2021). Safe in the city? Negotiating safety, public space and the male gaze in Kolkata, India. *Cities*, 117, 103321.

Sadler, A. G., Booth, B. M., Cook, B. L., & Doebbeling, B. N. (2003). Factors associated with women's risk of rape in the military environment. *American Journal of Industrial Medicine*, 43(3), 262–273.

Salahdine, F., & Kaabouch, N. (2019). Social engineering attacks: A survey. *Future Internet*, 11(4), 89.

Scatiggio, V. (2022). Tackling the issue of bias in artificial intelligence to design AI-driven fair and inclusive service systems. How human biases are breaching into AI algorithms, with severe impacts on individuals and societies, and what designers can do to face this phenomenon and change for the better. https://hdl.handle.net/10589/186118

Schaefer, R., Ziegler, M., & Mueller, W. (2006). Securing personal data in smart home environments. In *Workshop on Privacy-Enhanced Personalization (PEP2006)* (pp. 1–8). Institute for Software Research.

Schmitt, M. T., Branscombe, N. R., & Postmes, T. (2003). Women's emotional responses to the pervasiveness of gender discrimination. *European Journal of Social Psychology*, 33(3), 297–312.

Schomakers, E. M., Biermann, H., & Ziefle, M. (2021). Users' preferences for smart home automation–investigating aspects of privacy and trust. *Telematics and Informatics*, 64, 101689.

Selinger, E., & Leong, B. (2021). The ethics of facial recognition technology. SSRN Scholarly Paper ID 3762185. Rochester, Social Science Research Network, NY. https://papers.ssrn.com/abstract=3762185

Sharma, S., Salunke, D., Haldar, E., Mandlik, R., & Salke, N. (2022, November). A comprehensive survey on IoT based smart safety devices for women. In *2022 International Conference on Augmented Intelligence and Sustainable Systems (ICAISS)* (pp. 1101–1109). IEEE.

Silvers, A., Francis, L. P., & Badesch, B. (2016). Reproductive rights and access to reproductive services for women with disabilities. *American Medical Association Journal of Ethics*, 18(4), 430–437.

Singh, J., Pasquier, T., Bacon, J., Ko, H., & Eyers, D. (2015). Twenty security considerations for cloud-supported Internet of Things. *IEEE Internet of Things Journal*, 3(3), 269–284.

Sivan, R., Palaniswamy, S., & Pati, P. B. (2022a, December). Comparative study of deep learning models to recognize palm leaf Malayalam characters. In *2022 6th International Conference on Computation System and Information Technology for Sustainable Solutions (CSITSS)* (pp. 1–6). IEEE.

Sivan, R., Singh, T., & Pati, P. B. (2022b, December). Malayalam character recognition from palm leaves using deep-learning. In *2022 OITS International Conference on Information Technology (OCIT)* (pp. 134–139). IEEE.

Sorrentino, E., Vona, R., Monterosso, D., & Giammarioli, A. M. (2016). Gender issues on occupational safety and health. *Annali dell'Istituto superiore di sanita*, 52(2), 190–197.

Sundari, T. K. (2020). The untold story: How the health care systems in developing countries contribute to maternal mortality. *Women's Health, Politics, and Power*, 173–190.

Trench, S., Oc, T., & Tiesdell, S. (1992). Safer cities for women: Perceived risks and planning measures. *The Town Planning Review*, 279–296.

Tyer-Viola, L. A., & Cesario, S. K. (2010). Addressing poverty, education, and gender equality to improve the health of women worldwide. *Journal of Obstetric, Gynecologic & Neonatal Nursing*, 39(5), 580–589.

Uberoi, D., & De Bruyn, M. (2013). Human rights versus legal control over women's reproductive self-determination. *Health and Human Rights*, 15, 161.

van der Ham, M., Bolijn, R., de Vries, A., Ponce, M. C., & van Valkengoed, I. G. (2021). Gender inequality and the double burden of disease in low-income and middle-income countries: An ecological study. *BMJ Open*, 11(4).

Van der Wilk, A. (2021). *Protecting Women and Girls from Violence in the Digital Age*. Council of Europe. https://edoc.coe.int/en/violence-against-women/10686-protecting-women-and-girls-from-violence-in-the-digital-age.html

Velonis, A. J., Daoud, N., Matheson, F., Woodhall-Melnik, J., Hamilton-Wright, S., & O'Campo, P. (2017). Strategizing safety: Theoretical frameworks to understand women's decision making in the face of partner violence and social inequities. *Journal of Interpersonal Violence*, 32(21), 3321–3345.

Vesnic-Alujevic, L., Nascimento, S., & Polvora, A. (2020). Societal and ethical impacts of artificial intelligence: Critical notes on European policy frameworks. *Telecommunications Policy*, 44(6), 101961.

Vickery, L. (2012). Deepening disadvantages in housing markets for women. *Local Economy*, 27(8), 796–803.

Voss, W. G. (2013). Privacy law implications of the use of drones for security and justice purposes. *International Journal of Liability and Scientific Enquiry*, 6(4), 171–192.

Waks, E., Inoue, K., Santori, C., Fattal, D., Vuckovic, J., Solomon, G. S., & Yamamoto, Y. (2002). Quantum cryptography with a photon turnstile. *Nature*, 420(6917), 762–762.

Williams, E. J., Beardmore, A., & Joinson, A. N. (2017). Individual differences in susceptibility to online influence: A theoretical review. *Computers in Human Behavior*, 72, 412–421.

Yu, B., Montgomery, A. E., True, G., Cusack, M., Sorrentino, A., Chhabra, M., & Dichter, M. E. (2020). The intersection of interpersonal violence and housing instability: Perspectives from women veterans. *American Journal of Orthopsychiatry*, 90(1), 63.

Zimmerman, A. D. (1995). Toward a more democratic ethic of technological governance. *Science, Technology, & Human Values*, 20(1), 86–107.

Zimmermann, V., Gerber, P., Marky, K., Böck, L., & Kirchbuchner, F. (2019). Assessing users' privacy and security concerns of smart home technologies. *i-com*, 18(3), 197–216.

Žliobaitė, I. (2017). Measuring discrimination in algorithmic decision making. *Data Mining and Knowledge Discovery*, 31(4), 1060–1089.

12 Participation in the Community and Education

Devanand Bhonsle, Anu G. Pillai, Ruhi Uzma Sheikh, Sapna Singh Kshatri, Tanu Rizvi, and Manjushree Nayak

12.1. INTRODUCTION

Artificial Intelligence (AI) is the emulation of human intelligence processes which is used by computer systems. It is used to develop machine intelligence which is capable for various functions and can respond similar to the human beings (Shah et al., 2021). AI technique encompasses various areas viz. computer vision, machine learning (Chakraborty and Abougreen, 2018), natural language processing, etc. It can enable to the system to understand, analyse, and derive the knowledge from the data. In contrast, the Internet of Things (IoT) comprises a network of electronic gadgets which consists of various sensors (Chen et al., 2021), software, and memories to store the data (Hossain and Muhammad, 2016). They are physical items, and they can collect and exchange the data. IoT devices use the internet connectivity by which they can communicate with the other devices (Anisha et al., 2021). These IoT-based devices can be used to create smart homes, smart cities, smart education institutes, etc. (Bellini et al., 2022). Hence, they can participate in the community and education efficiently. AI-based IoT systems can improve the quality of life and enhance the productivity. Sensor-based IoT devices play an important role to collect the data from the surroundings which may be used for decision making for efficient management in the community and education system (Bhonsle et al., 2022). This chapter focuses only upon the use of AI-based IoT systems for the uplifting of community and educational institutes. A smart city has various places likes traffic signals, museum, railway station, school, colleges, government and private organisations' buildings, parking areas, banks, shopping malls, markets, police station, petrol and gas filling stations, etc. It is very important to protect these places to avoid any kind of mishap. India is now highest populous country, and it is really very difficult to provide the security without the use of technology. Many researchers developed various types of sensors which are to be used in IoT systems. These IoT systems are using AI for the smart, quick and accurate decisions (Rahman et al., 2021). For example, a sensor can analyse the traffic congestion and take the decision to control the traffic. Many metropolitan cities use air quality monitor to monitor the level of pollution. Shopping malls are full of various types of sensors for automatic applications. Banks also use automatic passbook printer, cash depositor, CCTV for surveillance,

 DOI: 10.1201/9781003538172-12

etc. Nowadays, almost all the important places are under surveillance using AI-based IoT devices which use different algorithms, image, and video processing techniques. A few year ago, when whole world was affected by COVID-19 diseases, AI and IoT were to be used in sustainable education (Barikova and Bernaziuk, 2022). They helped to run whole education system during pandemic. AI-powered chatbots efficiently address the inquiries of the students and provide personalised learning experiences (Embarak, 2022). IoT-based systems are used to track progress of the students and offer valuable feedback to the teachers. Moreover, students with special needs can benefit from AI-powered virtual assistants (Kamruzzaman and Alruwaili, 2022). Industrial IoT, combined with AI capabilities, can deliver tailored feedback and guidance to students and patients. Drawing from experiences in healthcare during the COVID-19 pandemic (Rizvi et al., 2022b), similar systems can be replicated to enhance education (Rahman et al., 2020). An example is depicted in Figure 12.1, showcasing an IoT-based education system.

This system facilitates the connection between teachers and students through a cloud-based teaching platform (Alhaidari et al., 2020; Yassine et al., 2018), enabling remote learning using student IDs based on RFID and mobile devices (Tan et al., 2018). Such a setup empowers teachers to monitor learners and their progress remotely, ensuring seamless educational delivery during challenging circumstances. Moreover, IoT-enabled devices offer the capability to track students' attendance, engagement, and progress, providing real-time data to teachers and administrators to optimise the learning experience. Overall, AI and IoT hold significant potential in facilitating distance learning and maintaining educational continuity during epidemics (Iqbal et al., 2020). However, despite their promise, several challenges need addressing. One critical challenge is the lack of standardisation in the development and implementation of these technologies. This can hinder educators' ability to effectively integrate AI and IoT into their teaching practices. Additionally, there are concerns about these technologies exacerbating existing inequalities in education, as not all students may have equal access to resources and opportunities. This study seeks to delve deeper into how AI and IoT can be effectively utilised in education systems during pandemics like COVID-19 (Rizvi et al., 2022a), addressing these challenges and exploring opportunities for their beneficial application (Raza, 2020).

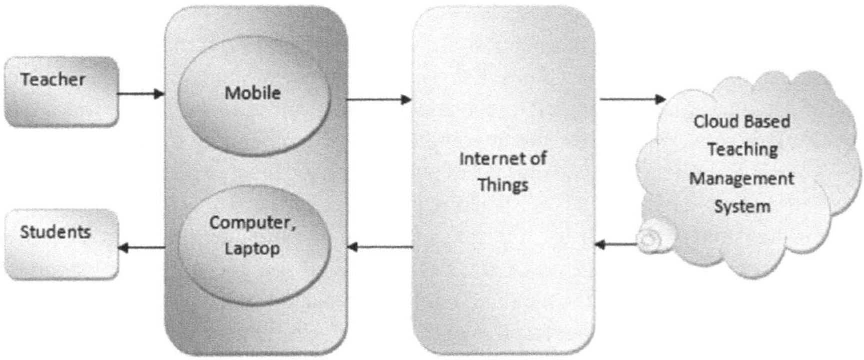

FIGURE 12.1 An IoT-based education system.

12.2. RELATED WORK

Several scholars have conducted research on the application of AI and IoT in sustainable education systems. The utilisation of AI and IoT in education has gained traction, offering potential benefits such as personalised learning and enhanced student engagement. The pandemic's onset accelerated the need for remote and online learning, leading to increased interest in incorporating AI and IoT into educational systems for smart cities (Mahdavinejad et al., 2018). One study delved into AI-assisted education's potential in smart cities during the pandemic, highlighting its ability to provide personalised and adaptive learning experiences while supporting remote and online learning (Li et al., 2021). Data privacy and security were emphasised as crucial considerations in implementing AI-assisted education systems (Li et al., 2022). Another study explored the IoT's role in educational systems for smart cities amid the pandemic, emphasising its capability for real-time monitoring, data collection, and support for remote learning. Challenges like cost and privacy concerns were acknowledged in IoT implementation (Rahman et al., 2019). Furthermore, it is also examined the use of AI and IoT in a smart campus system during the pandemic, highlighting benefits such as real-time monitoring of student progress and attendance, alongside challenges including data privacy and security. A systematic review analysed existing literature on AI and IoT in education during the pandemic, revealing benefits such as personalised learning and real-time monitoring, alongside challenges like data privacy and security. In terms of education, AI and IoT technologies have enabled remote learning and online education, including virtual reality, online tutoring, and e-learning platforms (Ahmad et al., 2021). These technologies have also enhanced online education accessibility for students with disabilities and improved efficiency through personalised learning and real-time feedback. However, challenges remain, such as the need for robust and secure systems and further research on long-term effects. In summary, research on AI and IoT-assisted education systems during pandemics like COVID-19 (Rizvi et al., 2022b) indicates their potential benefits, including personalised learning and real-time monitoring (Upadhyay et al., 2022). However, challenges such as data privacy and security must be addressed in their implementation.

12.3. MOTIVATION

Over the past decade, there has been significant research into AI, sparking interest in its future applications in smart cities. Integrating software systems enables the collection of data that can be leveraged to allocate capital, resources, and energy more efficiently. This trend aligns with the ongoing digitalisation, leading to a notable surge in AI and IoT applications. Various AI applications have been implemented in smart city operations, including advanced computing, neural networks, fraud detection, sensing technology, speech recognition, and human-computer interface software. Additionally, the COVID-19 pandemic has influenced specific AI and IoT applications. Studies indicate that the pandemic notably impacted video conferencing in the education sector. Students' accessed e-learning platforms, where video lectures were recorded, departing from traditional lecture delivery methods. Figure 12.2 illustrates

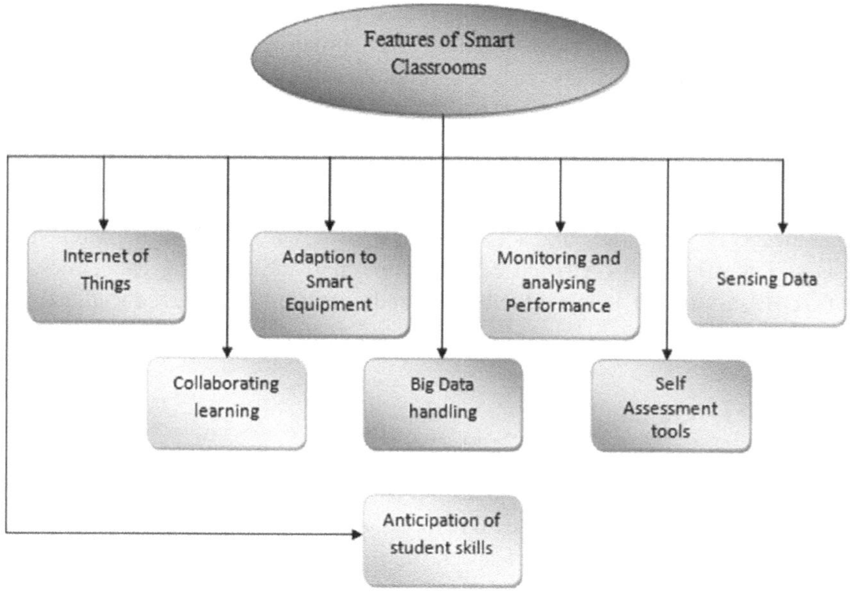

FIGURE 12.2 Features of smart classrooms.

the primary features of a smart classroom, showcasing how these classrooms enable students and teachers to benefit from internet tools for functions like self-assessment, e-learning, and consistent monitoring (Kim, 2018). Furthermore, incorporating AI technology and speech recognition algorithms can address language barriers by providing real-time translation of lectures using subtitles. This integration of language translation.

Advancements in technology have made learning a foreign language more accessible in smart cities, leveraging multi criteria analysis through internet technology. Real-time feedback is facilitated by AI and IoT systems (Ni and Cheung, 2022). It enhances student monitoring and progress evaluation. Automation of tasks such as grading and attendance through AI, ML, and IoT technologies streamlines educational processes (Mhlanga, 2022). Educational software aids in smart learning, even amidst the challenges posed by the pandemic, through e-learning platforms. The transition to wireless learning environments in smart cities presents challenges that require innovative solutions and the application of AI and IoT technologies to achieve sustainable education systems (Kamruzzaman et al., 2022). Remote-based learning systems have become imperative, especially during the pandemic era, as cities adopt smart city standards. AI and IoT technologies transform education systems, enabling personalised learning tailored to individual student needs. To address these challenges, there's a motivation to develop AI and IoT-assisted educational settings in smart cities (Bellini et al., 2022). Leveraging AI-powered robots, algorithms, and IoT devices can enhance educational tasks for both instructors and students, making education more effective and efficient. Furthermore, AI and IoT-based virtual and physical learning settings combine elements from virtual and physical environments to facilitate remote learning and communication. This system utilises technology such as virtual and augmented reality, smart devices, and data analytics to personalise learning experiences and provide real-time feedback. In smart cities, AI and IoT-assisted technology allow students to access learning resources using wearable technology, breaking the barriers of time and place (Nazaretsky et al., 2022). Integration of the metaverse into schools offers diverse learning opportunities for students (Bayani et al., 2017). The aim of the study is to provide comprehensive insights into AI and IoT-assisted education in smart cities during pandemics like COVID-19, aiming to enhance the quality and accessibility of the educational system (Zhang et al., 2022).

12.4. METHODOLOGY

In this section, specific application benefits of IoT-based applications in education are discussed. This discussion includes the challenges too. In the first phase, a survey in done on IoT-based educational institute applications such as smart classroom (Kim, 2018), smart library, smart learner, smart teacher, smart administration, smart hostel, smart healthcare, etc (Alshehri and Muhammad, 2020; Kshatri et al., 2022a). In the second phase, various challenges have been discussed which includes privacy and security, internet connectivity, bandwidth, cost of the IoT devices, battery life, device incompatibility, institutional policy, ethical concern, etc. Figure 12.3 shows the aforementioned benefits of IoT in education.

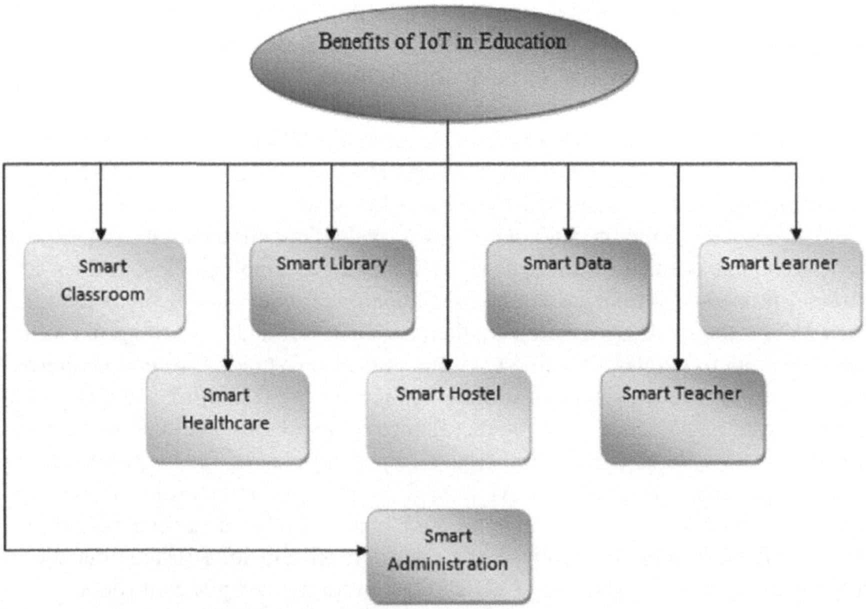

FIGURE 12.3 Benefits of IoT in education.

12.5. IoT-BASED EDUCATION SYSTEM

An IoT-based education system includes smart classroom (Kim, 2018), smart library, smart learner, smart teacher, smart administration, smart hostel, smart healthcare, etc. (Khan et al., 2023). The following is the description about each benefit:

12.5.1. Smart Classroom

Smart classroom uses different technologies and equipment capable of making the attendance of students automated. It also includes an interactive white board. This technology saves the time which may be wasted with marking of physical attendance (Kshatri et al., 2022). The smart board may be used to make class more interactive. It can be used to demonstrate complex design, pictures, technology, or algorithms easily. A smart classroom must have good internet connectivity.

12.5.2. Smart Library

A library plays an important role in uplifting academic institutes. The function of a conventional library includes issuing books to the students and faculty members, keeping records, classification of books in accordance with the subject, collecting the books, etc. Smart libraries use bar codes in the physical books to identify the book and all the details about the book along with its author(s), publication house, volume, etc. Smart libraries have computer systems which can be used to search books. They include all the information including their status, whether they are available in the library or issued to someone (Rizvi et al., 2022). More advanced libraries have soft copies of all the books. Students may request the specific book, and its soft version may be sent to him/her through email. A smart library allows user authentication and it creates an individual profile. It helps to give the notification about the due date, renewal, etc.

12.5.3. Smart Learner

The integration of IoT in education primarily aims to cultivate intelligent learners, which includes learner tracking, wearable technology, electronic books, etc. Within an IoT-enabled educational setting, students possess the capacity to discern novel skills and personalised learning methodologies through technological advancements and integrated analytics (Wang and Yu, 2022). The digitisation of education fundamentally shifts the educational paradigm from reactive to proactive learning, empowering learners to make informed decisions. The implementation of IoT in the educational landscape has proven instrumental in enhancing students' learning experiences and facilitating the monitoring of their activities (Al-Emran et al., 2020). The integration of IoT tools in online education can lead to a remarkable improvement in learners' performance and efficiency. Through IoT sensors, students now have the capability to track their progress individually, as these sensors can gauge fatigue levels and maintain cognitive engagement through continuous interaction. Furthermore, learners are increasingly benefiting from interactive online classes facilitated by smart phone-based platforms or e-classes.

E-books embedded with barcodes foster a dynamic reading environment, piquing learners' interest. An IoT device known as a scanmaker enables the extraction of editable text from various documents, including books, magazines, and articles, directly into computing devices. Moreover, IoT wearable technology plays a pivotal role in promoting seamless learner development. By integrating students' location data, exercise logs, and social media activities, IoT wearable devices generate vast amounts of big data for personalized learning. These wearable devices capture learners' interactions with educational content in the form of games, utilising IoT sensing devices.

12.5.4. Smart Administration

Smart administration increases the efficacy of day-to-day activities. It includes Human Resource (HR) management, accounts management, energy management, waste management, logistic monitoring, and security control. Smart HR management includes collection of resumes for conducting interviews after short-listing the eligible candidates. It also includes the promotion based on the performance of existing staffs. Teachers and other staffs can be monitored without a physically present manager. All these activities can be done with the help of mobile phones, laptops, smart watches, and IoT-based sensors and gadgets.

Smart account management involves collection of data and their analysis from the account section. Account sections are linked to the IoT devices via sensors to help the management to understand financial status of institutions. Smart energy management system helps to integrate school building with IoT for intelligent energy management. This system gathered the energy data from the classroom, offices, staff rooms and residential areas within the campus, and it analyses the data in real time (Veeramanickam and Mohanapriya, 2016). This smart system sends the notifications and recommendation so that energy consumption can be minimised, and cost must be reduced.

Smart security uses intelligent devices which are used for monitoring the school premises. The access of security system must be restricted to only authentic person's approach. This system also restricted the entrance of unauthorised person in the school area. For this purpose, students, teachers and other staffs may have sensor-based identity cards with unique IDs. Some institutes use biometric automatic attendance systems for login and logout purposes. These systems may use biometric information viz. fingerprints, face detection, or iris scanning, etc.

12.5.5. Smart Teacher

The smart teacher uses various technologies to improve teaching. Before introduction of AI and IoT-based learning only traditional methods like power point presentation and chalk and talk were using. But in the present era, teachers are using emerging technologies to improve the quality of their lectures. In the pandemic time, teachers had taken their classes online. In that situation mobiles and laptops were used required good internet connectivity. Various applications of mail have been used to give and submit the assignments.

12.5.6. Smart Hostel

In general, hostels in the educational institutes are accommodations for the students. Smart hostels are installed with IoT-based sensors with good connectivity of internet facilities. These gadgets may be used for surveillance so that any unauthorised person should not enter. Students can use internet facilities for their study, research and project purposes. The availability, room type, and price can be seen online. IoT-based sensors can be used to control energy utilisation too.

12.5.7. Smart Healthcare

One of the most important and basic requirement is the healthcare service in the institution premises (Rathi et al., 2021). In encompasses disease prevention, monitoring health condition, diagnosis and treatment etc.

12.6. CHALLENGES IN IMPLEMENTING IoT-BASED SYSTEMS

There are various challenges in implementation of IoT-based education systems. Some of the most common challenges are internet connectivity and its bandwidth, privacy and security, device cost and incompatibility, institutional policies, reliability and scalability, battery life, etc. The following is a discussion of the aforementioned challenges while implementing an IoT-based education system.

12.6.1. Internet Connectivity and Its Bandwidth

Internet connectivity is one of the significant challenges in India. Sometimes it is difficult to get good connectivity due to which various task are affected and become delayed.

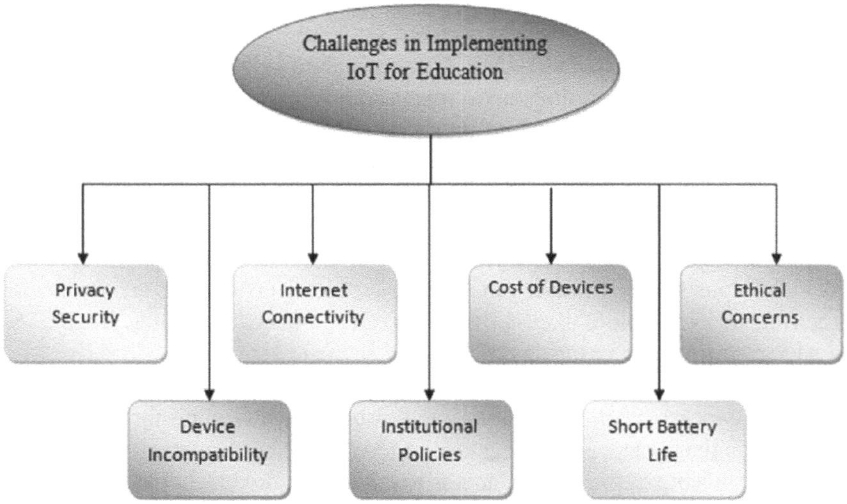

FIGURE 12.4 Challenges in implementing IoT for education.

IoT-based sensors require good internet connectivity, which helps for quick communication. Network bandwidth is the maximum amount of data transmitted over a network in fixed time. Bandwidth also plays an important role if the numbers of user are more.

12.6.2. Privacy and Security

In general, devices and systems are designed to be robust, reliable, and secure. Different algorithms and protocols are used for security purposes. But there are still the chances of the cyberattacks which may corrupt the system or steal the useful information. Most of the IoT-based devices are prone to cyberattacks and not hacked by the hackers. However, privacy and security is a prime concern so that personal, academic, and institutional information should be secured.

12.6.3. Device Cost and Incompatibility

In general, IoT-based devices are costly which increases with the campus area of the institution. Some of the parts of these devices are imported, which further increases the cost. These devices must be compatible against protocol and standards. If the devices are not standardised, then compatibility becomes a major problem.

12.6.4. Reliability and Scalability

Scalability is the capacity of a device to adapt the environment change. There is a continuous demand for the new technology in the education. IoT devices must be reliable so that they can adapt high dynamic environment.

12.7. FUTURE USE OF AI AND IoT

Artificial Intelligence (AI) and the Internet of Things (IoT) hold immense potential to revolutionise education, offering personalised learning experiences and enhancing instructional delivery. Integration of these technologies can create interactive, efficient, and engaging learning environments. One significant application of AI in education is through Intelligent Tutoring Systems (ITSs), which analyse student data and provide personalised learning experiences. ITSs utilise AI algorithms, natural language processing (NLP), and machine learning (ML) techniques (Kshatri et al., 2022a) to tailor content, assessments, and feedback to each student's learning style and pace. For example, the Carnegie Learning Cognitive Tutor employs AI to offer personalised instruction, resulting in improved student performance and motivation. Moreover, AI technologies like NLP and ML can automate the grading process, saving educators time and ensuring efficient and accurate assessment of student work. IoT-enabled devices such as smart cameras and microphones can further enhance the grading process by providing real-time feedback on student performance during exams or language classes. IoT technology also facilitates remote monitoring and grading of student work, enabling access to education for students unable to attend traditional classroom settings. Additionally, IoT technology in education enables access to digital resources and fosters collaboration among students and teachers.

Smart devices like smartphones, tablets, and smartboards facilitate interactive learning experiences. IoT-enabled monitoring of student progress provides real-time data on engagement, performance, and learning outcomes, enabling personalised instruction and adjustment of teaching methods. During pandemics like COVID-19, AI-powered virtual learning environments (VLEs) and virtual assistants offer personalised, self-paced instruction and real-time support to students. IoT technology further enables remote collaboration and communication among students and teachers, ensuring continuity of education. Intelligent Personal Learning Environments (PLEs), driven by AI and IoT, adapt to students' needs and preferences, providing personalised content and real-time feedback to improve engagement and learning outcomes. In conclusion, AI and IoT have the potential to transform education by providing flexible, adaptive, and personalised learning experiences. However, ethical and privacy considerations must be addressed, and educators need proper training to leverage these technologies effectively. The future vision of AI- and IoT-assisted education systems is depicted in Table 12.1.

TABLE 12.1
AI and IoT-Assisted Education System

Feature	Key Benefits	Technologies Used	Impact on Teachers	Impact on Students
Personalised Learning	Lesson plans for each student based on his own learning capability.	ML, NLP, and cognitive computing.	Effectiveness increases in teaching.	Academic performance improvement due to engagement in learning.
Intelligent Tutoring Systems	Guidance for problem-solving tasks and assessments for the students.	AI, NLP, and computer vision.	Less workload on teachers, increased ability to monitor the progress of students.	Improved problem-solving skills and increased self-directed learning.
Virtual and Augmented Reality	Interactive learning experiences for students by visualising the complex concepts.	Virtual reality and computer vision.	Increased ability to deliver interactive sessions.	Improved understanding of complex concepts.
Smart Classrooms	Classrooms with smart devices to teach, monitor and help the student.	IoT, sensors, and cloud computing.	Increased ability to monitor the students improved ability to make data driven decisions.	Improved ability to collaborate and communicate with classmates.
Adaptive Learning Platforms	Platforms that adapt the style of individual students.	ML, NLP, and big data.	Effectiveness in teaching and improved ability to monitor progress of the students	Motivation for learning, improved academic performance.

TABLE 12.2
Role of AI and IoT in the Education System

	Role of AI	Role of IoT
Remote Learning	AI algorithms personalise and optimise remote learning experiences through adaptive learning systems and intelligent tutoring systems, enhancing student engagement and performance.	IoT devices provide access to remote learning resources and monitor student participation and progress.
Classroom Management	AI algorithms monitor and manage student behaviour in real time, offering feedback and support to teachers for maintaining classroom discipline and engagement.	IoT devices monitor classroom conditions and provide data-driven insights for improving the learning environment.
Student Health and Safety	AI algorithms monitor student health and safety, identifying illness symptoms, tracking potential exposure to diseases like COVID-19, and providing early warnings of health risks.	IoT devices monitor student health and safety, track movement and interactions, and offer data-driven insights to enhance safety protocols.
Campus Management	AI algorithms optimise campus operations such as scheduling and resource allocation to ensure efficient resource use and cost reduction.	IoT devices monitor and control access to campus facilities, provide data-driven insights to enhance campus safety and security.
Parent–Teacher Communication	AI facilitates communication between parents and teachers through chatbots and virtual assistants, improving parent engagement and supporting student learning.	IoT devices provide real-time updates on student progress and activities, facilitating communication between parents and teachers.

AI (Artificial Intelligence) and IoT (Internet of Things) contribute to enhancing the education system at both the application and infrastructure levels. Based on the summarised insights provided in Table 12.2, here is a breakdown of how AI and IoT play significant roles at the application and infrastructure levels to strengthen the education system.

In summary, both AI and IoT technologies contribute significantly to various aspects of the education system, from enhancing remote learning experiences to improving campus management and communication between stakeholders. These technologies leverage data analytics and real-time monitoring to optimise educational processes and support student success.

12.8. CONCLUSION

This chapter discussed the integration of AI and IoT in sustainable educational systems, particularly focusing on their applications. Below is the conclusion based on aforementioned discussions.

1 AI and IoT Applications in Education during COVID-19:
AI based chatbots assist the students to connect with faculty and their academic performance records while IoT devices can monitor their progress and can provide real-time feedback to the faculty members. These technologies revolutionised the education sector by offering efficient, interactive, and learning environments.
2 Future Vision of AI- and IoT-Assisted Education:
AI techniques like NLP and ML are utilised in intelligent tutoring systems (ITSs) to adapt to individual student needs. NLP and ML both automate grading of student work. IoT devices provide access to digital resources and enable the communication between students and faculty members.
3 Role of AI and IoT in Pandemic Education:
In the pandemic, AI-enabled virtual learning systems which could be operated remotely. It offered real-time support viz. digital books, laboratories library, etc. Electronic gadgets like android mobile phones, tablets, laptops, and desktops enhance remote learning experiences by offering rich content using multimedia.
4 Transformation of Learning Experience:
AI and IoT together transform learning experiences by creating intelligent learning environments which adapt to each student's needs. It provides real-time feedback and guidance to improve engagement and learning outcomes.
5 Challenges and Considerations for Future Research:
The biggest challenges are privacy, security, and limited data sharing need to be addressed for better implementation of AI and IoT technologies in sustainable education systems.

Overall, this chapter emphasises the significant role of AI and IoT in enhancing education, particularly during the pandemic, and highlights the potential for creating personalised and engaging learning environments for students. However, it also acknowledges the challenges that need to be addressed for the effective implementation of these technologies in education systems.

REFERENCES

Ahmad, S.F.; Rahmat, M.K.; Mubarik, M.S.; Alam, M.M.; Hyder, S.I. Artificial intelligence and its role in education. *Sustainability* 2021, 13, 12902.

Al-Emran, M.; Malik, S.I.; Al-Kabi, M.N. A survey of Internet of Things (IoT) in education: Opportunities and challenges. In *Toward Social Internet of Things (SIoT): Enabling Technologies, Architectures and Applications*; Springer: Cham, Switzerland, 2020; pp. 197–209.

Alhaidari, F.; Rahman, A.; Zagrouba, R. Cloud of Things: Architecture, applications and challenges. *J. Ambient. Intell. Humaniz. Comput.* 2020, 1–9.

Alshehri, F.; Muhammad, G. A comprehensive survey of the Internet of Things (IoT) and AI-based smart healthcare. *IEEE Access* 2020, 9, 3660–3678.

Anisha, P.R.; Reddy, C.K.; Nguyen, N.G. Blockchain technology: A boon at the pandemic times—A solution for global economy upliftment with AI and IOT. In *Blockchain Security in Cloud Computing*; Springer: Cham, Switzerland, 2021; pp. 227–252.

Barikova, A.; Bernaziuk, Y. Electronic educational dimension of law enforcement in a pandemic and post-pandemic world. *ECS Trans.* 2022, 107, 18465–18477.

Bayani, M.; Leiton, K.; Loaiza, M. Internet of things (IoT) advantages on e-learning in the smart cities. *Int. J. Dev. Res.* 2017, 7, 17747–17753.

Bellini, P.; Nesi, P.; Pantaleo, G. IoT-enabled smart cities: A review of concepts, frameworks and key technologies. *Appl. Sci.* 2022, 12, 1607.

Bhonsle, D.; Bhale, Y.; Pillai, A.G.; Tiwari, S.; Moyal, V.; Fan, C.P. Applications and challenges of IoT-based smart healthcare systems that use cognitive sensors: An overview. In *Cognitive Sensors, Volume 1: Intelligent Sensing, Sensor Data Analysis and Applications*; IOP Science: Bristol, 2022; pp. 7–1.

Chakraborty, C.; Abougreen, A. Intelligent internet of things and Advanced Machine learning techniques for COVID-19. *EAI Endorsed Trans. Pervasive Health Technol.* 2018, 7, 168505.

Chen, M.; Liu, Y.; Tam, J.C.; Chan, H.; Li, X.; Chan, C.; Li, W.J. Wireless AI-powered IoT sensors for laboratory mice behavior recognition. *IEEE Internet Things J.*2021, 9, 1899–1912.

Embarak, O.H. Internet of Behaviour (IoB)-based AI models for personalized smart education systems. *Procedia Comput. Sci.* 2022, 203, 103–110.

Hossain, M.S.; Muhammad, G. Cloud-assisted Industrial Internet of Things (IIoT)—Enabled framework for health monitoring. *Comput. Netw.* 2016, 101, 192–202.

Iqbal, H.; Parra-Saldivar, R.; Zavala-Yoe, R.; Ramirez-Mendoza, R.A. Smart educational tools and learning management systems: Supportive framework. *Int. J. Interact. Des. Manuf.* 2020, 14, 1179–1193.

Kamruzzaman, M.; Alruwaili, O. AI-based computer vision using deep learning in 6G wireless networks. *Comput. Electr. Eng.* 2022, 102, 108233.

Kamruzzaman, M.; Hossin, M.A.; Alruwaili, O.; Alanazi, S.; Alruwaili, M.; Alshammari, N.; Alaerjan, A.; Zaman, R. IoT-oriented 6G wireless network system for smart cities. *Comput. Intell. Neurosci.* 2022, 2022, 1874436.

Khan, A.A.; Bourouis, S.; Kamruzzaman, M.M.; Hadjouni, M.; Shaikh, Z.A.; Laghari, A.A.; Elm, H. Data security in healthcare industrial Internet of Things with blockchain. *IEEE Sens. J.*2023, 23(20), 25144–25151.

Kim, P.W. Real-time bio-signal-processing of students based on an intelligent algorithm for Internet of Things to assess engagement levels in a classroom. *Future Gener. Comput. Syst.* 2018, 86, 716–722.

Kshatri, S.S.; Bhonsle, D.; Tiwari, S.; Mishra, R.; Rizvi, T.; Pandey, R. Sensor-based devices and their applications in smart healthcare systems. In *Cognitive Sensors, Volume 1: Intelligent Sensing, Sensor Data Analysis and Applications*; IOP Publishing: Bristol, 2022a; pp. 9–1.

Kshatri, S.S.; Bhonsle, D.; Verma, R.; Pillai, A.G.; Moyal, V. Crime detection approach using big data analytics and machine learning. *NeuroQuantology*2022b, 20(8), 1480.

Li, F.; He, Y.; Xue, Q. Progress, challenges and countermeasures of adaptive learning. *Educ. Technol. Soc.* 2021, 24, 238–255.

Li, Q.; Kumar, P.; Alazab, M. IoT-assisted physical education training network virtualization and resource management using a deep reinforcement learning system. *Complex Intell. Syst.* 2022, 8, 1229–1242.

Mahdavinejad, M.S.; Rezvan, M.; Barekatain, M.; Adibi, P.; Barnaghi, P.; Sheth, A.P. Machine learning for Internet of Things data analysis: A survey. *Digit. Commun. Netw.* 2018, 4, 161–175.

Mhlanga, D. The role of artificial intelligence and machine learning amid the COVID-19 pandemic: What lessons are we learning on 4IR and the sustainable development goals. *Int. J. Environ. Res. Public Health*2022, 19, 1879.

Nazaretsky, T.; Ariely, M.; Cukurova, M.; Alexandron, G. Teachers' trust in AI-powered educational technology and a professional development program to improve it. *Br. J. Educ. Technol.* 2022, 53, 914–931.

Ni, A.; Cheung, A. Understanding secondary students' continuance intention to adopt AI-powered intelligent tutoring system for English learning. *Educ. Inf. Technol.* 2022, 28, 3191–3216.

Rahman, A.; Hossain, M.S.; Alrajeh, N.A.; Alsolami, F. Adversarial examples—security threats to COVID-19 deep learning systems in medical IoT devices. *IEEE Internet Things J.* 2020, 8, 9603–9610.

Rahman, A.; Rashid, M.; Hossain, S.; Hassanain, E.; Alhamid, M.F.; Guizani, M. Blockchain and IoT-based cognitive edge framework for sharing economy services in a smart city. *IEEE Access* 2019, 7, 18611–18621.

Rathi, V.K.; Rajput, N.K.; Mishra, S.; Grover, B.A.; Tiwari, P.; Jaiswal, A.K.; Hossain, M.S. An edge AI-enabled IoT healthcare monitoring system for smart cities. *Comput. Electr. Eng.* 2021, 96, 107524.

Raza, K. Artificial intelligence against COVID-19: A meta-analysis of current research. *Stud. Big Data*2020, 78, 165–176.

Rizvi, T.; Bhonsle, D.; Rahangdale, R.; Bagga, J. A survey on behavioral change during the COVID-19 outbreak in India. In *Computational Intelligence and Applications for Pandemics and Healthcare*; IGI Global: Hershey, PA, 2022a; pp. 248–268.

Rizvi, T.; Bhonsle, D.; Uzma, R. Analysis and comparison of psychological constraints among various countries during COVID-19. In *Computational Intelligence and Applications for Pandemics and Healthcare*; IGI Global: Hershey, PA, 2022b; pp. 184–203.

Shah, H.; Shah, S.; Tanwar, S.; Gupta, R.; Kumar, N. Fusion of AI techniques to tackle COVID-19 pandemic: Models, incidence rates, and future trends. *Multimed. Syst.* 2021, 28, 1189–1222.

Tan, P.; Wu, H.; Li, P.; Xu, H. Teaching management system with applications of RFID and IoT technology. *Educ. Sci.* 2018, 8, 26.

Upadhyay, H.K.; Maggu, S.; Dhingra, G.; Juneja, A. Multi-criteria analysis of social isolation barriers amid COVID-19 using fuzzy AHP. *World J. Eng.* 2022, 19, 195–203.

Veeramanickam, M.R.; Mohanapriya, M. Iot enabled futurus smart campus with effective e-learning: I-campus. *GSTF J. Eng. Technol. (JET)* 2016, 3, 8–87.

Wang, J.; Yu, Z. Smart educational learning strategy with the Internet of Things in higher education system. *Int. J. Artif. Intell. Tools* 2022, 31, 2140101.

Yassine, A.; Singh, S.; Hossain, M.S.; Muhammad, G. IoT big data analytics for smart homes with fog and cloud computing. *Futur. Gener. Comput. Syst.* 2018, 91, 563–573.

Zhang, X.; Chen, Y.; Hu, L.; Wang, Y. The metaverse in education: Definition, framework, features, potential applications, challenges, and future research topics. *Front. Psychol.* 2022, 13, 108233.

13 Breaking Boundaries
AI Safeguards for Women and Transgender Individuals

Araya Tripathi and Parul Dubey

13.1. INTRODUCTION

There is a critical need to identify and address the unique security concerns of women and transgender people in the rapidly developing artificial intelligence (AI) landscape. The need of not just taking benefit of AI innovation but also ensuring the rights, protection, and well-being of these marginalised groups cannot be overstated as it becomes increasingly integrated into many aspects of our life. If we want a future that is more equitable and inclusive, this book chapter argues, we need to push the frontiers of AI development.

Some individuals may identify as transgender if their actual gender does not match the one they were given at birth. The term "gender identity" may refer to a person's subjective experience of identifying as male, female, or non-binary. The phrases "transgender", "transsexual", and "non-binary" are used by transgender persons to describe themselves.

Many options are available to transgender people, including hormone therapy and surgical transition, to help their bodies transition to their new sexual identity. However, not every transgender person is able or willing to do this. Using therapeutic treatments is not dependent on being transgender.

The term "transgender" is more accurately used as an adjective than a noun. It is essential to use people's actual words and to respect their given names and last names.

Segregation, poverty, and violence are some of the challenges that transgender people encounter.

Understanding transgender people's struggles and triumphs and being there for them as partners is crucial because of the fundamental contributions transgender people have made to society.

To push AI to new heights, we need to do more than just develop new technologies; we also need to carefully consider the moral principles that will govern these innovations (Nasare, 2020). It is critical that we guarantee the security and equity of AI systems for all users, particularly underrepresented groups like transgender people and women, as these systems become more pervasive in our everyday lives. Examining the three primary areas of transgender identity development, transgender crime statistics, and transgender legal safeguards, this chapter dives into crucial parts of AI safety. To further address the concerns raised by AI, we investigate novel

DOI: 10.1201/9781003538172-13

approaches like human noise detection models. By fixing these problems, we can make AI a tool that helps us all do better while still respecting our common principles of fairness and equality.

Transgender identity and expression may be very personal and unique to each person. Recognising and accepting transgender persons is essential, as is understanding and connecting with them via learning about the challenges they face. Transgender people are visible and active in many areas of the globe, but they also confront discrimination, poverty, and violence. As we strive for a more equitable and inclusive society, it is essential to support and promote transgender people.

13.2. LITERATURE REVIEW

Voice-Activated Insights into Counterfeiting (VAI) is becoming increasingly ubiquitous, popping up as conversational coworkers tailored to certain contexts or more personalised and summarised versions of Alexa or Siri. Many fields, including CSCW, have thought about the social impacts of VAI plans and arrangements, both good and bad. Particularly prominent have been inquiries on sexual orientation and the implications of the (typically feminine) gendering of VAIs for social norms and interactions with clients. Transgender (trans) people have been mostly left out of these discussions, with the rare exception being transgender clients whose demands have been predetermined in terms of representation (Enderling, 2019). The purpose of this study was to examine the experiences and needs of trans and non-binary VAI clients via a structured interview protocol. Our results suggest that these requirements go well beyond simple representational improvements; customers have valid concerns about the safety and privacy of their personal information when using VAI, the motivations of the massive for-profit corporations funding much of this research and development, and the fundamental nature of sexuality itself. Provide both short-term suggestions for creators and analysts aiming to create trans-inclusive VAIs and longer-term, more general suggestions for how analysts typically evaluate mechanical frameworks and appropriate intervention points.

Worldwide, women endure a great deal of sexually abusive domestic violence. The absence of an effective following system will cause this to be animated. This consideration revolved around an AI-based security system that provides protection to vulnerable women. In critical situations, this system may adapt and react manually. A speech recognition device, a GSM modem, and a few other locators, like beat discoverers and an accelerometer, are all part of the planned device to precisely track the condition of the casualty and Raspberry pi. Based on the criticality of the issue, avoidance or security measures can be implemented. Practical software, SWMS, provides a basic workflow for providing emergency assistance, as shown in this chapter. And make use of one application along with a few collar chain artefacts and appearances that are in common use (Katyal and Jung, 2021). To activate the yelling warning, the electric daze device, the screen, and the range of covert components of contacts and the nearest police station are brought to life for the purpose of self-defence, all via a button on the collar that controls the gadget. Shows that function as advanced technological devices also include elements that can impact women's lives, such as live video streaming and electric shock video cameras.

These days, women face a lot of obstacles in the modern global arena. Sexual harassment is an issue that affects women globally (Gehani and Ponnusamy, 2024). There are a lot of infractions against women in our country, even if it has great control and economic progress. The safety of women has become an international concern. The women-based security system and the Android-based system are shown in this project, which uses GPS (the following framework). Women may press a button on this safety device whenever they feel threatened. There, with the touch of a button, you may communicate the current location and area code of the nearest police station and crisis hotline. The device's female status data may be seen on Google Maps with the use of an exceptional programme. Two modules—GPS and GMS—are linked to this application. Women may rest easy knowing that the system is under their control and responds instantly.

13.3. SETTING OUT ON GENUINE SELFHOOD

Changing sexual orientation is also part of the method for some transgender individuals. This preparation is regularly called a sex move and can incorporate different changes, such as changing a person's title, appearance, and/or undergoing restorative methodologies to adjust their body to their sex characteristics. In any case, it ought to be noted that not all transgenders select to move or can move; transitioning isn't a necessity of being transgender (Iwamoto et al., 2019).

(Spielman, 2020) The choice to reassign sex is made when an individual feels that their sex does not match their sexual orientation identity at birth. Typically called "sex dysphoria" and may be a recognised medical condition.

Sex reassignment applies to people (Coutinho, 2023) who have experienced, are almost experiencing, or are currently experiencing sex reassignment (restorative and surgical treatment for body reassignment). One has no intention of getting medical treatments but needs to live until the end of time with a sexual orientation different from the one they were born with. This can include social, legal, and medical viewpoints, and it is diverse for each individual. A few individuals can select to socially move by changing their names and surnames, enhancing their lawful records, and showing themselves in a way that matches their sexual orientation identity (Rincón et al., 2021). Others may select hormone treatment or gender-affirming surgery to bring their bodies more in line with their sex identity.

The choice to move and specific steps are individual choices that ought to be discussed with medical and mental wellbeing professionals. Move can be a complex and proceeding process and is not continuously a straight or straight travel.

13.3.1. Move Journey Chronology

A move isn't essentially a straight line or a straight way (Pike, 2021). The move can be long and nonstop or it can happen in a brief period of time. A person can try different things to memorise what works best for the method of movement is to end up more completely dependable—in body, intellect, and connections. Subsequently, individuals now and then call the move "quiet".

Somebody can begin by learning almost diverse ways to alter or affirm sex.

Social moves can incorporate:

- Inside.
- Social.
- True blue.
- Physical (therapeutic and non-restorative).

Coming out to companions and family as transgender or non-binary, requires individuals to utilise pronouns that suit, go by another title, dress, or decorate in a way that feels suitable when other individuals can see them, and utilise voice in an unexpected way when talking to other individuals (Kidd et al., 2021).

A legitimate move changes data approximately sex in official records and government archives. In spite of the fact that laws shift from state to state, somebody can lawfully alter their title and/or sex personality on official records:

- Driver's permit, state ID or visa.
- Birth certificate.
- Social security number.
- Movement report, changeless inhabitant card, or recognisable proof.
- With school or manager.
- With a specialist or wellbeing protections.

A few shapes of legitimate movement require printed material and can be expensive. A few can be free and very simple. It depends on where they live and what they need to alter. A physical move changes the body briefly or forever to coordinate sex character (Spielman, 2020). Non-medical physical moves include ways to briefly alter the body without the assistance of a specialist. They are frequently cheap or free. These incorporate:

- Utilising clothing such as bras or sports bras to complement breasts.
- Utilising materials such as cushioned bras, clothing, or tissue paper to more completely uncover the breasts, breasts, or navel.
- Concealing private parts and/or scrotum to straighten bowels.
- To extend bowels by utilising things like packs, mugs, or socks.
- All these techniques are brief. So, somebody can do it routinely, on extraordinary events, fair once, or while holding up for a restorative pass.

A restorative physical move—a longer shape of move—includes working with a nurse or specialist. Therapeutic moves for trans men and a few androgynous individuals may incorporate any of the taking after.

SEX-AFFIRMING HORMONE TREATMENT

The use of hormones to induce a variety of secondary sex traits, including a deeper voice, thicker facial hair, larger muscles, a shift in fat distribution away from the liver and breasts, and the absence of menstruation; mastectomy, or "upper surgery," the removal of the breasts and associated tissue; and other similar procedures. Hormonal breast augmentation, which involves taking hormones to produce breasts and other auxiliary sex traits, redistributing fat to the breasts and thighs, and reducing hair growth, is also known as "best surgery" (a.k.a, inserts).

Voice preparation: work with a proficient to memorise how to utilise voice in an unexpected way; angioplasty: surgery that changes vocal strings.

Hysterectomy: evacuation of inside regenerative organs such as the ovaries and uterus.

Phalloplasty: development of the penis using the skin of another portion of the body.

Metoidioplasty: surgery to make the clitoris long and flexible like a penis.

Scrotoplasty: surgery that makes the scrotum and gonads;

Vaginectomy or vulvectomy: surgery to evacuate the vagina and/or vulva, frequently combined with other sex surgeries.

Extraction: an operation that stows away or expels all outside genitalia, such as the vulva, to make a smooth bowel; conservation of richness: sparing eggs that can be used to have organic children in the future. For trans ladies and a few non-binary individuals, therapeutic moves can incorporate any of the following:

- Angioplasty: surgery that changes vocal ropes.
- Laser hair evacuation: expelling hair from the face, neck, or other parts of the body.
- Tracheal clipping: contracting a man's throat.
- Facial feminisation surgery: surgery that changes the shape or size of a portion of the face, such as the nose, lips, cheeks, or chin.
- Orchiectomy: evacuation of the gonad.
- Vaginoplasty: ordinarily, invert the skin of the privates to form a vagina.
- Extraction: an operation that covers up or expels all the outside genitalia, making the bowel delicate.
- Conservation of richness: saving sperm that can be utilised to have natural children within the future.
- Sexual orientation: confirming therapeutic methods change in taken a toll and accessibility. A few strategies may be covered by protections, whereas others may not. It truly depends on where one lives and what therapeutic care they have access to.

13.4. TRUTHFULNESS PATHWAYS MADE PUBLIC

If one wants to be social, they don't need to resort to restorative passing, which can be accomplished by using one or, better still, a combination of the methods mentioned before. Alter one's gender identification and name on official papers; this procedure may or may not need a second review.

To be sex-neutral or indiscriminate, transitioning isn't necessary. Therapeutic approaches and other transitional measures are not necessary for all transgender people.

Therapeutic strategies can be costly, and not everybody can afford or have wellbeing protections. Transgender individuals who do not pass or don't pass in a certain way are just as genuine. The sex personalities of others ought to be continuously respected.

13.5. THREE STAGES OF TRANSGENDER EVOLUTION

Although each person's experience of coming to terms with their transgender identity is unique, there are three distinct phases that most people go through. The steps outlined here provide a useful foundation for comprehending the varied struggles that transgender people encounter on their journeys to acceptance and social acceptance (Brett, 2024). Our goal in outlining these phases is to provide light on the social, psychological, and emotional factors at work throughout. We want to shed light on the varied experiences of transgender people by tracing their growth through time. This will hopefully lead readers to a better understanding of transgender people and their struggles, as well as ideas on how support systems, such as AI, might be adapted to their specific requirements. In addition to highlighting the power of affirming and welcoming spaces, this conversation will focus on how transgender people may benefit from compassionate and knowledgeable assistance as they navigate the process of coming to terms with their identity.

13.5.1. Stage One (Discovery)

As shown in Figure 13.1, Stage One starts the gender questioning process and can occur at any age in life. This is a time of personal exploration; it's a time of searching for information, empathetic ears, and safe locations (Auer et al., 2014). Although conflict can exist between oneself and others, most of it is internal: questioning oneself about the validity of their own feelings and experiences. Good information and guidance can help the person begin to understand where they are on the gender spectrum, setting a foundation for how they want to move forward. Bad information and guidance can lead to guilt, anxiety, depression, self-loathing, and self-harm.

13.5.2. Stage Two (Transition)

Transition is a turbulent time, as shown in Figure 13.1. It is a mix of mountaintop highs tied to self-discovery, acceptance, and transition successes. It is also rife with social shame, family conflict, legal and bureaucratic roadblocks, financial challenges, and self-doubt. Navigating this stage needs a lot of love and support from friends, family, and support groups. A good therapist and primary care physician are essential in successfully navigating this stage to an outward gender identity that aligns with one's inner self.

13.5.3. Stage Three (Resolution)

The resolution stage, as shown in Figure 13.1, sheds light on the inner conflicts of gender identity, and most, or all, of the external conflicts with others about their

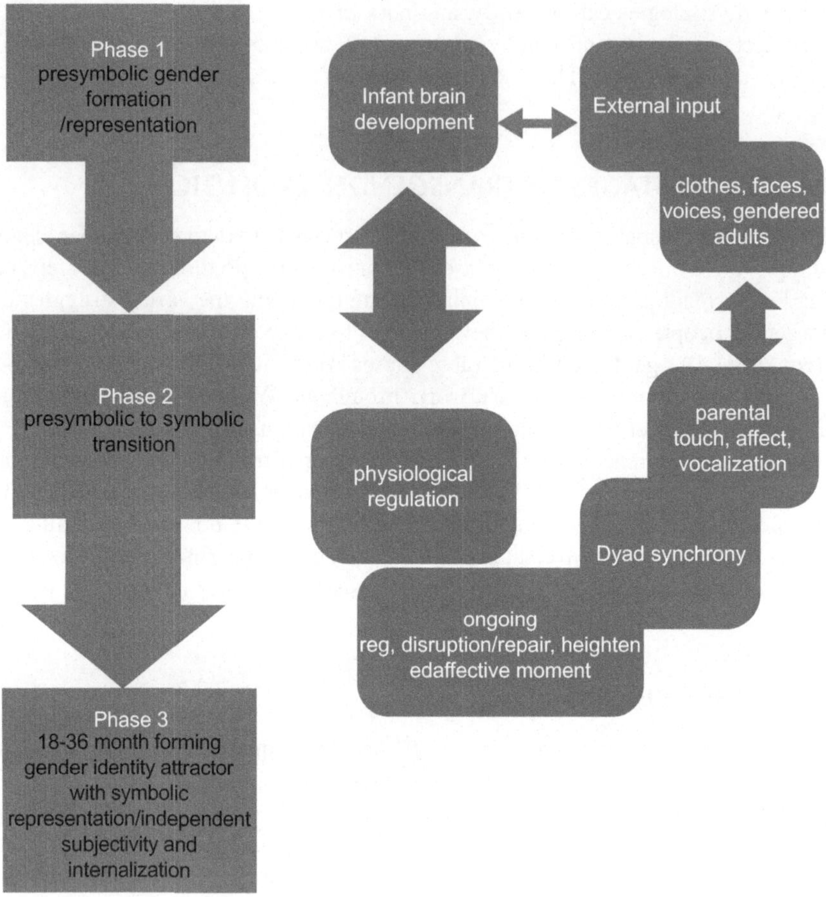

FIGURE 13.1 Representing three stages of transgender evolution.

authentic selves. What is left are the normal challenges that everyone faces in life. The difference is that this newly evolved person can now face those challenges as their authentic self, no longer hidden from the world. Inner peace and joy are either present or within reach. Life feels fresh and new, as though one has entered a new spring after a very long and dark winter.

13.6. SEX FREEDOM EPICENTRES

At 48%, the Netherlands had the greatest number of transgender persons who underwent gender-affirming surgery among all European nations, according to a 2019 poll. The fact that patients between the ages of 19 and 30 accounted for more than half of all treatments is another intriguing discovery. The practice of female genital mutilation is more common beyond the age of 40. Keep in mind that gender-affirming surgery isn't for everyone, and that the kinds of therapies accessible to transgender and non-binary persons may change as they go through transition. The United States, however, seems to be the top choice for those who choose for surgical procedures.

Transgender individuals have long ago made great strides in obtaining legal recognition and protection, according to the 2020 report of the ILGA (Universal Lesbian, Gay, Bisexual, Transgender, and Intersex Association). There is still a long way to go, and the level of acceptance and safety in various nations varies.

The report, which incorporates 193 UN part states:

- 43 countries allow legitimate sex recognition based on self-determination, which means transgender people may change their genuine sex without using restorative sex.
- 11 countries still mandate sterilisation as a condition for sex recognition.
- Ten countries have no legal recognition for transgender people.
- 68 countries have laws that specifically prohibit sex discrimination.
- 53 countries have legislation against gender-based segregation in education.
- 48 countries have legislation against gender discrimination in health care.
- 43 states prohibit sex-based segregation in hotels.
- 43 states prohibit sex-based segregation in hotels.
- 43 countries allow genuine sex recognition based on self-determination, implying transgender people may change their legitimate sex without restorative sex.
- 11 countries still mandate sterilisation as a condition for sex recognition.
- Ten countries have no legal recognition for transgender people.
- 68 countries have laws that specifically prohibit sex discrimination.
- 53 countries have legislation against gender-based segregation in education.
- 48 countries have legislation against gender discrimination in health care.
- 43 states prohibit sex-based segregation in hotels.
- 43 states prohibit sex-based segregation in hotels.

Additionally, the research highlights that although transgender people have gained legal protection in some countries and increased recognition overall, there are still significant obstacles to sexual orientation acceptance and safety from stigma.

People who identify as transgender often point to countries like Denmark, Argentina, and Malta as examples of those that have taken the lead in legally recognising and supporting transgender people. There are rules that prohibit sex-based segregation in many areas of life, and transgender people may legally change their sexual orientation via a simple regulatory process in many countries.

13.7. CRIME RATES WITH TRANSGENDER AND LAWS FOR THEM

Transgender persons in the United States face alarmingly high crime rates right now. Williams Institute researchers at UCLA School of Law found that transgender people had four times the risk of experiencing severe victimisation, including sexual assault, sexual ambush, disturbed or straight assault, and counting assault, compared to cisgender people. This study analysed combined data from the National Crime

Victimisation Survey (NCVS) for 2017 and 2018. The NCVS is the only survey of its kind that includes information on respondents' sex at birth and personality traits, making it the most complete and widely used dataset on crime victimisation. While the study did not find any differences between transgender men and women, it did find that transgender people had greater rates of violent victimisation compared to their cisgender counterparts. Hate crimes against transgender women were more common than those targeting cisgender women. There was an alarmingly high rate of property victimisation in transgender homes when contrasted with cisgender families (Progovac et al., 2021). These findings emphasise the urgent need for effective solutions and mediators that take into account the high rates of victimisation faced by transgender people. The authors of the research stress that experiences of victimisation are associated with mental health issues, including thoughts of or attempts at suicide. Beyond the contemplation, at least 41 transgender and gender-expansive people were reported to have been fatally shot or slain by various violent means in 2022, with a disproportionate number of transgender women of colour and Latinas being victims. These incidents highlight the extreme animosity directed towards the transgender community and the urgent need to do something about it. Transgender persons in India face significant discrimination, isolation, and high incidence of brutality and abuse. Williams Institute researchers at UCLA Law School found that transgender people in India are four times more likely than cisgender people to be victims of violent crimes such as sexual assault, assault, and sexual harassment. The National Wrongdoing Victimisation Overview, which includes information on respondents' gender identity and sex at birth, is the only complete and generally distributed criminal victimisation data set that this paper examined. The datasets for 2017 and 2018 were combined. Transgender people in India, who are often referred to as hijras, face discrimination in every area of life, including education, employment, and access to basic personal documents like passports, voter IDs, and driver's licences. Around 80% of transgender people in India are either forced into sex work or are begging for it, and many of them face brutality and mistreatment because of their gender, according to advocates. Under Narendra Modi's leadership, the Indian government passed the Transgender People (Security of Rights) Charge in 2019 to protect transgender people from discrimination and provide them with legal protections. However, community members and activists voiced their concerns about the accusation, arguing that the regulations being debated undermine the Act's framework. Additionally, transgender persons in India have the serious problem of obtaining economical and high-quality healthcare. Costing anything from 300,000 to 800,000 Rs, gender-affirmation surgery is beyond of reach for many trans people. Although campaigners acknowledge that 480,000 is a huge understatement and suggest that 1.5 million may be a more accurate number, the 2011 census confirms that there are transgender people inside the country. On the other hand, very few people are on the government's 2020 Division of Social Equity & Strengthening National Entrance for Transgender People. If an enrolled person wants to apply for government funding for gender-affirming surgery, they will require the internationally recognised transgender certificate and ID card that they get.

13.8. WOMEN

Since social circumstances have never been static, social change is inevitable in any civilisation. Societal change, whether by legislation or judicial representation, reveals an accepted shift in lifestyle, perhaps leading to a much better, stronger, and enhanced living. Changing social, economic, and political trends, as well as community activities, need comparing variable designs with the laws of a particular culture while simultaneously maintaining the essential adjustment between rights and obligations. Therefore, equality and the rule of law may serve as a check on the progress of social change. The Middle Ages were a period of great strife for the privileged Indian women of yesteryear. A crucial aspect of concealing is the social, economic, and political components. Disruptions to social norms and harmful practices continued. The "aware" and "civilised" eras are where the grandiose things happen (Auer et al., 2014). Achieving parity in social standing for women was a goal of the autonomous executive and the activity. To guarantee and maintain balanced segregation against women based on their qualities and human society's position, the structure is the fundamental statute from the constituent assembly.

13.8.1. Women's Security

13.8.1.1. Indian Situation

There is a gender gap in every area of education, from classroom teaching to access to financial opportunities to administrative representation and beyond. Women in India are less protected due to the many forms of violence they face at home, in their communities, and even from the government on occasion. Some further measures taken with respect to women include:

As far as the G-20 nations go, India is the worst place for women to live (according to Thomson Reuters' Hope Law). In 2010, a bride was murdered per hour due to demands for endowments (Office for the Accounting of Misconduct). Premature marriage occurs in at least 45% of Indian adolescent females. One out of five Indian women, a large number of them are mothers, live through this, according to the World Centre for Research on Women Pregnancy and Delivery. Female infanticide and feticide have resulted in the "loss" of as many as 50 million girls and young women in the last century.

66 percent of women who have been physically abused in their lives have been abandoned, widowed, or split from their spouses. Among the women who reported brutality, 85.3% blamed their present husbands. An increase of 7.1% from 2,13,585 incidences in 2010 to 2,28,650 occurrences in 2011 was recorded in the country in terms of misconduct against women (under both the IPC and SLL). There is a heightened risk of gender-based violence against women and girls in metropolitan India. Scanning the daily newspapers in Delhi, the capital of the nation, reveals shockingly high numbers of instances of brutality against women. As more and more women and girls leave rural areas in search of economic opportunities and better education,

road violence in urban centres becomes an increasingly pressing issue for them. Experiencing physical brutality, social exclusion, and marginalisation is common for women and girls from northeastern India residing in metropolitan centres like Delhi. The North East Back Middle reported that out of 100,000 northeastern residents of Delhi in 2005, 86% experienced detailed racial segregation and 41% were victims of sexual abuse.

13.8.2. Trafficking of Women

The exact number of young women involved in human trafficking and prostitution in India is impossible to determine, since it may include both victims and perpetrators from a variety of countries and international organisations. According to the National Human Rights Commission's "missing children" report, some 44,000 children go missing every year in the country. 11,000 of these remain unchecked. Amazing "missing child" cases are often the product of human trafficking, but that's not always the case; the situation is like a "lost and found". Nobel laureate financial analyst Amartya Sen calculated that there were over 100 million "lost" women in the globe. According to an unanswered question posed by Indian financial experts Sivan Anderson and Debra Beam, almost 2 million women disappear annually. According to experts in the field of finance, around 12% of females die during childbirth.

13.8.3. Sexual Badgering and Assault Cases

The number of reported assaults in India increased 3.6%. After reaching a countrywide wrongdoing rate of 21,397 in 2009, the number of cases increased to 22,172 in 2010. Roughly 68,000 rape instances have been reported nationwide, with 16,000 of them occurring between 2009 and 2011. His appearance in inconvenient photos of sex guilty parties led to his sentencing to prison. According to the National Crime Records Bureau, 5,724 people were rejected for assault in 2011, out of 24,206 incidents registered in the country. Once again, in 2010, there were 22,172 rape incidents, and 5,632 people were apprehended for the crime. A total of 21,397 transactions have taken place. There may have been 5,316 layoffs in 2009, but that was before the numbers were adjusted. Sexually violent acts account for 40% of all incidents in India, with family members implicated in 94% of all sexual assaults. Compared to last year's (9,961) situation, the number of such instances decreased by 14.0%. In 2011, Andhra Pradesh reported 42.7% (3,658) of all instances, with Maharashtra following closely after at 12.5% (1071) of all cases. Andhra Pradesh has the highest rate of wrongdoing (4.3% vs. 0.7% nationally). Assault instances are going upwards. Assaults that occurred between 2008 and 2011 were observed in 2007 and 2008. Its 2008 detailing reveals a 3.5% expansion. In 2007, there was a 0.3% decline from 2008. In 2010, there was a 3.6% increase, and in 2011, there was an additional 9.2% growth. With 3,406 reported assaults in 2010, Madhya Pradesh accounted for 14.1% of all assaults in the country. Mizoram had a 7.1% crime rate, far higher than the national average of 2.0%. Crimes involving sexual assault and other violent incidents are categorised as rape.

13.8.4. Seizing and Snatching

The number of cases increased to 35,565, 19.4% annually, in comparison to the previous year's total of 29,795 instances. Uttar Pradesh has a total of 7,525 occupational cases nationwide, accounting for 21.2% of the total. Compared to the highest percentage of misconduct, which was 12.4, Shop UT reported at 2.9, it ranks third nationally.

13.8.5. Victory Over Tragedy

Recommendations from the Equity Verma Committee Following the public outcry following Narbada's horrific gang attack in Delhi on November 16, the Equity J. S. Verma Committee has rejected the plea to present a passing for assault and, in response, has increased the penalty threshold for a broad range of current and prospective sexual offences. Legal action over the last five decades has led to the recommendation in the report released on January 23, 2013, to codify a harsh alternative to the life sentence. The following are the main recommendations put out by the Equity Verma Committee:—A. In its current form, the Board does not support the death penalty for assault but does support the existing punishment of 7–14 years in prison with the possibility of release after 14 years under government supervision. However, the Board recommends a 20-year prison term in the event that an assault results in the death of a victim or puts them in a vegetative state. A 20-year prison sentence or the remainder of a life sentence if convicted of pack assault. Offenders should get life sentences without the possibility of parole if gang rape results in the death of a victim or their placement in a vegetative condition. The same punishment for repeat offenders. The board recommends a minimum of 10 years in prison, with the possibility of a life sentence, in cases when the victim is a juvenile. If the victim is a minor and dies as a result of the attack or goes into a vegetative condition, the term should be increased from 20 years to life in prison without the possibility of parole. Modern offences such as stalking, human trafficking, and exposing a woman are recognised by this board. The new crime of "breach of command responsibility" may land a top security officer in jail for 7–10 years if their subordinates commit violence. As a crime punishable by the worst penalty for 5 years, "intentional touching" is considered sexual ambush. Assault at a correctional facility carries a mandatory minimum sentence of 10 years and a maximum life sentence (Witt, 2022). The specific offence of exposing a woman's undergarments in public places carries a sentence of 3 to 7 years in prison. "Voyeurism" or "peeping toms" may result in a lengthy jail sentence for three people. The crime of stalking, often known as "eve teasing", is a specific offence. Gender neutrality in assaults should be achieved. Assault on either sex, regardless of how rough or restricted, is considered sexual. The juvenile equity framework must be strengthened, but the board does not mandate lowering the age of juvenile responsibility. All ages of women should be considered victims of conjugal violence. Adopted the practice of handling assault matters via the regular court system rather than the Court Marshal system. Because it violates the victim's right to live in dignity, corrosive assault should be considered a special offence punishable by at least ten years in jail.

13.8.6. Effects of Gender and Personality on AI Noise Detection

Creating models of human noise detection is one way to address the possible risks of AI technology. Deep, inconsistent fraud, which disproportionately affects vulnerable populations, may be identified and filtered using this technique. A mix of deep learning, computer vision, and natural language processing methods are used by the model to identify and filter out fraud (Naved et al., 2022). Gender norms in society may impact noise detection algorithms that aim to identify and react to distress signals. Figure 13.3 shows how these patterns might show up in the model's training data,

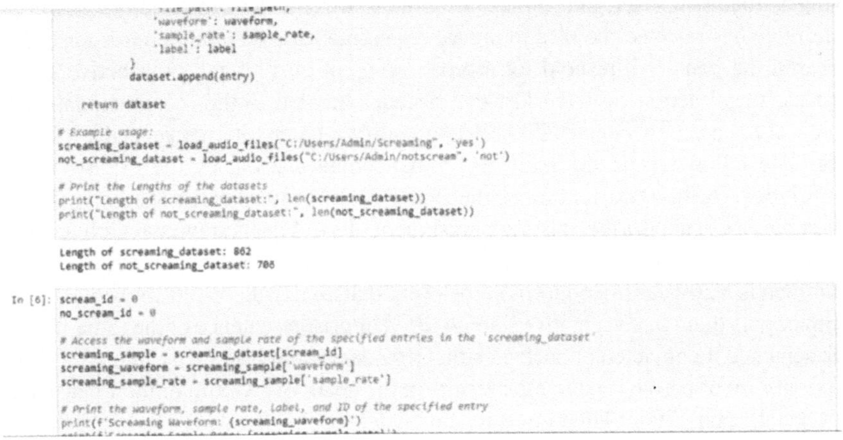

```
            'waveform': waveform,
            'sample_rate': sample_rate,
            'label': label
        }
        dataset.append(entry)

    return dataset

# Example usage:
screaming_dataset = load_audio_files("C:/Users/Admin/Screaming", 'yes')
not_screaming_dataset = load_audio_files("C:/Users/Admin/notscream", 'not')

# Print the lengths of the datasets
print("Length of screaming_dataset:", len(screaming_dataset))
print("Length of not_screaming_dataset:", len(not_screaming_dataset))

Length of screaming_dataset: 862
Length of not_screaming_dataset: 708

In [6]: scream_id = 0
        no_scream_id = 0

        # Access the waveform and sample rate of the specified entries in the 'screaming_dataset'
        screaming_sample = screaming_dataset[scream_id]
        screaming_waveform = screaming_sample['waveform']
        screaming_sample_rate = screaming_sample['sample_rate']

        # Print the waveform, sample rate, label, and ID of the specified entry
        print(f'Screaming Waveform: {screaming_waveform}')
```

FIGURE 13.2 Length of dataset.

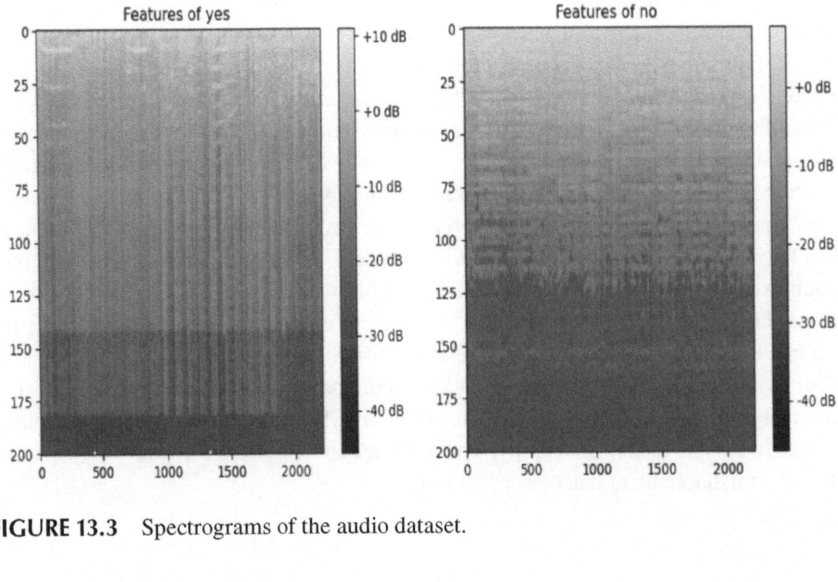

FIGURE 13.3 Spectrograms of the audio dataset.

```
60/60 [==============================] - 21s 352ms/step - loss: 0.0000e+00 - accuracy: 1.0000 - val_loss: 0.0000e+00 - val_ac
curacy: 1.0000
Epoch 6/10
60/60 [==============================] - 22s 363ms/step - loss: 0.0000e+00 - accuracy: 1.0000 - val_loss: 0.0000e+00 - val_ac
curacy: 1.0000
Epoch 7/10
60/60 [==============================] - 23s 384ms/step - loss: 0.0000e+00 - accuracy: 1.0000 - val_loss: 0.0000e+00 - val_ac
curacy: 1.0000
Epoch 8/10
60/60 [==============================] - 22s 360ms/step - loss: 0.0000e+00 - accuracy: 1.0000 - val_loss: 0.0000e+00 - val_ac
curacy: 1.0000
Epoch 9/10
60/60 [==============================] - 22s 365ms/step - loss: 0.0000e+00 - accuracy: 1.0000 - val_loss: 0.0000e+00 - val_ac
curacy: 1.0000
Epoch 10/10
60/60 [==============================] - 23s 378ms/step - loss: 0.0000e+00 - accuracy: 1.0000 - val_loss: 0.0000e+00 - val_ac
curacy: 1.0000
15/15 [==============================] - 2s 125ms/step - loss: 0.0000e+00 - accuracy: 1.0000
TensorFlow Test Accuracy: 1.0
```

FIGURE 13.4 Accuracy of the model.

which can cause it to provide biassed findings. If the screams in the past were mostly male, for instance, the model could have an easier time identifying and reacting to cries that were feminine or transgender. The efficacy and equity of noise detection systems might be compromised as a result of this perpetuation of gender prejudice.

13.8.6.1. Contrast and Discrimination in Noise Detection Algorithms

Women and transgender people are particularly vulnerable to discriminatory outcomes caused by variations in gender identification algorithms. These differences, if not resolved appropriately, can cause false alarms based on specific gender traits or, conversely, the misidentification of crisis signals. These disputes have far-reaching effects that go beyond technology constraints; they have the potential to deepen social inequality and make already vulnerable marginalised groups even more so. Figure 13.2 shows the total number of audios in the dataset, which is 15,68. Figure 13.3 shows the spectrogram that is generated from this dataset. Training and testing are then conducted using this spectrogram. Many different algorithms are used, including CNNs, SVMs, Random Forests, K-Nearest Neighbours (KNN), etc.

13.9. CONCLUSION

In conclusion, it is essential to address the security concerns of women and transgender people in the AI environment. In this chapter, we stress the need of advancing AI research while putting the safety and well-being of vulnerable populations first. To emphasise how important it is to make sure that everyone using AI is safe, we look at important parts of transgender identity and legal protections, and we provide creative solutions, including models that identify human noise. In order to create a more accepting society, it is critical to support transgender rights and include their viewpoints while designing AI.

REFERENCES

Auer, M. K., Fuss, J., Höhne, N., Stalla, G. K., & Sievers, C. (2014, October 9). Transgender Transitioning and Change of Self-Reported Sexual Orientation. *PLoS ONE*, 9(10), e110016. https://doi.org/10.1371/journal.pone.0110016

Brett, S. (2024, February 20). Exploring the Three Stages of Transgender Evolution. *Medium*. https://medium.com/@abbasarms22/exploring-the-three-stages-of-transgender-evolution-1b56d 0b6b809

Coutinho, K. (2023). What Is Gender Reassignment. *Equality, Diversity & Inclusion*. www.equality.admin.cam.ac.uk/training/equalities-law/protected-characteristics/gender-reassignment/guidance-gender-reassignment-0

Enderling, H. (2019, May 28). Towards a Quantitative Personalised Oncology. *Research Outreach*, 107, 130–133. https://doi.org/10.32907/ro-107-130133

Gehani, H., & Ponnusamy, S. (2024). Mobile Application-Based Women's Safety and Security System Using AI. In *Impact of AI on Advancing Women's Safety* (pp. 200–215). IGI Global.

Iwamoto, S. J., Defreyne, J., Rothman, M. S., Van Schuylenbergh, J., Van de Bruaene, L., Motmans, J., & T'Sjoen, G. (2019). Health Considerations for Transgender Women and Remaining Unknowns: A Narrative Review. *Therapeutic Advances in Endocrinology and Metabolism*, 10, 2042018819871166.

Katyal, S. K., & Jung, J. Y. (2021). The Gender Panopticon: AI, Gender, and Design Justice. *UCLA Law Review*, 68, 692.

Kidd, K. M., Sequeira, G. M., Paglisotti, T., Katz-Wise, S. L., Kazmerski, T. M., Hillier, A., . . . & Dowshen, N. (2021). "This Could Mean Death for My Child": Parent Perspectives on Laws Banning Gender-Affirming Care for Transgender Adolescents. *Journal of Adolescent Health*, 68(6), 1082–1088.

Nasare, R. (2020, February 29). Women Security Safety System Using Artificial Intelligence. *International Journal for Research in Applied Science and Engineering Technology*, 8(2), 579–590. https://doi.org/10.22214/ijraset.2020.2088

Naved, M., Fakih, A. H., Venkatesh, A. N., Vani A., Vijayakumar, P., & Kshirsagar, P. R. (2022). Artificial Intelligence Based Women Security and Safety Measure System. *Recent Trends in Science and Engineering*. https://doi.org/10.1063/5.0074211

Pike, J. (2021). Safety, Fairness, and Inclusion: Transgender Athletes and the Essence of Rugby. *Journal of the Philosophy of Sport*, 48(2), 155–168.

Progovac, A. M., Tran, N. M., Mullin, B. O., De Mello Libardi Maia, J., Creedon, T. B., Dunham, E., . . . & Cook, B. L. (2021). Elevated Rates of Violence Victimization and Suicide Attempt Among Transgender and Gender Diverse Patients in an Urban, Safety Net Health System. *World Medical & Health Policy*, 13(2), 176–198.

Rincón, C., Keyes, O., & Cath, C. (2021). Speaking from Experience: Trans/Non-Binary Requirements for Voice-Activated AI. *Proceedings of the ACM on Human-Computer Interaction*, 5(CSCW1), 1–27.

Spielman, R. M. (2020, April 22). 10.3 Sexual Behavior, Sexuality, and Gender Identity—Psychology 2e. *OpenStax*. https://openstax.org/books/psychology-2e/pages/10-3-sexual-behavior-sexuality-and-gender-ide ntity

Witt, H., & Medina-Martinez, K. (2022). Transgender Rights & The Urgent Need for Social Work Advocacy. *Social Work in Public Health*, 37(1), 28–32.

14 Empowering Safety Through Innovation

Understanding the Role of Technology in Women's Safety

Kailash Kumar Sahu and Pushkar Dubey

14.1. INTRODUCTION

The issue of women's safety remains a critical concern worldwide, reflecting deep-rooted societal challenges and gender inequalities. Despite progress in some areas, the global landscape of women's safety is marked by persistent threats ranging from physical violence and sexual assault to cyber harassment and socio-economic discrimination. According to a report by the United Nations (UN Women, 2022), around one in three women globally have experienced physical or sexual violence, primarily by an intimate partner. This statistic underscores the pervasive nature of gender-based violence, affecting women across all countries, cultures, and socioeconomic groups (UN Women, 2022). Women's safety is not only a matter of physical security but also encompasses psychological well-being, freedom from harassment, and equal access to public spaces and resources (UN Habitat, 2020). The rise of digital platforms, while offering new avenues for connectivity and empowerment, has also introduced novel forms of cyber violence against women, including online harassment, doxing, and non-consensual sharing of intimate images (Chen et al., 2021). These digital threats further complicate the landscape of women's safety, necessitating a multifaceted approach to understanding and addressing them (Chen et al., 2021).

Historically, women's safety has been compromised by systemic gender inequalities embedded within legal, social, and political frameworks. Traditional norms and practices in many cultures have perpetuated women's vulnerability by restricting their rights and freedoms. For example, laws governing property rights, inheritance, and marital relations have often placed women at a disadvantage, impacting their safety and autonomy (United Nations Office on Drugs and Crime, 2021). However, the past few decades have witnessed significant advancements in improving women's safety. Feminist movements and advocacy campaigns have played a pivotal role in raising awareness and pushing for legal reforms (Yuval-Davis, 2006). Milestones

DOI: 10.1201/9781003538172-14

include the establishment of international frameworks such as the Convention on the Elimination of All Forms of Discrimination Against Women (CEDAW), adopted in 1979 (United Nations, 1979), and the Beijing Declaration and Platform for Action adopted in 1995 (United Nations, 1995), which have galvanised global efforts to protect women's rights and safety.

Advancements in technology have also contributed to enhancing women's safety, offering tools for personal security, emergency response, and community support (Lindquist & Wolak, 2020). Moreover, societal shifts towards greater gender equality have led to changes in attitudes and behaviours that support women's rights to live free from violence and harassment (United Nations Women, 2021). Societal and cultural factors play a crucial role in shaping perceptions and realities of women's safety. Cultural norms and values influence attitudes towards gender roles, violence, and justice, affecting both the prevalence of violence against women and the responses to it (Jewkes et al., 2016). In societies where traditional gender roles confine women to the domestic sphere and prioritise male dominance, violence against women may be normalised or tolerated to a greater extent (Messinger, 2016). This can be seen in cultures with practices like honour killings or female genital mutilation, which are justified based on cultural beliefs and traditions. Conversely, societies that promote gender equality and female empowerment are more likely to have lower rates of violence against women and more robust support systems for victims (World Health Organization, 2018).

Social factors, including family structure, community cohesion, and economic conditions, also impact women's safety. For instance, women facing economic dependency on their partners may be more vulnerable to domestic violence and less able to leave abusive relationships (Junge et al., 2009; Straus et al., 1997). Community attitudes towards gender-based violence can either reinforce silence and stigma or promote support and intervention (Moya et al., 2016; Jewkes et al., 2016). Hence, it can be stated that understanding and addressing women's safety concerns requires a comprehensive approach that considers the global context, historical challenges, and the complex interplay of societal and cultural factors (Bermúdez Figueroa et al., 2023). Recognising the multifaceted nature of women's safety is essential for developing effective strategies to protect and empower women worldwide.

14.2. EXISTING TECHNOLOGICAL SOLUTIONS

In response to the pressing need for improved women's safety, a variety of technological solutions have been developed and deployed across the globe. These technologies span from personal safety apps to wearable tech, each designed to offer women more control over their safety in diverse situations. Personal safety apps, such as bSafe, Noonlight, and Circle of 6, enable users to alert selected contacts or authorities in case of an emergency, share real-time location data, or set up fake calls to escape uncomfortable situations (Lindquist & Wolak, 2020). Many of these apps feature a simple interface that allows for quick activation, like a panic button that sends out alerts with the user's location (Perreault & Davidson, 2018). Wearable technology also plays a significant role in enhancing women's safety. Devices like smart jewellery, watches, and keychains can be programmed to perform similar functions as safety apps, sending SOS messages or location data to predefined contacts with subtle gestures or presses (Rai et al., 2019). These wearables are designed to blend in with everyday accessories, providing a discreet method for seeking help (Gupta & Jain, 2019).

In addition to personal devices, public and private sector initiatives have explored the use of surveillance systems, AI-powered monitoring, and IoT devices to enhance community safety. These technologies aim to deter potential offenders, facilitate faster response times during incidents, and provide evidence that can aid in criminal proceedings (Wang et al., 2020). The effectiveness of these technological solutions varies widely, influenced by factors such as user adoption, accessibility, and situational context (Xu et al., 2018). Personal safety apps and wearable tech have been praised for giving users, particularly women, a sense of security and autonomy. They offer practical tools for prevention, immediate response, and assistance in emergencies. Anecdotal evidence and user testimonials suggest that these technologies can and do deter attackers, aid in the swift arrest of perpetrators, and provide a lifeline in critical situations (Lindquist & Wolak, 2020; Perreault & Davidson, 2018). However, the impact of these technologies is difficult to quantify at scale, and there is a dearth of comprehensive studies that evaluate their long-term effectiveness in reducing incidents of violence against women (Krohn-Hansen & Nielsen, 2018). While individual success stories highlight their potential, the overall reduction in gender-based violence attributed to technology remains hard to determine (Smith et al., 2017).

Despite the potential benefits, existing technologies aimed at enhancing women's safety face several challenges and limitations. One major issue is accessibility; not all women have access to the necessary devices or the internet connectivity required to use these solutions effectively. Economic and geographical barriers thus exclude a significant portion of the global female population from benefiting from these technological advancements (Lindquist & Wolak, 2020; UNESCO, 2021). Another concern is the reliance on user activation in emergencies, which may not always be feasible in high-stress or dangerous situations (Perreault & Davidson, 2018). Furthermore, privacy concerns arise with the collection and handling of sensitive data, such as real-time location tracking, which could be misused if not adequately protected (Smith et al., 2017). Technological solutions also cannot address the root causes of violence against women, which are deeply embedded in societal and cultural norms. While they can provide immediate help or deterrence, they do not replace the need for comprehensive education, legal reforms, and societal change aimed at eradicating gender-based violence (Jewkes et al., 2016). Moreover, the effectiveness of public surveillance and monitoring systems in enhancing safety has been a subject of debate. Critics argue that such systems may lead to over-surveillance and infringement on individual freedoms without significantly improving safety outcomes (Bennett & Lynch, 2019; Krohn-Hansen & Nielsen, 2018; Furedi, 2017). Hence, while existing technological solutions offer valuable tools for enhancing women's safety, they are not standalone solutions. Their effectiveness is contingent upon broader societal efforts to combat gender-based violence as well as ongoing improvements to address their inherent challenges and limitations.

14.3. TECHNOLOGICAL TRENDS AND INNOVATIONS

The landscape of technologies aimed at improving women's safety is rapidly evolving, with new innovations offering promising solutions to age-old problems. Emerging technologies such as Artificial Intelligence (AI), the Internet of Things (IoT), and blockchain have the potential to significantly impact the field of women's safety, each bringing unique capabilities that can be adapted for safety applications (World Economic Forum, 2020).

- **Artificial Intelligence (AI)**: AI technologies, including machine learning and natural language processing, can be used to enhance threat detection, predict potential incidents, and provide personalised safety recommendations (Wang et al., 2020). For example, AI-powered surveillance systems can analyse video footage in real time to identify suspicious behaviours or incidents and alert authorities or individuals nearby (Hassan & Jin, 2020). AI can also power chatbots that provide support and guidance to victims of violence, offering resources and helping them navigate legal and medical processes (Rani & Sharma, 2021).
- **Internet of Things (IoT)**: IoT devices, which encompass a wide range of internet-connected gadgets and sensors, can be integrated into public and private spaces to enhance safety (Gubbi et al., 2016). Smart lighting, motion sensors, and emergency alert systems can be deployed in urban areas to improve the safety of public spaces, especially during nighttime (Boyle et al., 2019). Wearable IoT devices can be designed not only to send alerts in emergencies but also to monitor vital signs, potentially detecting signs of distress (Sun et al., 2022).
- **Blockchain**: Known for its security and decentralisation, blockchain technology can be applied to create tamper-proof records of incidents, providing a secure and anonymous way for victims to report crimes (Casino et al., 2019). Blockchain can also support the creation of secure digital identities, protecting the identity of users while enabling them to access services and support anonymously (Jewkes et al., 2016).

The adaptation of these technologies for safety applications involves innovative approaches to leverage their strengths for preventing violence and aiding victims.

- **AI for Predictive Analytics and Support Systems**: AI is being adapted to analyse patterns and trends in data related to violence against women, aiming to predict and prevent incidents before they occur (Dakalbab et al., 2022). It is also used in developing intelligent personal assistants that can discretely activate emergency protocols, ensuring help is on the way without alerting potential aggressors (Ermolina & Tiberius, 2021).
- **IoT for Enhanced Personal and Public Safety**: IoT devices are increasingly integrated into smart city initiatives to enhance public safety through improved lighting, surveillance, and emergency communication systems (Ullah et al., 2024). Personal safety devices, such as smart jewellery or

keychains that trigger alerts and record audio or video, offer immediate ways for individuals to seek help (Nast, 2024).
- **Blockchain for Secure Reporting and Support Networks**: Blockchain applications are being developed to facilitate the secure and anonymous reporting of incidents, making it easier for victims to come forward without fear of stigma or reprisal (Casino et al., 2019). They also support the creation of decentralised networks that connect victims with legal, psychological, and medical support in a secure manner (DS Legends Pte. Ltd, 2023).

14.3.1. Innovative Case Studies or Pilot Projects

- **AI-Powered Safe City Projects**: Several cities around the world have initiated pilot projects that use AI algorithms to analyse surveillance footage in real-time, identifying potential threats and improving the response times of emergency services (Lum & Isaac, 2020).
- **Smart Jewellery for Personal Safety**: Companies like Nimb and invisaWear have developed wearable devices that look like everyday accessories but serve as personal safety devices, capable of sending SOS messages with the location to predefined contacts or emergency services (*Nimb, n.d.*).
- **Blockchain-Based Reporting Platforms**: Platforms like Guardian Circle use blockchain to enable users to create a private network of guardians who can be alerted in an emergency, providing a secure and rapid response system. Similarly, initiatives are exploring blockchain for securely documenting and storing evidence of sexual assault, helping to streamline the reporting and judicial process while protecting the victim's identity (Guardian Circle, n.d.; Casino et al., 2019).

These technological trends and innovations represent a frontier in the ongoing effort to enhance women's safety. By harnessing the power of AI, IoT, and blockchain, new solutions are being developed that could significantly reduce the risk of violence against women and improve the support systems available to victims. However, the success of these technologies in enhancing safety will depend on their accessibility, user adoption, and integration with broader societal efforts to combat gender-based violence.

14.4. ETHICAL AND PRIVACY CONSIDERATIONS

The integration of technology into efforts to improve women's safety brings to the forefront critical ethical and privacy considerations. As technological solutions become more pervasive, striking a balance between enhancing safety and protecting individual privacy emerges as a paramount concern. The implications of surveillance, data collection, and the ethical deployment of safety technologies are areas requiring careful deliberation (Zhao et al., 2021).

The use of technology in enhancing safety often involves the collection and analysis of personal data, including real-time location tracking, personal identifiers, and even biometric data in more advanced systems (Apthorpe & Fagan, 2019). While these measures can significantly improve response times in emergencies and aid in the prevention of violence, they also raise concerns about privacy and consent. Individuals may feel apprehensive about the extent of data being collected, who has access to this information, and how it is being used or potentially shared (Smith et al., 2017). The challenge lies in developing systems that provide essential safety features while also respecting the user's right to privacy. This requires transparent practices regarding data collection, clear user consent protocols, and robust data security measures to prevent unauthorised access or misuse of personal information (Zhao et al., 2021).

The use of surveillance technologies and data collection in public spaces and through personal devices has profound implications for individual privacy (Apthorpe & Fagan, 2019). While intended to deter crime and enhance public safety, such measures can lead to a surveillance culture where individuals feel constantly monitored (Lyon, 2001). This can infringe on personal freedoms and may have a chilling effect on the free movement of women in public spaces, ironically counteracting the aim of such technologies to enhance freedom and safety (Bennett & Lynch, 2019). Moreover, the collection of sensitive data, especially without explicit consent or inadequate protection, exposes individuals to risks such as identity theft, stalking, or misuse of data (Furedi, 2017). The ethical deployment of surveillance and data collection technologies must, therefore, include stringent safeguards against abuse, mechanisms for accountability, and the option for individuals to opt-out or control the extent of their participation (Jobin et al., 2019; *UN Office of the High Commissioner for Human Rights, 2018*; *Center for Democracy & Technology, 2023*).

The development and deployment of technologies for women's safety are fraught with ethical dilemmas that require careful consideration:

- **Inclusivity and Accessibility**: Ensuring that safety technologies are accessible to all, regardless of socio-economic status, geography, or technical literacy, is essential. This includes addressing language barriers, the cost of technology, and the need for devices that do not rely solely on smartphone access (Zhao et al., 2021).
- **Consent and Control**: Users must have control over their data, including what is collected, how it is used, and who it is shared with. Consent should be informed and easily revocable, ensuring users understand the implications of data sharing (European Commission, 2016).
- **Bias and Discrimination**: Technologies, especially those reliant on AI and machine learning, must be developed to avoid reinforcing societal biases or discrimination. This includes careful training of AI systems to recognise diverse populations and scenarios fairly and accurately (Apthorpe & Fagan, 2019).
- **Accountability and Transparency**: Developers and deployers of safety technologies must be accountable for their ethical use, including the implementation of measures to prevent misuse and the provision of clear, transparent policies regarding their operation and data handling practices (Jobin et al., 2019).

- **Security and Data Protection**: Robust security measures are essential to protect against data breaches and unauthorized access. This includes encryption, regular security audits, and protocols for responding to data breaches (Council of Europe, 2018).

Hence, it can be stated that the ethical deployment of technology in enhancing women's safety involves a delicate balance between effective protection measures and the safeguarding of individual privacy and rights. Addressing these ethical considerations requires a multi-stakeholder approach, involving technology developers, policymakers, civil society, and the users themselves, to ensure that safety technologies are both effective and respectful of the ethical and privacy concerns they raise (Center for Democracy & Technology, 2023).

14.5. FUTURE PERSPECTIVES AND POTENTIAL IMPACT

As we look towards the future, the evolution of technology in the context of women's safety holds significant potential for transformative change. This evolution is likely to influence not only the direct mechanisms of ensuring safety, but also societal norms and behaviours related to gender and safety. To fully realize this potential, however, it is crucial to develop strategies that ensure technological solutions are inclusive, accessible, and responsive to the needs of diverse populations (Zhao et al., 2021).

The future of technology in enhancing women's safety is likely to see advancements in several key areas:

(a) **Integration of AI and Machine Learning**: Further integration of artificial intelligence and machine learning will enable more sophisticated prediction and prevention strategies, offering personalised safety recommendations and identifying risk patterns with greater accuracy (Apthorpe & Fagan, 2019).
(b) **Advancement in Wearable Technology**: Wearable devices will become more discreet, powerful, and versatile, offering a range of functions from emergency signalling to health monitoring, potentially detecting signs of physical or emotional distress (Smith et al., 2017).
(c) **Expansion of IoT in Public Safety**: The Internet of Things will play an increasingly significant role in public safety, with smart cities integrating sensors and devices into urban infrastructure to improve lighting, surveillance, and emergency response systems (Center for Democracy & Technology, 2023).
(d) **Blockchain for Secure Reporting and Services**: Blockchain technology will likely see increased application in creating secure, anonymous platforms for reporting incidents and accessing support services, protecting victims' identities while ensuring accountability (Jobin et al., 2019).
(e) **Cross-Sector Collaboration**: Greater collaboration between tech companies, non-profits, governments, and communities will drive the development of comprehensive safety solutions that address both immediate risks and long-term societal change (Zhao et al., 2021).

Technology has the power to influence societal norms and behaviours significantly, particularly concerning women's safety:

a) **Raising Awareness and Educating**: Technology can play a key role in educating the public about gender-based violence, promoting empathy, and challenging harmful stereotypes and norms (Apthorpe & Fagan, 2019).
b) **Empowering Individuals**: By providing tools for personal safety and reporting, technology empowers women and marginalised communities, potentially shifting power dynamics and reducing vulnerability to violence (Smith et al., 2017).
c) **Facilitating Open Dialogue**: Digital platforms can facilitate discussions on gender and safety, enabling survivors to share their stories and communities to engage in dialogue, fostering a culture of respect and equality (Zhao et al., 2021).
d) **Supporting Legal and Policy Changes**: Technological evidence and data can support advocacy efforts for legal and policy changes, strengthening protections against gender-based violence and enhancing accountability (Jobin et al., 2019).

Ensuring that technological solutions are inclusive and accessible requires intentional design and implementation strategies:

- **User-Centred Design**: Technologies should be developed with input from diverse user groups, ensuring they are user-friendly, culturally sensitive, and accessible to people with disabilities (Zhao et al., 2021).
- **Affordability and Accessibility**: Solutions must be affordable and accessible to those in lower-income regions, including options that do not require the latest smartphone or constant internet access (Center for Democracy & Technology, 2023).
- **Education and Training**: Providing education and training on the use of safety technologies can help ensure that a wider audience can benefit from these tools, regardless of their technical expertise (Smith et al., 2017).
- **Partnerships for Distribution and Support**: Collaborations with local organisations, governments, and community groups can help distribute technologies more widely and provide support and training to users (Zhao et al., 2021).
- **Ongoing Evaluation and Adaptation**: Technologies should be continuously evaluated for effectiveness and adapted based on user feedback and changing needs, ensuring they remain relevant and impactful (Apthorpe & Fagan, 2019).

Therefore, the future of technology in enhancing women's safety is fraught with both challenges and opportunities. By prioritising ethical considerations, inclusivity, and accessibility, and leveraging the potential for technology to drive societal change, we can work towards a future where technology plays a pivotal role in creating safer environments for women worldwide.

14.6. CHALLENGES AND BARRIERS

While technological solutions offer promising avenues for enhancing women's safety, their development and implementation are fraught with challenges and barriers. These obstacles range from technical difficulties to societal, cultural, and legal hurdles, each affecting the adoption and effectiveness of safety technologies.

14.6.1. Technical Challenges in Developing and Implementing Safety Technologies

- **Interoperability and Standardisation**: One of the significant technical challenges is ensuring interoperability between different devices, platforms, and systems. The lack of standardisation across technologies can hinder their effectiveness, making it difficult for emergency services, apps, and devices to communicate seamlessly with each other (Center for Democracy & Technology, 2023).
- **Data Security and Privacy**: Ensuring the security and privacy of data collected by safety technologies is a paramount concern. Developers must implement robust encryption and data protection measures to guard against hacking, unauthorised access, and data breaches, which can compromise user safety and trust (Jobin et al., 2019).
- **Reliability and Accuracy**: Safety technologies must be reliable and accurate to be effective. Issues such as false alarms, malfunctioning devices, or inaccuracies in location tracking can undermine trust in these technologies and potentially put users at greater risk (Smith et al., 2017).
- **Accessibility and Usability**: Designing technologies that are accessible and user-friendly for a diverse population, including those with disabilities, non-native language speakers, and individuals with limited technological literacy, presents another layer of complexity (Zhao et al., 2021).

14.6.2. Societal and Cultural Barriers to Adoption and Effectiveness

- **Stigma and Privacy Concerns**: Societal stigma and privacy concerns can deter individuals from adopting safety technologies, especially in communities where reporting violence or seeking help is stigmatized (Zhao et al., 2021), or where surveillance is viewed with suspicion (Lyon, 2001).
- **Gender Norms and Inequality**: Deep-rooted gender norms and inequalities can impede the effectiveness of safety technologies. In cultures where women's autonomy is limited (Apthorpe & Fagan, 2019), gaining access to and control over personal safety devices or apps may be challenging.
- **Digital Divide**: The digital divide, or the gap between those who have access to modern information and communication technology and those who do not, limits the reach of safety technologies. Economic disparities (UN Women, 2021), rural-urban divides (Center for Democracy & Technology, 2023), and differences in technological infrastructure across regions can exacerbate this challenge.

14.6.3. Legal and Regulatory Considerations

- **Compliance with Privacy Laws**: Safety technologies must navigate complex privacy laws and regulations, which vary significantly across jurisdictions. Ensuring compliance, especially for technologies that operate internationally, can be a daunting task (European Commission, 2016).
- **Liability Issues**: Determining liability in cases where safety technologies fail to prevent harm or where false alarms lead to unwarranted emergency responses is a legal challenge. Establishing clear terms of use, disclaimers, and legal protections is necessary to address these concerns (Jobin et al., 2019).
- **Regulatory Approval**: For certain safety technologies, especially those that involve surveillance or the collection of sensitive data, obtaining regulatory approval can be time-consuming and challenging. Developers must work closely with regulators to ensure their solutions meet all legal requirements (Council of Europe, 2018).
- **Ethical Guidelines and Standards**: The lack of clear ethical guidelines and standards for the development and use of safety technologies can lead to ethical dilemmas (Jobin et al., 2019) and controversies (Furedi, 2017), undermining public trust and acceptance (Bennett & Lynch, 2019).

Overcoming these challenges requires a multifaceted approach involving collaboration between technology developers, policymakers, legal experts, and communities. By addressing technical, societal, and legal barriers, we can enhance the adoption and effectiveness of safety technologies, ultimately making strides toward improving women's safety globally.

14.7. RECOMMENDATIONS FOR STAKEHOLDERS

The development, implementation, and promotion of technologies for women's safety involve multiple stakeholders, each playing a crucial role in ensuring these technologies are ethical, effective, and widely accessible. The following recommendations are designed to guide technology developers, policymakers, community leaders, and other key stakeholders in their efforts to enhance women's safety through technology.

14.7.1. Guidelines for Technology Developers

- **Adopt User-Centric Design**: Engage with potential users from diverse backgrounds during the design process to ensure technologies meet their needs and preferences. Accessibility should be a priority to accommodate users with disabilities and those with limited technological literacy.
- **Ensure Ethical and Privacy-Conscious Development**: Implement robust data protection measures and transparent privacy policies. Users should have control over their data, including what is collected and how it is used or shared.
- **Test for Reliability and Accuracy**: Rigorously test technologies in various scenarios to ensure they are reliable and accurate. Address potential issues

such as false alarms and inaccuracies in location tracking to build trust and dependability.
- **Promote Interoperability and Standardisation**: Work towards interoperability and standardisation to enhance the compatibility of different safety technologies, facilitating seamless communication and response coordination with emergency services and other platforms.

14.7.2. Recommendations for Policymakers and Community Leaders

- **Support the Development and Adoption of Safety Technologies**: Provide funding, incentives, and regulatory support for the development and deployment of innovative safety technologies. This includes supporting startups and SMEs focused on safety technologies.
- **Foster Public Awareness and Trust**: Launch public awareness campaigns to educate the community about the benefits and limitations of safety technologies. Address privacy and ethical concerns transparently to build public trust.
- **Implement Policies that Enhance Accessibility**: Advocate for policies that ensure safety technologies are accessible and affordable to all segments of the population, reducing the digital divide and promoting inclusive safety solutions.
- **Establish Partnerships and Collaborative Networks**: Facilitate partnerships between technology developers, non-profit organisations, law enforcement agencies, and community groups to create a cohesive ecosystem that supports the effective use of safety technologies.

14.7.3. Suggestions for Further Research and Collaboration

- **Encourage Cross-Sector Collaboration**: Promote collaboration among tech companies, non-profits, academia, and government entities to foster innovation, share best practices, and leverage diverse expertise in enhancing women's safety.
- **Invest in Research on Impact and Effectiveness**: Support research to assess the impact and effectiveness of safety technologies in reducing gender-based violence and improving women's safety. This includes longitudinal studies and data analysis to inform future developments.
- **Explore New Technologies and Approaches**: Encourage exploration and experimentation with emerging technologies (e.g., AI, IoT, blockchain) for potential applications in women's safety. This involves staying abreast of technological advancements and adapting them to safety solutions.
- **Promote Global Standards and Guidelines**: Work towards the development of global standards and ethical guidelines for the creation and use of safety technologies. This can help ensure consistency, reliability, and ethical integrity in technologies deployed worldwide.

By following these recommendations, stakeholders can contribute to the development of effective, ethical, and inclusive technologies that enhance women's safety.

Collaboration, innovation, and a steadfast commitment to addressing the multifaceted challenges of gender-based violence are key to realizing the full potential of technology in creating safer communities for women.

14.8. CONCLUSION

This chapter has explored the multifaceted role of technology in enhancing women's safety, delving into current solutions, emerging trends, and the challenges and opportunities that lie ahead. It has highlighted how technologies such as personal safety apps, wearable devices, AI, IoT, and blockchain offer promising avenues to improve safety measures for women globally. However, the effectiveness of these technologies is contingent upon overcoming significant technical, societal, cultural, and legal barriers. Reflecting on the potential of technology to make a meaningful difference in women's safety, it's clear that while technological solutions can provide powerful tools for prevention, response, and support, they are not solutions. Their true value lies in their ability to complement broader efforts aimed at addressing the root causes of gender-based violence and fostering societal change towards greater equality and respect for women's rights. Therefore, this chapter calls for continued innovation, research, and collaboration among all stakeholders involved in the development and implementation of safety technologies. Technology developers, policymakers, community leaders, non-profits, and academia must work together to ensure that technological solutions are ethical, effective, inclusive, and accessible to all women, regardless of their background or circumstances. By prioritising user-centric design, addressing privacy and ethical concerns, and fostering an environment of collaboration and cross-sector partnership, we can leverage technology to make significant strides towards creating a safer world for women. The journey towards enhancing women's safety with technology is ongoing, and it requires the collective effort, creativity, and commitment of society as a whole to realise its full potential.

REFERENCES

Apthorpe, N., & Fagan, M. (2019). The ethics of AI and big data in the context of violence against women and girls. In A. Cavallaro & N. Ruddick (Eds.), *The Routledge Handbook of Technology and Society* (pp. 261–272). Routledge.

Bennett, S., & Lynch, M. (2019). *The Politics of Surveillance from Foucault to Big Data*. Edinburgh University Press.

Bermúdez Figueroa, E., Dabetić, V., Yuste, R. P., & Saeidzadeh, Z. (2023). Gender and structural inequalities from a socio-legal perspective. In *Gender-Competent Legal Education* (pp. 95–142). Springer. https://doi.org/10.1007/978-3-031-14360-1_4

Boyle, M., Pervan, S., & Watson, M. (2019). Smart city lighting: An assessment of lessons learned from large scale trials. *Energy Policy, 134*, 1101–1110. https://doi.org/10.1016/j.enpol.2019.06.020

Casino, F., Fiore, M., De Mauro, A., & Thoenens, M. (2019). A blockchain-based system for secure and trustworthy reporting of gender-based violence. *2019 IEEE International Conference on Blockchain (Blockchain)*, 126–133. https://doi.org/10.1109/Blockchain48018.2019

Center for Democracy & Technology. (2023). *Designing for Choice and Control in the Digital Age*. Retrieved from https://cdt.org/

Chen, J., Hinduja, S., & Waxman, B. (2021). Cyberbullying and cyberstalking: A review of the literature. *Aggression and Violent Behavior, 59*, 101466. https://doi.org/10.1016/j.avb.2020.101466

Council of Europe. (2018). *Convention for the Protection of Individuals with regard to Automatic Processing of Personal Data and Its Additional Protocol*. Retrieved from https://rm.coe.int/1680078b37

Dakalbab, F., Abu Talib, M., Elmutasim, O., Bou Nassif, A., Abbas, S., & Nasir, Q. (2022). Artificial intelligence & crime prediction: A systematic literature review. *Social Science and Humanities Open, 6*(1), 100342. https://doi.org/10.2139/ssrn.4039691

DS Legends Pte. Ltd. (2023). The role of Web3 in creating decentralized mental health support platforms. *Medium*. Retrieved from https://dslsingapore.medium.com/the-role-of-web3-in-creating-decentralized-mental-health-support-platforms-dd5143ded099 (Accessed date 02/08/2024)

Ermolina, A., & Tiberius, V. (2021). Voice-controlled intelligent personal assistants in health care: International Delphi study. *Journal of Medical Internet Research, 23*(4), e25312. https://doi.org/10.2196/25312

European Commission. (2016). *General Data Protection Regulation (GDPR)*. Retrieved from https://eur-lex.europa.eu/eli/reg/2016/679/oj

Furedi, F. (2017). *First Draft: A Manifesto Against Surveillance*. Bloomsbury Publishing.

Guardian Circle. (n.d.). Retrieved from https://theindexproject.org/award/nominees/2978

Gubbi, J., Gupta, D., & Bhattacharya, S. (2016). Internet of Things (IoT): A vision, architectural elements, and future directions. *Future Generation Computer Systems, 56*, 166–184. https://doi.org/10.1016/j.future.2015.05.002

Gupta, D., & Jain, A. (2019). A survey of wearable security devices for women's safety. *2019 9th International Conference on Cloud Computing, Data Science & Engineering (CONFLUENCE)*, 672–677. https://doi.org/10.1109/CONFLUENCE.2019.8975384

Hassan, M. F., & Jin, W. (2020). A survey on deep learning-based approaches for anomaly detection in video surveillance. *Pattern Recognition, 101*, 107053. https://doi.org/10.1016/j.patcog.2019.107053

Jewkes, R., Flood, M., & Garcia-Moreno, C. (2016). What is the relationship between intimate partner violence and gender inequality? A systematic review of ecological and individual-level studies. *The Lancet Global Health, 4*(4), e280–e288.

Jobin, A., Ienca, M., & Vayena, E. (2019). *The Ethics of Artificial Intelligence.*Cambridge University Press.

Junge, M., Dhingra, K., & Dodge, H. (2009). Economic dependence and intimate partner violence among low-income women: A review of the literature. *Violence Against Women, 15*(11), 1336–1362. https://doi.org/10.1177/1077801209348563

Krohn-Hansen, C., & Nielsen, B. (2018). The limited effects of CCTV surveillance: A review of the scientific evidence. *European Journal of Criminology, 15*(1–2), 22–40. https://doi.org/10.1177/1477370816632202

Lindquist, C. S., & Wolak, J. (2020). Safety apps for women: A review of functionalities and the potential for unintended consequences. *Violence Against Women, 26*(11–12), 1422–1443. https://doi.org/10.1177/0886243318818742

Lum, C., & Isaac, W. (2020). To predict and serve? Discrepancies in risk prediction between police stops and future violent crime. *ArXiv preprint arXiv: 2002.04218.*

Lyon, D. (2001). *Surveillance Societies: From the Panopticon to the Digital Age*. Polity Press.

Messinger, D. (2016). *Gender Violence in a Global Context*. Routledge.

Moya, R. R., Velasquez, N. R., & Bevacqua, L. (2016). Building community capacity to prevent intimate partner violence: A review of the intervention literature. *Aggression and Violent Behavior, 28*, 126–137. https://doi.org/10.1016/j.avb.2015.11.003

Nast, C. (2024). The best personal safety devices, apps, and wearables. *WIRED*. Retrieved from www.wired.com/story/best-personal-safety-tech/ (Accessed date 02/08/2024)

Nimb. (n.d.). Retrieved from www.nimb.com.np/services/eservices/ebanking

Perreault, S., & Davidson, J. (2018). Safety and security apps for women: A critical review. *Violence Against Women, 24*(11), 1321–1342. https://doi.org/10.1177/0886243317748742

Rai, A., Chi, H., & Xu, Y. (2019). Security and privacy in wearable health monitoring systems. *IEEE Design & Test, 36*(4), 70–80. https://doi.org/10.1109/MDT.2019.2904224

Rani, S., & Sharma, G. (2021). A review on the role of AI chatbots in mental health support. *Artificial Intelligence in Medicine, 123*, 114373. https://doi.org/10.1016/j.artmed.2021.114373

Smith, S. G., Patel, N. V., & Mahalik, J. R. (2017). Does technology empower or endanger? A review of safety apps for women. *Violence Against Women, 23*(1), 74–95. https://doi.org/10.1177/0886243315592252

Straus, M. A., Gelles, R. J., & Sugarman, D. B. (1997). Physical violence and marital rape in the United States: Prevalence and implications for mental health. *Journal of Consulting and Clinical Psychology, 65*(4), 1044–1055. https://doi.org/10.1037/0022-006X.65.4.1044

Sun, F., Zhang, S., Xu, Y., Yang, Z., Li, S., & Zhang, X. (2022). Deep learning-based wearable health devices for real-time stress monitoring: A review. *Sensors (Basel), 22*(1), 208. https://doi.org/10.3390/s22010208

Ullah, A., Anwar, S. M., Li, J., Nadeem, L., Mahmood, T., Rehman, A., & Saba, T. (2024). Smart cities: The role of Internet of things and machine learning in realizing a data-centric smart environment. *Complex & Intelligent Systems, 10*(1), 1607–1637. https://doi.org/10.1007/s40747-023-01175-4

UNESCO. (2021, April 8). *Women's Access to and Participation in Technological Developments*. Retrieved from https://en.unesco.org/artificial-intelligence/gender

UN-Habitat. (2020). *The Global Assessment on Women's Safety*. Retrieved from https://unhabitat.org/the-global-assessment-on-womens-safety

United Nations. (1979). *Convention on the Elimination of All Forms of Discrimination Against Women*. Retrieved from www.ohchr.org/Documents/ProfessionalInterest/cedaw.pdf

United Nations. (1995). *The Beijing Declaration and Platform for Action*. Retrieved from www.un.org/womenwatch/daw/beijing/pdf/BDPfA%20E.pdf

United Nations Office on Drugs and Crime. (2021). *Global Study on Homicide 2019*. Retrieved from www.unodc.org/documents/data-and-analysis/gsh/Booklet1.pdf

United Nations Women. (2021). *Transforming Our World for the 50–50: An Agenda for Sustainable Development.*Retrieved from https://sdgs.un.org/goals

UN Office of the High Commissioner for Human Rights. (2018). *The Right to Privacy in the Digital Age*. Retrieved from www.ohchr.org/en/privacy-in-the-digital-age

UN Women. (2021). *Women and the Digital Divide*. Retrieved from https://unsdg.un.org/latest/stories/bridging-digital-gender-divide-technically-empowered-young-women-share-their

UN Women. (2022). *Facts and Figures: Ending Violence Against Women*. Retrieved from www.unwomen.org/en/what-we-do/ending-violence-against-women/facts-and-figures

Wang, H., Zhang, A., Liu, Y., & Liu, W. (2020). AI-powered intelligent surveillance for public safety. *IEEE Transactions on Industrial Electronics, 67*(7), 5858–5867. https://doi.org/10.1109/TIE.2019.2950802

World Economic Forum. (2020). *Shaping the Future of Technology Governance: Global Risks Report 2020*. Retrieved from https://centres.weforum.org/centre-for-the-fourth-industrial-revolution/home

World Health Organization. (2018). *Preventing Intimate Partner Violence and Sexual Violence Against Women: Protecting Health and Promoting Equality*. Retrieved from www.who.int/teams/social-determinants-of-health/violence-prevention

Xu, Y., Li, Z., & Yang, Y. (2018). A comprehensive survey on internet-of-things security: Standards, protocols, and open research issues. *Journal of Network and Computer Applications, 117*, 1–28. https://doi.org/10.1016/j.jnca.2018.04.011

Yuval-Davis, N. (2006). *Gender & Nation*. Sage Publications.

Zhao, I. Y., Ma, Y. X., Yu, M. W., Liu, J., Dong, W. N., Pang, Q., Lu, X. Q., Molassiotis, A., Holroyd, E., & Wong, C. W. (2021). Ethics, integrity, and retributions of digital detection surveillance systems for infectious diseases: Systematic literature review. *Journal of Medical Internet Research*, *23*(10), e32328. https://doi.org/10.2196/32328

15 Successful Implementations
Case Studies

Parul Dubey, Ajinkya Tamhankar, and Biswajeet Mallick

15.1. INTRODUCTION

When it comes to making cities safer places to live, the incorporation of technology has been a game-changer, changing the way people think about and do urban safety measures. Safetipin is one such groundbreaking programme that is examined in this chapter. By looking at Safetipin's fresh perspective, we can see how technology and city safety are coming together, and we can see how certain cities throughout the globe have benefited from these efforts.

When it comes to dealing with safety issues in metropolitan areas, Safetipin signifies a radical change in thinking. With the use of data analytics, community participation, and technology, Safetipin provides a one-stop solution to make cities safer places to live and work in.

This chapter explores Safetipin's foundational concepts and methodology, looking at case studies that show how it works in different types of urban environments. The multi-faceted strategy of Safetipin exemplifies creativity and teamwork, improving lighting infrastructure and mapping safety checks. It serves as a model for successful urban safety efforts worldwide.

This chapter intends to inspire and inform politicians, urban planners, and technologists who are tackling safety issues in their own communities by thoroughly analysing Safetipin's effect and lessons learnt. Our goal is to build a better understanding of how technology can be used to make cities safer and more inclusive for everyone by presenting examples of successful implementations and emphasising the power of technology-driven solutions (Safetipin | Safetipin, Creating Safe Public Spaces for Women, 2023). Women, in particular, feel the effects of urban safety worries, which limit their options. With its multi-pronged strategy, tech-driven solution Safetipin seeks to reimagine urban safety. In this case study, we take a look at Safetipin and how it uses data-driven maps and real-time warnings to create inclusive cities with programmes like "She Rises". We also see how it affects people and communities. Additionally, we explore Safetipin's robust data approach and how it might enable safer city development.

 DOI: 10.1201/9781003538172-15

15.1.1. Empowering Navigation With Key Features

1. Data-Driven Safety Maps: By combining state-of-the-art AI with user-generated data, Safetipin creates dynamic, color-coded maps, completely changing the game for urban navigation. Users are able to confidently explore urban landscapes with the help of these maps, which show both safe and dangerous locations, allowing them to make educated judgements (Viswanath & Basu, 2015).

2. Collaborative Safety Audits: Safetipin offers a fresh perspective on community safety, so user may embrace the position as an agent of change. Volunteers assess vital aspects like lighting and accessibility as part of group safety audits of public areas. Communities are given the authority to improve safety standards and cultivate a feeling of ownership over public areas via this grassroots effort (Manazir et al., 2019).

3. Vigilant Real-Time Alerts: With Safetipin's watchful real-time warning system, one'll always be one step ahead. So users may be prepared and stay alert, users can get alerts when there are events or possible safety problems in the area. Users may be aware and prepared to react to new dangers with this helpful tool.

4. Instantaneous Emergency Response: With Safetipin's lightning-fast emergency response capabilities, users can rest easy like never before. A user may quickly inform pre-selected contacts and local authorities in an emergency by activating an SOS alert with a single press. This quick and effective response system gives peace of mind and guarantees that assistance is always close by.

5. Secure Guardian Circles: Safetipin allows users to establish private guardian rings, allowing them to travel with confidence and peace of mind, and establish a connection with dependable loved ones, so they may monitor the whereabouts in real-time and get emergency notifications. In particular, for those exploring dangerous or unknown places, this priceless support network provides an additional degree of protection (Le, 2022).

6. Safe Routes: Count on Safetipin as your reliable companion for navigating metropolitan areas. The software finds the most secure paths for users to walk, ride a bike, or drive using sophisticated AI analysis and their own data. Users are empowered to comfortably navigate urban settings while minimising possible threats by maximising awareness and comfort with Safetipin's safe pathways feature (Gupta et al., 2022).

All of these new elements work together to make city life safer and more comfortable for everyone, especially those who are already at a disadvantage, including women and people of colour. The importance of Safetipin in creating more welcoming and secure communities is shown by its dedication to using technology for social benefit. Figure 15.1 shows the regions where SafetiPin app is used.

15.1.2. Transforming Lives: The Impact of Safetipin

When it comes to Safetipin, it's not just an app; it's a force for positive change in communities. A safer atmosphere is being created and people are being empowered in the following ways:

1 Empowering Fearless Navigation: When it comes to navigating metropolitan environments, Safetipin gives women a new feeling of confidence.

FIGURE 15.1 World map highlighting the SafetiPin app user regions.

Through addressing safety issues, the app empowers women to fearlessly pursue opportunities and enhance their lives.

2 Amplifying Awareness: Safetipin serves as an effective platform for bringing attention to important community safety concerns. This increased awareness motivates those in charge and others with a stake in the matter to act swiftly in response to safety issues, creating an atmosphere free of harm.
3 Driving Data-Driven Progress: Government officials and urban planners are able to make better decisions because to Safetipin's use of crowdsourcing data. The software helps execute effective safety measures that are customised to each community's requirements by offering useful information regarding safety perceptions and issues.
4 Fostering Collaborative Spirit: In order to make the world a safer place for everyone, especially women, Safetipin promotes a cooperative spirit across communities. As a group, we are better able to accomplish our goals and bring about positive change, which strengthens our bonds as people and as a community.

Safetipin affects more than just its users; it weaves a safer web for whole communities by responding to safety issues, increasing awareness, and encouraging collaborative action. The revolutionary way it improves safety highlights how technology can revolutionise society for the better.

15.1.3. Safetipin: Building Inclusive Cities for All

Safetipin creates fair society, not only applications. Their approach to filling important gaps is as follows:

15.1.3.1. Gender-Responsive Urban Planning

- Women make up half of the population; thus, it's important that Safetipin creates environments that are welcoming and safe for them.
- Their data-driven approach has guided actions in places worldwide, addressing the barriers to women's mobility.
- From a female point of view, the "She Rises" paradigm takes a comprehensive approach to many facets of city life.

15.1.3.2. Empowered Youth, Thriving Cities

- Many urban youths, particularly young women, face obstacles due to outdated social standards, and insufficient public services.
- By advocating for their health, safety, and participation in urban planning, Safetipin is extending their "right to the city".
- Empowering adolescents to map their experiences and advocate for their needs, they combine data, technology, and human-centred research.
- By addressing many issues at once, this strategy empowers youth-led citizenship models and gives them a stronger voice.

Safetipin builds inclusive, thriving cities by tackling these areas of attention, which has a domino effect.

15.1.4. Safetipin: A Multi-Pronged Approach to Urban Safety Assessment

Safetipin uses an all-encompassing approach to make cities safer by collecting, analysing, and presenting data from a variety of sources.

15.1.4.1. Data Collection

- Crowdsourcing:
  - Users generate safety rankings for sites by conducting audits and providing real-time feedback using the MySafetipin app.
  - The Safetipin Site App is a project-specific data collector that takes note of specifics like usability and accessibility.
  - Safetipin Nite App: Skilled workers collect information by taking pictures and doing site inspections.
- City-Wide Data:
  - The Safetipin Nite app uses machine learning algorithms and cameras installed on vehicles to gather data scalable.
  - Using Preexisting GIS Data Layers for Integration: More accurate conclusions by combining new information with previously collected data.

15.1.4.2. Data Processing and Presentation

- Analysis and Coding: Data is classified, examined, and presented visually via individualised maps and reports (Kartik et al., 2017).
- Results That Matter: Stakeholders get straight talk and practical advice based on the research.

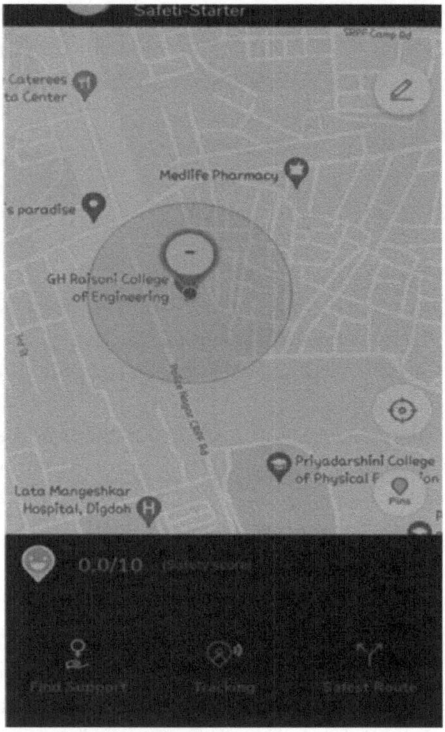

FIGURE 15.2 Real-time safety score check.

- The ability to continuously see and analyse data is made possible by dynamic GIS environments and dashboards, which are used in urban modelling.

KEY BENEFITS

- **Data-Driven Decision-Making:** The safety audit ratings for different areas are generated by Safetipin using crowdsourced data. Urban planners and politicians greatly benefit from this impartial data. They may prioritise the distribution of resources and identify regions with significant safety concerns using these findings.
  - Make data-driven modifications based on an evaluation of the efficacy of current safety measures.
  - Monitor development over time and assess the results of actions taken.
- **Community Engagement:** By inviting locals to take part in safety inspections, Safetipin promotes an attitude of active citizenship. Because of this, communities are able to fight for betterment and take charge of their own health. The app makes this possible through:
  - Provision of an easy-to-use system for the reporting of lighting, infrastructure, and social safety factors by citizens.

    - Providing a more thorough awareness of safety risks in particular places by allowing people to offer comments and solutions.
    - Making everyone feel that they have a part to play in making the city a better, more welcoming place for everyone.
- **Scalability and Adaptability:** When it comes to city surroundings and demographics, Safetipin knows that safety issues might vary a lot. Because of this, we ensured that the software could expand and adapt to the needs of the business. I'll demonstrate:
    - The parameters of the safety audit are adaptable to the particular requirements and priorities of each municipality.
    - By integrating the application with pre-existing city management systems, data collection and analysis can be streamlined.
    - Safetipin provides a diverse range of data visualisation tools that enable stakeholders to conduct analyses of safety data across various geographical dimensions.
- **Actionable Outcomes:** Data is only useful when it inspires tangible actions. Safetipin facilitates constructive transformation by surpassing the mere dissemination of information. In the following methods, it accomplishes this:
    - The safety audit reports are disseminated to pertinent governing bodies, including law enforcement and municipal departments, stimulating them to implement essential measures to mitigate safety issues.
    - By analysing the data, it is possible to pinpoint potential infrastructure enhancements, such as improved public transportation or street illumination.
    - The insights provided by Safetipin have the potential to guide the creation of focused safety awareness campaigns and community programmes.

Through the integration of these components, Safetipin presents a resilient and adaptable approach to the development of safer, more inclusive urban environments that benefit all.

15.1.5. Services of Safetipin

Safetipin implements a comprehensive approach to urban safety, which encompasses a wide range of services spanning various departments. These services have been purposefully developed to tackle multiple facets of safety improvement, community involvement, evidence generation, knowledge development, access to open data, and technical support. Safetipin endeavours to facilitate positive societal transformation, promote technological empowerment, and encourage community collaboration through the utilisation of data-driven insights. This section will provide a comprehensive analysis of each of the aforementioned service categories, emphasising their importance, influence, and contributions to the establishment of urban environments that are safer and more inclusive. By conducting a comprehensive analysis of Safetipin's products and services, we shall reveal the application's multifaceted strategy for tackling intricate safety issues and enabling users to traverse urban environments with assurance and protection. Figure 15.3 shows the list of Services offered by SafetiPin App.

Capacity Development:

1 Safety Audits: By allowing users to evaluate aspects like illumination and accessibility, Safetipin enables community safety assessments. By taking part in these audits, individuals of the community improve their ability to spot safety issues and make a difference in their own neighbourhoods.
2 Emergency Response Training: The app's emergency response training and resources provide users the tools they need to respond successfully in times of catastrophe. Individuals and society as a whole benefit from this training since it improves people's ability to react to catastrophes.
3 Safe Routes Education: Learn how to navigate safely with the help of Safetipin's instructional materials and advice, including how to choose routes that won't put user at risk. Users' ability to make educated judgements and reduce risks is improved by the app's education on safe navigation methods.

Community Engagement:

1 Collaborative Safety Audits: By encouraging people to work together to evaluate the security of public areas, Safetipin promotes community involvement. The software encourages community involvement in these audits, which gives people a voice in resolving safety issues and strengthens communities as a whole.
2 Guardian Circles: Users may establish virtual guardian circles with their chosen contacts using the app. These circles can then be used to receive emergency warnings and monitor the user's position. By facilitating the use of social networks to improve individual security and mutual aid, this function promotes participation in the community.
3 Real-Time Alerts: By keeping users aware of local occurrences or dangerous circumstances, Safetipin enables them to remain proactive and respond accordingly. The app encourages community involvement and gives people the ability to make a difference in their own and others' safety by involving them via timely warnings.

Evidence Building:

1 Safety Maps: Using user-generated data and AI technology, Safetipin creates safety maps that show where it is safe to be in metropolitan areas and where it is not. These maps are valuable tools for stakeholders and policymakers since they show the current state of safety and help with decision-making.
2 Data-Driven Progress: City planners and lawmakers may use the app's crowdsourced data on safety perceptions and occurrences to make evidence-based decisions. Safetipin helps develop evidence and allows for the adoption of effective safety measures by analysing this data.

3 Crowdsourced Data Analysis: In order to find patterns and trends in safety perceptions and occurrences, Safetipin analyses data that has been crowdsourced. Building targeted interventions and better understanding community safety dynamics are both bolstered by this finding.

Knowledge and Innovations:

1 AI-Powered Safety Maps: Innovative methods for improving urban safety are offered by Safetipin, which uses AI to generate dynamic safety maps. Using this knowledge-driven method of mapping, users may get vital insights to make educated decisions.
2 Innovative Safety Solutions: App developers are always thinking of new ways to make the app safer and more secure for users. Safetipin promotes progress in knowledge and encourages improvements in safety measures via the introduction of novel solutions.
3 Continuous Improvement Initiatives: Safetipin is always looking for ways to better serve its users and stakeholders by listening to their suggestions for how the service can be improved and new safety issues that may arise. A dynamic strategy for improving safety is encouraged by this culture of innovation and learning, which also supports the exchange of information.

Open Data Platform:

1 Crowdsourced Data Sharing: Users are able to view and contribute to crowdsourced safety data using Safetipin's open data platform. Stakeholders are able to use shared information for safety improvement projects thanks to this open data strategy, which encourages openness and cooperation.
2 Transparent Safety Information: Safety data, such as maps and incident reports, is easily accessible via the app. Stakeholders are empowered to make educated choices and accountability is promoted by Safetipin's open access to safety data.
3 Accessibility for Stakeholders: Stakeholders, such as academics, community groups, and legislators, are guaranteed access to Safetipin's data and services. With the help of this open data platform, stakeholders are able to share information and work together to achieve shared safety objectives.

Technical Assistance:

1 Emergency Response Support: Users are guaranteed access to aid in an emergency with Safetipin's technical assistance and support for responding. Both user safety and the efficacy of emergency response operations are improved by this technological assistance.
2 App Training and Support: To ensure that users get the most out of the app's features and functions, it offers training and support services. Safetipin makes sure that users can make the most of the software to improve safety by providing instructions and support.

FIGURE 15.3 List of services offered by SafetiPin app.

3 Safety Solutions Consultation: When stakeholders need advice on safety improvement projects, they may turn to Safetipin for consulting services. The goal of this technical assistance is to help communities find answers to their unique safety problems and put them into action.

15.1.6. Conclusion

To sum up, Safetipin's groundbreaking services have revolutionised urban safety. Safetipin has changed the game when it comes to improving city safety by giving people the tools they need, encouraging community involvement, and providing data-driven insights. A key player in making communities safer and more welcoming for everyone, it is dedicated to openness, responsibility, and constant development. In the future, we may build upon Safetipin's achievements to make even greater strides in urban safety via the use of technology and community involvement.

REFERENCES

Gupta, S., Janicki, S., Casula, P., & Parvin, N. (2022, June). Rethinking safe mobility: The case of Safetipin in India. In *Proceedings of the 2022 International Conference on Information and Communication Technologies and Development* (pp. 1–6). https://gupta-shubhangi.github.io/Publications/Rethinking%20Safe%20Mobility.pdf

Kartik, P., Jose, S., & MK, G. K. (2017). Safetipin: A mobile application towards women safety. *Rajagiri Journal of Social Development*, *9*(1), 5–12.

Le, T. (2022). Crowdsourcing women's experiences of space: Empowerment, (in)visibility, and exclusions—a critical reading of Safetipin map. *PLATFORM: Journal of Media & Communication*, *9*(1).

Manazir, S. H., Govind, M., & Rubina. (2019). My Safetipin mobile phone application: Case study of e-participation platform for women safety in India. *Journal of Scientific Research*, *8*(1), 47–53.

Safetipin | Safetipin,Creating Safe Public Spaces for Women. (2023). https://safetipin.com/

Viswanath, K., & Basu, A. (2015). SafetiPin: An innovative mobile app to collect data on women's safety in Indian cities. *Gender & Development*, *23*(1), 45–60.

Index

T

V

W